Karin —

Inspire & Be Inspired! :)

Beyond Happiness

How Authentic Leaders Prioritize
Purpose and People for Growth
and Impact

Jenn Lim

GRAND CENTRAL
PUBLISHING

NEW YORK   BOSTON

Copyright © 2021 by Jennifer Lim

Cover design by Derek Thornton
Cover copyright © 2021 by Hachette Book Group, Inc.

Grand Central Publishing
Hachette Book Group
1290 Avenue of the Americas, New York, NY 10104
grandcentralpublishing.com
twitter.com/grandcentralpub

First Edition: October 2021

Grand Central Publishing is a division of Hachette Book Group, Inc. The Grand Central Publishing name and logo is a trademark of Hachette Book Group, Inc.

The publisher is not responsible for websites (or their content) that are not owned by the publisher.

The Hachette Speakers Bureau provides a wide range of authors for speaking events. To find out more, go to www.hachettespeakersbureau.com or call (866) 376-6591.

Personal photos on page iii provided by Jenn Lim.
Images throughout the book created by Delivering Happiness.

Library of Congress Control Number: 2021939220

ISBN: 9781538736883 (hardcover), 9781538736890 (ebook), 9781538707364 (international trade)

Printed in the United States of America

LSC-C

Printing 1, 2021

Dad, Tony, Travis, and everyone I've loved who's passed—wherever you're existing now—I hope you can do so with even more peace and happiness, knowing we're all on brighter paths of wholeness in the greenhouses you've helped architect. Until the next...I love you and miss you so.

Contents

Part IV

RIPPLE TO YOUR COMMUNITY

Part V

THE NEW RIPPLES: SOCIETY + PLANET

Why I Wrote This

Do not fear death, but rather the unlived life.
—TUCK EVERLASTING

I was five weeks out from this book's deadline when my phone started blowing up one night, in a way that lets you know either something amazing just happened or something on the furthest other end from that. The way it was buzzing nonstop, it felt like my phone was furious, and I had a sinking feeling.

Tony Hsieh had died.

The world had lost a kindhearted imagineer and entrepreneur, and I had lost one of my soulmates and partners in positivity. Having been through death before, most painfully the passing of my dad seventeen years prior, I was familiar with the feelings and the five stages of grief, but this was so different.

His passing sent me into one of the most raging tailspins I've experienced. The only salve that brought the occasional calm was the outpouring of love, support, and grief shared with so many others who had been affected and inspired by Tony's life too. We couldn't physically be together because of the pandemic, but as his family, his friends, and the world mourned his loss, I was struck by the feelings of solace and love that can still be felt in a digital age when technology is usually cast as the enemy. In this case, it became a trusted friend.

I'll be forever grateful to everyone who shared their humanity with me and each other. My friends and family, who took the baton to make sure I was eating and sleeping; my Delivering Happiness (DH) work family, who gave me all the time I needed to grieve; and people far and wide who sent heartfelt messages that helped me get by, one moment at a time.

But there was still a book to write. One that reassures us of the deep meaning in the work we do and that could inspire leaders to understand scientific happiness in the workplace and what's beyond it. At times, I had doubts that I could pull it off. But as each day passed from a blur to moments of a slight smile tied to a warm memory, it reminded me how the lights eventually get brighter again and I realized the irony of it all. Tony's death—with the heavy media storm and cynical, at times heartless, questions—was testing *all* the lessons I'd learned about highs, lows, happiness, and beyond.

On some days, it was impossible to focus because his passing was so public. On other days, I'd look at the picture of me and Tony on Mount Kilimanjaro and hear his words: "Anything is possible." I wasn't sure how things were going to turn out, but I did know Delivering Happiness was a part of Tony. Overnight, it had transformed from a company we'd cofounded ten years before to one of the ways that his legacy would live on. I was reinspired to live out our company's purpose with even more impact on the world.

As things cleared in my head, I knew the core messages of this book—the relationships among purpose, people, and profits for growth and impact—were still the same as before he died. Even though the world without a physical Tony would never be the same, the "why" behind this book and the reasons it had to be written grew in its strength.

As Buddhists believe, and American political journalist Norman Cousins wrote, "Death is not the greatest loss in life. The greatest loss is what dies inside us while we live." We have no way of telling what forms our bodies and souls will transition to next, so we might as well live fully and wholly in the here and now, or, as Tony liked to say, unapologetically true to our weird selves.

I learned this when my dad died, and now that Tony's passed, it couldn't be a bigger truth to me. We all eventually lose the things we love, including ourselves, but if we can accept this truth, the why behind our existence is clear: holding space for ourselves and others to be truly who we are while feeling belonging and love. If there's anything in the world that can slow the metastasis of divisiveness, it's the celebration of what unites us. We all want to love and be loved while being true to our (weird) authentic selves, whether at work or in life.

This book is about understanding the authentic self in our work/life journeys. It shares how we can get back to the core of who we are and live the purposeful life we want through the *work we do every day*. It shows how we can adapt to unknowns by applying Purpose + Values to navigate the future. It shines light on some of the defining questions of our time: How can individuals have a greater effect on business growth and success? How can companies modernize org design so we can each do our best work because we love it? How can we find meaning and create a positive impact in our work and communities—regardless of the challenges the world throws our way?

During our *Delivering Happiness* book tour back in 2010, Tony and I had one of our many random conversations that turned out not to be so random at all. Things still felt surreal as we were traveling around cross-country with our book team on a bus we had bought from the Dave Matthews Band, our goal to share the message and one of our core values: inspire and be inspired (and have fun while doing it). We were excited that the book was doing well, but it was also one of the most stressful times in our lives. Being on the road, trying to deliver happiness to others, took a toll on everyone on that bus.

In this particular conversation, both Tony and I acknowledged there was something missing in the book. It talked a lot about the ups and downs that he and Zappos had to go through, but it was focused on the company level. The book showed that happiness as a business model can sustain a company, but it didn't highlight that the business model really has to start with the sustainable happiness of the individual. It was obvious to us that healthy companies prioritize culture and purpose, but in order to get there, people have to first know their personal purpose, then connect it to why they show up at work every day.

While Tony and I didn't predict that *culture* and *purpose* would eventually become common words in boardrooms and lunchrooms, that conversation seeded one of DH's biggest learnings between then and now: that the building blocks of a company's sustainable success start with every *individual* member's Purpose + Values being aligned with those of the company.

For the next ten years, in workplaces around the world, the DH team and I gained a deeper understanding of how true systemic change comes down to those building blocks that enable companies to grow. Creating this bridge between the company level and the individual level has been one of our main focuses at DH for years now. That means leaders at *all levels* need to get real with themselves first. Whether you run a Fortune 500 company, manage multiple teams, own a small business, or sit on the front line as a receptionist, we can all be leaders of our own lives at work. If we choose to be.

To illustrate this point, I love sharing Rachel's story. She's a receptionist at a doctor's office in Manhattan. Genuinely caring, with an authentic smile to greet even the grumpiest New Yorker having a bad day, she's the highlight of every patient's visit. People wonder how someone could love her job that much and be unaffected by other people's moods and the inevitable hassles of the work. There are many reasons, but one of them is the title she chooses to print on her business card: director of first impressions. She knows how her work matters to the organization and absolutely owns her role, and everyone can tell she loves it. She is a leader of her life at work.

Companies will go through their natural ups and downs, but we also need to own our personal highs and lows, light and shadow sides, strengths and blind spots. As leaders, as much as we need to work on the company, we need to work on ourselves too. When it all aligns, we see the beauty of a ripple effect that starts from the individual and ripples first to the team and company, then to the community of customers, partners, and vendors. And as an added bonus, when we do this right, the society and planet that we live on benefit too.

The conversation Tony and I had in 2010 is where this book is taking the baton. I've often said Tony was tenaciously true to himself, which was likely the reason we connected so well. We both thought authenticity to ourselves and others was one of the most important values to live by. It grounded our relationship a majority of the time and annoyed the hell out of us when it didn't. But our mutual respect and trust came from that shared value. When I was trying to make sense of what to think, what to write, and what to process after he passed, I realized I already knew where I had to take the baton.

Tony used to bring up the concept of "greenhouses" from time to time. It was his belief that true leaders were building greenhouses for others to grow in rather than trying to be "the tallest plant." He'll forever be one of the best greenhouse architects the world has seen—one of the many legacies he lived and left behind.

Tony proved to be the expert architect for others, but what does it mean to build greenhouses for ourselves too? How can we truly be ourselves at work and in life, grow our greenhouse *and* others? How do we create sustainable environments where we can all meaningfully connect and feel a sense of belonging? What people ecosystems can we cultivate to bring happiness, embrace wholeness, and nurture new ways to feel more human at work?

DH's work has always been around work/life integration, and now it's time to realign our personal and professional lives in even more profound and purposeful ways.

What you will find in these pages is an explanation of why focusing on people is the way to futureproof your work and your orgs. This includes an overview of our latest model, stats and stories (because you need both), how the model affects the bottom line, and how the new ROI is your "ripple of impact" (not just your return on investment). That's Part I. The next three sections walk you through how to create people ecosystems no matter what leadership role you have—whether you lead the whole company, your team, or your own life. Part II focuses on the ME or the individual, Part III on the WE or the team and org, and Part IV on the immediate COMMUNITY, with ripples going all the way out to our SOCIETY and PLANET in Part V.

There are lessons I've learned along the way, practical exercises to help you bring inspiration and purpose to work and life, and stories of globally recognized brands like Starbucks, Toyota, and WordPress transforming their businesses during a pandemic, as well as of folks around the world finding their purpose in companies of diverse sizes and industries. I also tell stories that spotlight personal ups and downs in the hope that you're inspired to live a more fulfilling life, both at work and outside it.

I know we can all attest that life can be fucking hard. Sometimes in unrelenting ways that make us wonder if the waves will ever stop crashing. At times we question if there's enough strength left that our legs won't give out under us, let alone enough to keep us grounded. But I also know that if we do the work, for ourselves and others, we'll be more than OK. We'll know what it means to truly live and not fear the life unlived.

I hope this book inspires and supports you in building your own greenhouse and enables you to help others build theirs. I hope it supports people, teams, and companies in doing the reflective work required to understand highs and lows so we can get to a place where we're showing up as our authentic selves. By staying curious, with courage and calmness, I hope to show how we can grow to love ourselves and each other, and the work we do every day.

WHY DOES THIS MATTER?

Everybody has a plan until they get punched in the mouth.

—MIKE TYSON

2020: The Reset on Humanity (and Ourselves)

When the context of the world instantly changed in 2020, and we all had to adapt, fast, it was obvious that shifts were happening at work and at home like never before.

We all moved to Zoomland overnight, closets became our conference rooms, and parents realized TikTok wasn't an app for telling time. Without a glimmer of light at the end of the tunnel, it felt like 2020 wouldn't stop 2020-ing and every day felt like we were waking up on Blursday.

Over the course of a year, the button that reset humanity was pushed a few times, and there was no turning back. The income disparity gap widened, hundreds of millions of people around the world lost their jobs and homes, and people lost more and more loved ones as the relentless virus kept spreading. The world saw the haunting realities of racism and social injustice, climate change, and elections that threw back the curtain over how divided our countries and their citizens really were. And it seemed that we were all left to fend for ourselves.

Historically, sharing a common enemy is one of the best ways to bring people together. Before 2020, I would've considered "global pandemic" to be a pretty safe bet to be that enemy. Instead, it just revealed how fractured we were. As 2020 roiled on, the world showed us too many different enemies to choose from, and people struggled to agree on what the real "enemy" was. Real or fake news. Science or superstition. Populists or elites. Left or right. We were confronted with a spectrum of tough decisions in an increasingly uncertain and complex society. Questions like: "What do I stand for? What would I fall for?" (couldn't resist the megafan of *Hamilton* in me) made us eventually realize the answers weren't binary. The volume of opinions kept getting louder, and the strength of even the best relationships between friends, family, and neighbors was being tested—let alone relationships between enemies.

But we also found things that united us—simple kindnesses, the power of community, and a golden age of creatively hilarious memes. The reset button helped us pause even as life continued. Parents who used to travel a majority of their time got to hear their kids' first words or attend their high school graduation in person, most likely in the luxury of their own living room. Many of us rediscovered nature and came to viscerally understand why a hug or a handshake is different from an elbow bump or air hug. But the biggest pause was found in the gravity of the questions we were asking ourselves.

Take a moment to reflect…where were *you* in 2020 BC (Before COVID)? What questions were you asking yourself after it came into your life? Perhaps they sounded something like these:

- What are the things most important to me, and why do I do anything but focus on them?
- Am I living an authentic life that's true to myself and not what others expect of me?
- How do I know if I'm spending the minutes of my day meaningfully?

Or maybe you were thinking in the stark terms that Steve Jobs used when he framed it so well. In his famous 2005 commencement speech at Stanford University, Jobs said that he looked in the mirror every morning and asked himself, "If today were the last day of my life, would I want to do what I'm about to do today?"[1]

People were dying, and life-and-death questions entered most of our minds in some form or another. Being in lockdown or sheltering in place gave us ample time to consider what clarity could mean amid chaos. And it became clearer to a lot of people what was worth expending energy on and what should be tossed in the bullshit bin.

SURPRISE...IT WAS COMING ALL ALONG

Some people were shocked at the state of the world that was laid bare by COVID, doubting they even knew what reality was anymore, but others had predicted that a set of massive changes was coming. They might not have guessed that the enormity of it all would be crammed into an extraordinary year, but they knew something was imminent. Futurists like Vernor Vinge had predicted it decades before. In his 1993 article "The Coming Technological Singularity," he wrote about how the world was changing faster than ever: "We are on the edge of change comparable to the rise of human life on Earth."[2] Unsurprisingly, futurists were already making projections about what this new internet thing would do, how limited the resources on our planet actually were, and how our globally changing demographics would affect us all.

The World Economic Forum calls the period we're living in the Fourth Industrial Revolution.[3] We've seen an evolution of the Industrial Age roughly every hundred years—from mechanization and steam power in the 1800s to mass-production assembly lines in the early 1900s to automation and computers in the late 1990s, which led to the Internet of Everything and distributed networks today. The only difference between previous revolutions and our current one is that the change we're now seeing is *exponential*, with rates and frequencies faster than we've ever seen before. It took seventy-five years for the telephone to reach fifty million people in the world. Guess what took only nineteen days to reach the same number of people in 2016?

Pokémon Go.

Although big changes were looming, it didn't mean we had to

expect doom and gloom. Peter H. Diamandis, another futurist and author of *Abundance: The Future Is Better than You Think*, believed technology would liberate us in such a way that resources could go from scarce to abundant, and that abundance wouldn't just provide the world with lives of luxury, but with lives of possibility instead.[4]

By "possibility," these futurists weren't just referring to coming up with solutions to poverty and climate change to help a billion people at a time; they were also thinking about those existential questions that I mentioned before. Whether it's in our scientific journals or the latest sci-fi stories, there's a growing belief that there will come a time when AI will allow our consciousnesses to live on even after our bodies quit. If you're into the hypothesis as well, just don't forget to upgrade your iCloud and Google storage accounts to the Eternity Package before it's too late.

But to get to that point of possibility, do humans need to evolve exponentially too? Most would say that in itself is impossible. The human race has been evolving at a pretty steady rate since we appeared on this Earth; it just doesn't make logical sense that we would wake up one morning and start evolving as quickly as technology is developing.

The documentary (or, some might argue, very realistic horror movie) *The Social Dilemma* shows what our physiological inability to evolve as quickly as technology means for our daily lives today. What *The Social Dilemma* reminds us is that we're not getting anything for free and that what we're paying is much more important and valuable than money—it's data about us, our kids, and even our pets that is feeding into something that's beyond our control. At the same time, technology lets us reconnect with friends, meet the love of our life, or express ourselves. The dilemmas we face of weighing these risks are real and with us every day.

So if technology is outpacing us, what is left for us to do? Whether at home or at work, we have little choice other than to double down on the things that computers might not ever be able to do.

Things like be empathetic. Exercise creativity. Act with a sense of ethics, inclusion, and equity. Keep solving problems through a lens of humanity as situations get more unpredictable and unknown. Feel happiness and sadness and every emotion we can possibly experience, knowing they will pass. As humans, let's do what humans do best. Be human.

By now, we expect that AI and automation will continue to disrupt the way we live and work forever. The prospect is a little terrifying given how movies have planted the seeds of the idea that it's just a matter of time until the role of who's boss flips. Instead of Alexa and Siri responding in their singsongy voices it'll be HAL 9000 from *2001: A Space Odyssey* with the persona of Hannibal Lecter saying, "I'm sorry, I'm afraid I can't do that for you right now. I'm virtually having an old friend for dinner." While it may seem like tech is slowly overtaking our lives, the more automated we get, the more we should be reminded that we have a choice as to what we believe in and pray to—perhaps it's nature, some form of spirituality so we can better understand this world and what might come after, or the inner voice that speaks to us from within. Or, more likely, a combination of them all.

Sometimes we forget that the driving forces behind AI and automation are *also people*. People who want to feel love, be loved, and might show up as the villains in the next movie sensationalizing the notion of AI taking over the world. But if we do what we've been doing so far—staying smart with empathy, intentionality, and vigilant ethics as the world progresses—we won't have to worry so much about Alexa, Siri, or being at the beck and call of HAL.

Even though it's daunting to keep up with the unpredictable, exponential change around us (things we can't control), it just highlights that it's never been more important to control what's *within us*—our beliefs, purpose, values, and ability to adapt.

We're Living in the Adaptive Age

They say optimism is knowing life is uncertain.

With the uncertainty we've experienced in the world, our level of optimism should be at the highest it's ever been. But, of course, our realities paint a different picture.

Accepting that life is uncertain might be the hardest thing to do, even though it would be the wisest. People can spend their lifetimes trying to find peace with every unplanned event that happens to them—divorce, illness, losing loved ones—but never actually get there. And with the world changing at exponential rates around us, we can expect the level of VUCA (volatility, uncertainty, complexity, ambiguity) to keep rising too.

It's almost impossible to ignore how things seem to get more unstable with every sound bite we hear on the news and social media. Everyone wanted to believe the end of an unrelenting year would make all the unimaginable events in the world go away. But days into 2021, watching a mob raid sacred ground at the US Capitol made the world's jaw drop and reminded us the turn of a calendar year has nothing to do with what might come next.

We're still jarred by brands that we thought would be permanent fixtures in our lives disappearing or filing for bankruptcy: JCPenney,[5] Cirque du Soleil, 24 Hour Fitness, and Sizzler (sorry, Dad, I'll miss our memories of cheese toast too), just to name a few.

Then there's the most heartbreaking news: news of friends and relatives becoming ill or losing their jobs and businesses, or, worst, losing their lives. As I write this, over half a million people have died from COVID in the US alone (about the number of US soldiers who died in World War II, the Korean War, and the Vietnam War combined), and over two million have died worldwide (about equal to the population of Slovenia). Our communities look and feel different—we can't walk into our favorite local restaurants and watering holes, knowing someone will know our name. Over one hundred thousand US small businesses had to shut down permanently just in the first six months of the pandemic. This is especially upsetting if you know that small businesses make up 44 percent of the US economy, create two-thirds of our country's jobs, drive innovation to keep big corporations on their toes, and keep competition alive and kicking. It hurts that the biggest blows are hitting the passionate people who are trying to make a living and taking the risks to dream.

All the predictions about the future of work—the rise of remote working, automation and AI "taking over" and displacing hundreds of millions of jobs (aka people) in the global workforce—aren't so much of a speculation anymore. The reset button accelerated the future to show up at our doorstep now.

With the rise of VUCA, it's no wonder we also saw the rise of FUD—fear, uncertainty, and doubt—in the forms of stress and anxiety, depression, suicide, and addiction. And it's inevitable that what's happening in our lives gets brought into our workplaces.

FUD takes us below our line of psychological safety and stability. We feel overwhelmed and exhausted, struggling to get through our days. FUD is at its worst in work environments that lack trust, don't allow open and honest communication, and don't foster the freedom we need to do our jobs. It makes us insecure, less resilient, and less productive as it increases and we feel our energy and happiness spiral down. It's a dreadful feeling. You begin to wonder why someone else got a higher bonus than you. You begin to hear murmurs about another round of layoffs, but it's a guessing game as to who's going next. You wake up every day wondering why you should even bother going to work if it wasn't the need to pay the bills.

With so many uncontrollable events, how can anyone plan for the future of their career with confidence? How can we even start thinking about designing a dream job and loving the work we do when it might be gone the next day? Where do we go to find answers to questions in an increasingly unpredictable world?

As with most challenging questions, the answer is usually the simplest one. We don't turn to anyone else because the answer is within ourselves. And although that might sound far-fetched for a business book—or remind you too much of a Mariah Carey song about being your own hero—I'll share in Part II exactly why it makes so much sense and how to begin that journey. For now, the most important things to do when all looks grim and bleak in the world are these:

> *Control and change what we can. Embrace and*
> *adapt to what we can't.*

That's why I say that businesses are operating in what I call the Adaptive Age.

ADAPTIVE ORIGINS

The notion of the Adaptive Age is in many ways inspired by Charles Darwin. His work is often boiled down to the statement "It is not the strongest species that survive, nor the most intelligent, but the ones most responsive to change." As someone who gets inspired by how much we can learn from nature, I wondered how we might apply the concept of adaptiveness so that orgs and (more important) the people within them are more resilient—to the degree that they're not just more likely to survive the times but able to find ways to thrive too.

Ten thousand years ago, Mother Nature decided to give us humans a little breather by changing our world's weather patterns to be more consistent and predictable. Without the need to keep roaming the land to hunt and gather, we were able to plant seeds and become farmers in the agrarian age. Fast-forward thousands of years, and with the advent of steam and coal, capitalists employed us to start working in the Industrial Age. Then, with the birth of the microchip, the computer, and the interwebs, we moved our livelihoods into the technological age, and eventually the Information Age.

Agrarian Age ➡ Industrial Age ➡ Technological/Information Age ➡ ADAPTIVE AGE

Which brings us to where we are today—the Adaptive Age.

In the previous section, I mentioned that the World Economic Forum calls our current era the Fourth Industrial Revolution. But to me that's looking at it from an economic point of view. Observing ourselves as cogs in the global economic machine doesn't really answer those existential questions that seem to get louder in our heads every day. "Am I spending my hours at work with meaning and purpose? Or am I just listening to the chatter in my mind telling me what's expected of me so I can get by?"

One of the things I've learned over these last decades of working with orgs around the world is that the clichés of humankind are true. We all generally want the same basic things—to be our best selves living our best lives, be with the people we love, make a contribution to the world to help others, and go *beyond* happiness by being true to our *whole* selves.

Even in the darkest days of the divisiveness we've seen over the last several years, I held faith for brighter ones because I've seen the other side. Beyond all the differences we have in geography, society, and culture, I've seen the beauty of what's shared in the core of people. Our will to do what's right. Not just for ourselves but for others too. I've witnessed what it means to have humanity and humility at work. Of course, every person, company, and country has its nuances, but they're like different types of pudding—vanilla, tapioca, pandan, Yorkshire, malva, kheer, [insert your favorite international pudding here]. The basic ingredients are pretty much the same.

Research has shown there is universality in the things that mean the most to us. The nonshocking truth is that what matters most isn't the fleeting, "rock star" highs of happiness like getting the most likes you've ever had on Instagram, bingeing on another series on Netflix, or getting a fat bonus to afford a new adult toy (feel free to interpret that however you'd like). Those dopamine rushes are fun and may seem like the most important thing in that moment, but unfortunately, they don't last. It's the oxytocin and serotonin surges of what moves us *intrinsically* (purpose, values, love, well-being, and belonging) that we deem more important than what motivates us *extrinsically* (praise, fame, and money).

If it doesn't seem that these basic, universal needs are easy to obtain, it's because they're not. The external forces of greed, power, and inequities will always stand guard to keep us from getting them.

But if we see this as the Adaptive Age, we begin to own the answers within ourselves. By being present and observing instead of assuming. By using our analytical thoughts and grounded instincts instead of turbulent emotions to guide our decisions. By being aware of our heads and hearts—the mindset and feelings showing up within us. Then by asking ourselves, "Which of these things are within my control and which are outside of it?" By only focusing on the things that can be affected by our actions, by changing what we can and letting go of what we can't, we're actively adapting.

Being adaptive is easier said than done, of course. It isn't always intuitive; at times it can be uncomfortable if not downright terrifying.

We have a tendency to try to fix things when we're not even sure what needs to be fixed. To be emotionally reactive to situations beyond our control. Or to cling to the past and resist change, hoping we can hit rewind to the "good ol' days."

But in an Adaptive Age, we must accept that uncontrollable factors like AI, natural disasters, and global recessions will continue. However, their impact can only go so far if we reframe and develop our own form of AI—adaptive intelligence. It's an alternative kind of AI based on fortifying what's within our control and most meaningful to us (our beliefs and values) while getting over the fear of failure and experimentation. It involves setting aside pride by doing what others (or even you) might consider "beneath" you and adopting a beginner's mindset, turning your attention to all there is still to learn. With this form of AI we become more resilient and assured that—with determination and a dash of luck—we'll get through the lows to reach a new high.

Adaptiveness and Humanity at Work

While most others were bleeding money or shutting down during the pandemic, companies like Amazon, Netflix, Domino's, and Ace Hardware were poster children for companies that could adapt. Of course, having billions in the bank helped their pivots, but they still deserve kudos—large companies making moves isn't too different from big sumo wrestlers outmaneuvering the smaller ones.

There were also entrepreneurs and smaller enterprises that hit reset on their businesses, reimagined, and adapted. Denmark's Michelin-starred restaurant Noma flipped its model to make burgers instead. The Talent Shack, a theater school in Wales, turned to TikTok to put its classes online; producers in Hollywood and on Broadway started contacting it for advice. Namevents in LA went from producing fashion shows and fundraisers for groups of ten thousand to putting on yoga retreats for eight women at a time, an activity inspired by the owner's side passion, which she adapted for a stripped-down livelihood until the pandemic passed.

On the level of individuals within companies, I've been inspired time and time again by how resilient and adaptive we humans can be. A few years ago, Turkey experienced a series of terrorist bombings, a coup attempt, and an economic recession…all in one year. VUCA was at an all-time high when Murat Özcan, the VP of Canpa (a construction materials company) decided to control what he could and adapt to what he couldn't. Sales were plunging, turnover was high, and beyond the need to conduct layoffs, close offices, and eliminate departments, leadership wasn't even sure if the thirty-year-old company was going to survive.

On top of it all, it was a family-owned business, and even he didn't want to show up to work anymore. So he sneaked out to San Francisco to attend DH's master class on culture. He wasn't sneaking around because of the government; it was because his leadership team would dismiss a program on happiness as a waste of time during a period of civil unrest and financial crisis. But he had to do something—not just for Canpa but for himself too.

Eight months later, I opened my inbox to find the longest email I'd ever received in my life. It was from Murat, detailing every project he'd launched and all the positive outcomes he'd seen at a time of extreme FUD in his country. He said some of leadership was still skeptical, but he had enough evidence to go all in. And he continued to share Canpa's progress following that email. Its turnover dropped from 30 percent to a negative percentage because employees actually returned to the company after seeing its new priority on people. He saw a seven-fold increase in revenue and, even more impressively, streamlined operational costs and improved margins to increase profits fourfold. The cherry on top was another email I received a couple of years later: Murat was beaming with pride because the organization Great Place to Work awarded Canpa first place in its category, sharing the ranks with larger, big-brand companies like eBay, Vodafone, and Hilton.

Needless to say, the rest of his leadership team is now 100 percent on board with prioritizing happiness and culture.

So why do some companies adapt and thrive more than others? Even when the external factors of instability and chaos swirl around them, the companies most successful *and respected* for adaptiveness are those that choose to double down on their people.

When life gives us lemons, companies in survival mode just pass out the lemons until they run out. If they're thinking slightly longer term, they'll build a lemonade stand. But if they're adapting and thriving, they'll use the seeds to plant more lemon trees so everyone can have a stand of their own. Even in the hardest times of FUD, leaders don't just think about what's at stake for the execs or shareholders, they think about every stakeholder in the ecosystem.

In April 2020 Brian Chesky, CEO of Airbnb, wrote a heartfelt letter to his teams, telling them that the company had finally come to a point where it had to lay people off. What impressed me most about the letter was that it not only felt earnest and transparent, it also addressed everyone's FUD. To people who were being cut, he said that it wasn't their fault, they were still highly skilled and appreciated for all they'd done. And he identified the resources Airbnb was providing to help them find their next jobs. For those who were staying, he shared specifics about what the company was going to do to adapt while FUD and VUCA were still running around.

Following that letter, Airbnb was one of the most effective companies at adapting and bouncing back even while COVID infections were still on the rise. Its sales were unaffected between 2019 and 2020, a remarkable feat for a company in the hospitality industry (as opposed to well-known hotel chains, which dropped well below their 2019 sales). Going from the brink of extinction to a $106 billion dollar valuation isn't bad for one of the worst financial years since World War II.

At Gravity Payments, a financial services company, revenues dropped by 55 percent when COVID hit. It was on a trajectory to be out of business within four to five months. Decisions had to be made. Fortunately, CEO Dan Price had already set a precedent for making big moves a few years before.

You may remember what Dan did, because he made headlines in publications like *Forbes* and *Inc.* after announcing a $70,000 minimum wage for everyone at the company.[6] It caused all forms of reactions. Some cried tears of joy because it was about time people got paid fairly. Others, including some who worked at the company, protested because the raise wasn't merit based. It was a question of why someone else's grass suddenly got greener even though they didn't do anything different. It was a bold move on Dan's part to restructure the financials, take a pay cut, and show his commitment to prioritizing people.

The risk paid off, with revenue and profit doubling just six months after the announcement in 2015. In the end, only two employees quit, which meant Gravity Payments had an increase in its retention rates, from 91 percent to 95 percent. According to Dan, the outcome didn't mean people are purely motivated by pay: "In reality, removing money as a stressor let them bring their full selves to work. CEOs don't need an extra million. Low-pay workers need to be lifted up." The team surprised Dan with the gift of a Tesla in gratitude. He ultimately made less money personally, but between his employees' taste in gift giving and the benefits to the company, it wasn't too bad a trade.

Five years later, Gravity Payments's revenue dropped by over 50 percent amid the pandemic, and Dan was faced with a different dilemma: raise prices, lay people off, or both. Just before he was going to make the decision on his own, he decided to share his predicament with the whole company. By the end of that all-hands meeting, 98 percent of employees volunteered to temporarily cut their pay by between 5 and 100 percent. "Instead of looking at our employees as expenses, we acknowledged their humanity and the vital role they play in our business," Dan explained.

As a result, people were more productive than ever. Sales went up 31 percent from the year prior, despite no increase in head count and an unknown economic environment, and everyone's salary was restored to 100 percent. Dan's belief in prioritizing people was reinforced yet again: "CEOs don't get you out of a crisis. Employees do. Trust them."

Companies that have invested significant time, money, and resources to build a solid company culture—including our DH clients—were equally challenged to adapt. In times of VUCA, culture-minded leaders can't help but ask the hard, honest question of whether they're still able to prioritize people. It's difficult to make that choice because there's no culture to think about if the company can't weather the instability and ceases to exist.

Still, as hard as it was, it was those companies that prioritized people that were able to adapt (and recover) more quickly (and sustainably) than those that didn't. DMG, a real estate and construction client in Egypt, decided to forego revenue opportunities when it needed them because it wanted to take care of its people first. It immediately ordered all construction to stop until there was more information as to what the safety protocols should be. Rasha El Gama, the CPO (chief people officer) was grateful that her leadership team walked the talk with its decision. Their motto had been "Keep our people safe." DMG was able to avoid layoffs after the company agreed to take cuts across the board so it could keep the team together until people felt safe and projects resumed again. Later in the year, it became one of the fastest-growing companies in the industry.

Vietnam was one of the first countries to go into lockdown, and our client/partner I Can Read, a chain of language schools, quickly responded by committing to timely and transparent communication as things felt like they were changing by the day. When the company reluctantly announced that it had to close its doors for an unknown time, Executive Director Ha Van Phan emailed me afterward: "[It's early, so we don't] know where exactly everyone is at emotionally, but we're happy and ready to deal with whatever comes." While the pandemic was still raging around a year later, I Can Read was able to keep all of its centers open (while similar institutions were closing) and launched DH Vietnam, a new joint venture to help other businesses instill a culture of happiness too.

Companies had to think long and hard about if (and how) they were going to prioritize people in times of crisis. I don't think they would be well-balanced, well-led companies if they didn't. But by taking the extra time to truly consider people an asset (instead of an expense) *and treat them with humanity* in times of VUCA, they were able to bounce back and rebuild quicker with their culture intact than they would've otherwise.

Behind Every Brand, People Are Adapting

When we read all these stories about companies, sometimes we forget that the headlines come from people—individuals and teams feeling emotions and making decisions. I hope bringing in the story of one of the most ubiquitous brands in the world will help illustrate how much is going on behind the scenes in people's lives when you take your next sip of coffee.

Most of us know what Starbucks is all about thanks to Howard Schultz—a visionary who repurposed the passion of Italian café culture into a convenient, affordable American luxury that got habituated into our everyday lives. Starbucks regularly lands on various "best companies to work for" lists and is understandably proud about its longtime mission statement: "To inspire and nurture the human spirit—one person, one cup and one neighborhood at a time."

Starbucks was a pioneer in putting its people first—it has given full benefits to eligible employees (whom it calls partners) regardless of part-time or full-time status since 1988,[7] as well as providing programs to give partners more access to higher education and to support veterans. But as it goes with every company, even the most purpose-driven ones, Starbucks has had its fair share of challenges too. When

Schultz announced his departure from his CEO role in 2017, investors wondered how big a void would be left and whether his experience and knowledge could be replaced.[8] Not too long afterward, in 2018, the arrests of two Black men in one of the downtown Philadelphia stores ignited a #BoycottStarbucks hashtag on Twitter, raised questions about the company's training in racial bias and discrimination, and elicited an official statement by Schultz's successive CEO, Kevin Johnson: "You can and should expect more from us. We will learn from this and be better."[9] That same year, Starbucks dropped to its lowest consumer-perception level since November 2015.[10]

Even with all of these challenges, Starbucks was being lauded by analysts and the market, as evidenced by its stock price spiking in 2019 just months before the pandemic hit.[11] The business was such a contrast to most clients we work with. Most companies bring us on to help them examine their DNA and origins to articulate a purpose that can inspire people to show up and stay on as loyal customers and employees. Starbucks, on the other hand, was in the enviable position of being a world-renowned mission-driven company already.

Before COVID hit, we were just about to kick off an aspirational project: to be archaeologists of Starbucks's admirable fifty-year existence and envision an enduring brand for the future. With a new leadership team evolving, it was time to hear what the Starbucks siren was now singing. Starbucks was going to depart from the model of a sole visionary to the vision of many. Starbucks was going to deep dive into researching the future trends of cities, community, coffee, retail, well-being, purpose, and work. To rapidly prototype new ways to engage with its customers and partners from a people-centered design point of view. We were about to support and help define a vision for Starbucks. It was a giant undertaking, but we were ready to tackle it—until, of course, the pandemic punched us all in the mouth.

During 2020 all companies were put to the test in an unprecedented situation. A globally recognized brand with four hundred thousand "green apron" partners* and thirty-two thousand physical locations worldwide, Starbucks was thrown into instability and confusion as a virus infected the world. Like so many other companies, it entered a mode of triage, scrambling to figure out which fire was biggest, knowing the answer might change the next second. Companies such as Uber, Hilton, Southwest, Ford, and Disney were announcing layoffs and furloughs.[12] So many companies were downsizing that it was hard to distinguish if I was reading the news or watching a reality show of companies fighting to survive another day.

The world's FUD factor was reaching an all-time high, people and revenues were in major distress, and no one was sure what the next day would bring. At Starbucks, revenue was at a loss of $3.2 billion in the first quarter that the pandemic hit,[13] and some store partners openly worried that their health would be at risk if they had no choice but to return to work.[14] Amid a time of extreme uncertainty, CEO Kevin Johnson and Starbucks did what some might think was unexpected. Instead of prioritizing the salvage of profits first, they doubled down on their mission and values.

They announced that they were going to prioritize the health and well-being of all their partners and customers, support health and government officials to mitigate the spread of the virus, and show up in a positive way to serve their communities.[15] They adapted by learning from what their stores in China (where COVID was first identified) successfully did to safely reopen. At the height of the pandemic, Johnson showed he was listening to partners' concerns by committing to pay workers even when they were closing stores down.[16]

I did a double take.

Doubling down on mission and values meant he was prioritizing purpose instead of the bottom line. In effect, he understood the greater

---

* "Green apron" partners include employees who work in stores that are licensed by Starbucks; e.g., a Starbucks-licensed store is one you'd see in a supermarket, grocery store, or airport.

ripple of impact that Starbucks could actually have—where purpose-led, profitable companies could make an even bigger ripple for people and the planet. The revelation led him to announce, "It's time to build a company that gives back more than it takes," at the hardest possible time to do it.

There was a new abnormal coming out of COVID, and the race was on for every company: adapt or die. Starbucks rallied in a way that you would never imagine such a large corporation could do. Politics and tenure are expected barriers to getting shit done in any company, especially a behemoth with a $125 billion market cap in 2020. But Starbucks realized the gravity of how its stakeholders could be impacted by a global pandemic and economic crisis. It took instant action to address the triage and help steer how Starbucks should respond.

It's important to remember that all big decisions, both good and bad, you read about in the headlines come from a singular source... people. Sometimes people are doing their best to live their most authentic, purposeful ME (self), aligned with WE (teams and their company), and greater COMMUNITY (customers, partners, and everyone in a company's ecosystem). Sometimes people are at the opposite end of that.

There are also times these decisions are made in the best of circumstances, but oftentimes they're suboptimal. It's been said that the worst of times reveal the true character of a person. I believe that to be true of companies as well.

Someone who was living their authentic ME was COO Rosalind (Roz) Brewer. She made everyone in the room feel as if they belonged. She was the kind of person who asked if anyone would like a pastry before jumping into the meeting's agenda—making space for a moment of graciousness to let everyone know humanity had a seat at the table. Her belief was in the servant-leadership style of getting good people together and then getting out of their way so they could be their best and just do their thing. As risky as that proposition could be at times, she was grounded in that. In her belief in people.

Roz had already taken a risk on Danny Brooks.[†] He was a chef at Michelin-star restaurants and a consultant on human-centered design from IDEO, and he came on board at Starbucks to help redesign their culinary menu. The scope was specific, but when he started digging around to understand the strategy and source of where the menu should come from, the archaeologist in him came up empty-handed. Things weren't making sense, so he decided to take on the hard questions that everyone seemed to be asking and see how he could contribute. Danny was eventually asked to help the company collectively articulate what the brand stands for—i.e., in a post-Schultz Starbucks, what's the real DNA of the company and what does the brand stand for now?

Danny was born to invert the status quo. That kind of bravado only goes so far in typical corporate culture and he was aware of the risks; even with a Teflon sense of personal ambition, he had his share of self-doubt. But Roz believed in him, which helped his belief in himself too. She got out of his way so he could do his thing.

He started "his thing" by bringing together the dream team he needed to make it happen. I'm not sure he even knew what "it" was entirely, but he knew he'd need people to get there. Serendipitously he met Annie Richmond, at the time a manager in corporate strategy. Danny was instantly Annie's "brother from another mother," and they finished each other's thoughts without even speaking them out loud. At that point, they also brought other passionately experienced people on board (which was when DH joined the team). Their mind meld motivated us to trust that the team they were building was something special, even though we had little idea of what the outcome was going to be.

Danny and Annie were curious to see what magic they could make from a human-centered point of view. In a miraculously short couple

---

† It's worthwhile to share that Danny Brooks and Annie Richmond (to be introduced) are no longer Starbucks partners as of April 2021. More will be shared later as to why!

of years, our team helped the company codify their founders' intuition into a singular brand promise (to *Uplift the Everyday*) that scaled and unified the company globally. The team redesigned strategy and systematized new ways of working through a people-centered process by helping other teams understand their roles in the company's bigger picture and articulate their purpose and behaviors. Our team had a direct hand in helping the company improve working conditions like pay, housing/transportation security, and mental health benefits for their partners.

But when the pandemic hit the fan, the stakes literally became life and death. With stark rawness, Danny reframed the question for all of us: "It's in times of crisis when you see [what a company stands for]. What are you—what are *we*—going to cling to? Which boat are we going to cling to? The money boat? The people boat? The purpose boat?"

This wasn't a question just for Starbucks but for every company in the world. Were they going to choose profitability or people...society or politics...technology or the human hands that were surviving, trying to adapt, and hoping to thrive? We'll take that deep dive in Part III.

I've introduced Kevin, Roz, Danny, and Annie because companies are basically people making choices. What so many of us forget is that the reason some companies succeed and others fail starts at the cellular level of what makes up these orgs—the most basic unit of them all—YOU. Whether you're someone who works on the front line, a manager, a CEO, a founder, an investor, and/or on the board, it's only fair to ask *why* you are doing what you do.

And what did the reset button on humanity mean for you?

Throughout the years, DH has been testing and refining its models of systemizing happiness in the workplace. From Starbucks to Sallie Mae and Northwell Health to the government of Dubai, we've seen how these models work. And by that, I mean work for *all* levels—individuals, teams, and companies. You'll see how your personal contributions ripple out to your communities, and, when you do it right, you'll see your impact on society and our planet too.

The idea of loving our work and nudging the world to a better place is no longer a utopian concept. It's a path that works when we dare to ask questions, test if they're true, learn, and repeat the cycle all over again. The process isn't too different from the one in the science classes we took in school. When I was in twelfth grade, I gained so much knowledge by applying the scientific method with my cadaver cat, Mandu (see what I did there?). The only difference is that we're applying the scientific method of hypothesizing, experimenting, and analyzing to business, work, and our lives.

Now that you've heard several stories of what adaptiveness and humanity at work can look like, let's take the next step and see how they might apply to you and your workplace.

Futureproof Your Work/Life

Hearing your alarm go off in the morning and feeling you can't wait to get to work may seem like a fantasy for most, but we've seen these modern miracles happen within people and workplaces all the time. It comes down to implicitly knowing that no matter what happens, we'll spend the rest of the day with a sense of purpose, doing something greater than ourselves, while being authentically true to ourselves too.

Taking that a step further, imagine if you were able to do that with confidence that no matter what happens in your external world, your internal world is grounded in a way that the unknowns of the future won't shake. Because we recognize we're living in an Adaptive Age and want to minimize the shock and stress of an unpredictable future, the most important thing to continuously work on is futureproofing ourselves—making sure that we stay relevant and do not become obsolete. Learning new skills so that we're always growing and developing is important, but that's just a part of the bigger equation.

As James Key Lim, founder of exec coaching company FUTURE-PROOFx and one of the original members of DH (and my brother from the same mother ☺) puts it: our world is evolving into "a global community of people living better lives because they know how to futureproof themselves and their business."

FUTUREPROOFING BUSINESS

Even though VUCA has accelerated the arrival of the future of work, it turns out that's not so bad. Now that there's more data and evidence (instead of speculation) of what the future will bring, we know the use of automation and AI will only keep advancing, we see the pros and cons of remote teams working at scale, and we can note how institutions are more aware of the value of human capital. The value of people.

The software review company TechJury reports, "By 2025, the global AI market is expected to be almost $60 billion. Already 77% of the devices we use feature one form of AI or another."[17] The World Economic Forum states that "the time spent on current tasks at work by humans and machines will be equal" by 2025 too.[18] And in a pretty historic move, The US Securities and Exchange Commission (aka the SEC) just made new rules requiring companies to include descriptions of their measures in three areas, "attraction, development, and retention of personnel,"[19] so there can be more transparency in human capital.

Every day we're learning more about the future of work and what it means for the relationship between humans and automation. Here's a little cheat sheet of the top ten "how might we" questions rooted in a positive approach to people and systems change. They're things to keep in mind and be curious about as we learn how to be adaptive in the future of work… with purpose, profits, and people prioritized.

How might we…

1. Answer "What's in it for me?" and "What's in it for all?"
2. Make more profits to have a more purposeful impact?
3. Evolve transactional relationships into meaningful ones by creating triple wins (benefiting yourself, others, and the community at large all at the same time)?
4. Inspire and align people with Purpose + Values?
5. Treat people as assets, not expenses?

6. Strategize for long-term (not just short-term) gain?
7. Measure what matters to all, not just the few?
8. Honor people as individuals within a system that rewards collaboration?
9. Reward and recognize every stakeholder, not just the shareholders?
10. Stop focusing on doing things right for efficiency and focus on doing the right things for people?

FUTUREPROOFING OURSELVES

To futureproof ourselves as individuals, we need to see ourselves constantly learning and growing toward our most authentic selves. We need to figure out how to meet our basic physiological needs, feel a sense of safety, love, and belonging, and live our higher purpose. Futureproofing is about understanding the gamut of what's possible, and then, with self-awareness, working to fill our needs—physically, mentally, financially, and spiritually—no matter what job we might currently have.

If you think this sounds like Maslow's hierarchy of human needs,[20] you're spot-on.

In the book *Delivering Happiness*, Tony shared Maslow's hierarchy of human needs because he believed that once people's basic survival needs are met, they're more motivated by nonmaterialistic needs like achievement, creativity, and relationships. It was a nod to how important psychology is in building successful businesses with people (and happiness) prioritized. It was a smart basis to grow businesses but the world keeps shifting.

Since Maslow published his theory on the hierarchy of human needs in 1954 there's been a lot of conversation, and sometimes controversy, around it. It's impressive that it still holds up after all this time, but a lot has changed since then too. For it to stay relevant in today's world, some concepts have to evolve.

MASLOW'S HIERARCHY: ORIGINAL

So let's revisit Maslow's theory with the current state of humanity, and how DH has expanded our model, in mind:

- **Change from bidirectional to unidirectional**—Maslow's original idea was that the pyramid is a ladder that needs to be climbed to the peak of self-actualization, but it's really more of a spectrum. People who don't have everything at a given level of the pyramid (like job security) can be more self-actualized than someone who has all their needs met. Our existence is more complex than a hierarchy.

- **Expanded levels of love/belonging**—A sense of belonging is not just about our immediate relationships to friends, family, coworkers, and groups of affiliation anymore. Now that we're hyperconnected with technology, that sense includes a bigger scope of diversity, equity, inclusion, and belonging (DEIB) that applies to every interaction within the global society at large (something we'll do a deep dive on when we come to Part V).

- **Expanded levels of self-actualization**—Self-actualization is still about seeking fulfillment and change through personal growth.

MASLOW'S HIERARCHY: EVOLVED

Seeking our full potential hasn't changed; it's *how* we see that potential that has evolved. Rather than just doing all that we're capable of and achieving what Maslow called the "peak" experiences of joy and euphoria, self-actualization in the forms of fulfillment and authenticity can come from understanding our valleys (i.e., lows and shadow sides) too.

- **New addition of transcendence**—This was an addition made by Maslow himself in the years before his death in 1970; it means people are motivated by values not just for personal benefit but by experiences with nature, spirituality, and the selflessness of helping others self-actualize too. I'll expand on this when I talk about the greenhouse model and how we all have an ability to make a ripple of impact by helping others build their greenhouses.

- **New addition of Wi-Fi and the internet**—If he were still alive to update the model, I'm sure Maslow would add these as the basis of all human needs (wink).

Understanding the ways in which Maslow's hierarchy has evolved helps us envision what it means to futureproof our own lives. Even during times of high VUCA, we know that the things we can do toward self-actualization, purpose, and fulfillment are intrinsically within us. Even if we don't have every level of Maslow's pyramid completely checked off, we can still be fulfilled in what we do for work and how we live our lives. On the flip side, even if we have most of the levels checked off, we're not automatically self-actualized. In both scenarios, it still takes work to truly be our authentic selves.

Futureproofing our businesses and individual work/life may seem complex, but the greenhouse model I'll be sharing was designed to simplify it. With all the noise in our busy lives and shrinking attention spans, who has time to ponder existential questions every day if their first name isn't Plato and their last name isn't Nietzsche? Instead of spending precious time questioning our lives, we can use the time toward living it...in the best, biggest, and most meaningful ways.

The goal is to get to a point where following the model will become as natural as drinking when we're thirsty and sleeping when we're ready for bed. Rather than asking ourselves, "Wait. Was all that time I spent on [x] worth it?" we can more easily know if it was or wasn't. We'll be more confident that our everyday actions are aligned with our purpose, and bad days won't feel as debilitating. Instead of questioning if we are where we're supposed to be—as a leader of our lives, an entrepreneur, an executive, and most importantly a human being—we'll know we're on the right path, going in the direction we've chosen for ourselves (and not the one others expect of us).

Before I get to the model that shows *how* to implement these ideas at the ME, WE and COMMUNITY levels, I want to talk about *why* the model works.

As we all know, businesses need to be fueled by profit to survive and grow. For centuries we've seen the pros and cons of capitalism, and we know they're not going to disappear overnight. On the negative side, we've seen inequalities in the widening income and wealth gap around the world and the stresses that we feel when our financial well-beings are threatened.[21] At the same time, there's a rising, more conscious form of capitalism that reframes what the ultimate goals are in making more profits. Instead of an unending vicious circle, we now see more virtuous ones in the form of what I call the double ROI.

The Double ROI

Since money is already being spent on people costs, we can look at that spending in one of two ways: as an expense or as an investment. Billions of dollars are already being invested by companies that know the future of work has already arrived. JPMorgan Chase, Accenture, Verizon, Google, and Microsoft are actively reskilling and upskilling because they're looking at people as the latter—investments for their long-term, sustainable futures.[22]

In the Adaptive Age, smart companies know people are no longer considered workers on the assembly line or cogs in the machine of capitalism. They also don't want to see them displaced by automation and AI because they know humans are *needed* for businesses to adapt and grow. Long-term thinkers like Microsoft CEO Satya Nadella and Zoom Video Communications CEO Eric Yuan realize how important taking care of their people is for the sustainability of their businesses, the strength of their companies' culture, and the impact they can scale to the world.

Something that should go without saying—but unfortunately still needs to be said—is that workers are also people with hopes and dreams, parents and loved ones, and desires for full and purposeful lives. People just like you and everyone else on this planet.

What this means is that in the Adaptive Age, we can scale meaningful impact by *measuring what matters to all, not just the few.*

The risk of not doing this shows up in social unrest, a widening economic divide, and the disproportionate devastation a pandemic and climate change have on the poor, the elderly, and people of color. The rich get richer and the poorer get more reasons to resent them. The impact of the growing socioeconomic divide applies whether people are conservatives or liberals, as we saw in the storming of the US Capitol in 2021, Black Lives Matter protests in 2020, and the #MeToo movement in 2017. *In its simplest form, people don't like the feeling when they're not heard, understood, or treated fairly.*

But businesses can play a major role in social change by measuring beyond traditional financial metrics. They can take into account how prioritizing people holistically ends up creating more sustainable and profitable businesses while also contributing to a more equitable society and more meaningful, purposeful lives for their employees.

THE TRADITIONAL ROI: RETURN ON INVESTMENT

One of the most rewarding things we've witnessed is how companies are realizing that culture- and people-focused strategies are necessary if they are to adapt to thrive in the future of work. From a numbers point of view, the past several years of data continue to speak for themselves. As researched by Jacob Morgan in *The Employee Experience Advantage* (Wiley, 2017), companies that invested in employee experience "led not only to happier employees but also to larger talent pipelines and greater profitability and productivity." Companies that land on *Fortune* and Glassdoor's lists of best places to work continue to consistently outperform the S&P 500 and NASDAQ.[23, 24] When comparing the difference between the companies that invest in people for the long term, every dollar has shown at least a twofold return in stock price as a result.[25]

We've seen growth in investment funds as well. The founder of Parnassus Investments, Jerome Dodson, was inspired by the idea of "creating a fund that only invested in organizations where employees were really happy." Since it was launched in 2009, the Parnassus Endeavor

STOCK PRICE: Based on a $1,000 investment

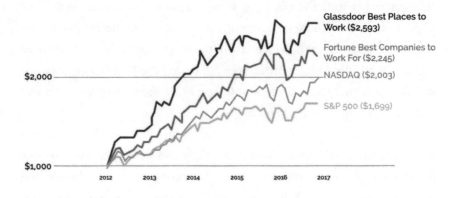

Source: The Employee Experience Advantage by Jacob Morgan (Wiley, 2017)

Fund's returns have also surpassed those of the S&P 500 (indicated by the gray in the graph), and in 2017 it was outperforming the S&P 500 by approximately 30 percent. Mark C. Crowley at *Fast Company* can't help but agree: "Workplace happiness may seem like a fuzzy concept when it comes to financial value. But as the Parnassus Workplace Fund has proven, dignity has—and creates—value."[26]

The CEO of BlackRock (Larry Fink) is the world's largest asset manager with $7.4 trillion of investments as of 2019, and he's one of the most respected investors in the world. People eagerly anticipate his annual CEO reports to hear his predictions about growth and profit. Over the last few years, he's been fine-tuning his message of corporate responsibility to include making "positive contributions to society" by looking at the impacts of climate change, and he's been underscoring that "purpose is not the sole pursuit of profits but the animating force for achieving them. Profits are in no way inconsistent with purpose—in fact, profits and purpose are inextricably linked."[27]

Harvard Business Review (HBR) has also identified purpose as a critical driver of high-growth companies, admitting it wasn't even on its radar just eight years ago. It states that most companies with an average of 30 percent annual growth in the previous five years had moved

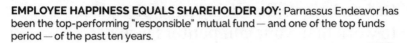

EMPLOYEE HAPPINESS EQUALS SHAREHOLDER JOY: Parnassus Endeavor has been the top-performing "responsible" mutual fund — and one of the top funds period — of the past ten years.

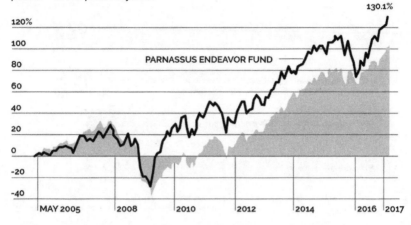

Source: Bloomberg

purpose from the periphery to the core of their strategy.[28] In 2020 data from HBR Analytical Services showed that a majority of leaders believe in prioritizing workplace happiness. An average of 95 percent believe that increased workplace happiness makes it easier to attract and retain talent; 87 percent think it gives them a significant competitive advantage. What I find most interesting in the survey is that most leaders agree employees are realistic in expecting to be happy.[29]

Whether the metric you're tracking is retention, attraction, engagement, or growth, the odds are that purpose will correlate to profits too.

From DH's own set of clients, we've seen the ROI as well:

- A 45 percent to 91 percent increase in employee engagement at Northwell Health (one of the largest healthcare systems in the US) over the past five years. After we helped launch a culture of C.A.R.E. (connectedness, awareness, respect, and empathy) across 23 hospitals, 850+ ambulatory facilities, and 75,000 employees, their success rippled out. The systemic changes that Northwell Health adapted over time has earned them a well-deserved spot on

Do you believe that being a happier place to work than your competitors would:

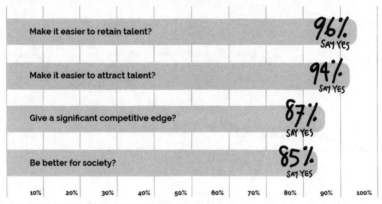

Make it easier to retain talent?   **96%** SAY YES

Make it easier to attract talent?   **94%** SAY YES

Give a significant competitive edge?   **87%** SAY YES

Be better for society?   **85%** SAY YES

10% 20% 30% 40% 50% 60% 70% 80% 90% 100%

Source: *Harvard Business Review* analytic survey. February 2020

Fortune's 100 Best Companies to Work For list for the second year, moving up the list to rank number 19 in 2021.

- A sales increase of 20 percent at BI Group, one of the largest construction companies in central Asia, which is now scaling across the world. Its NPS (Net Promoter Score) jumped by 12 percent as a result of an increase in its employee happiness

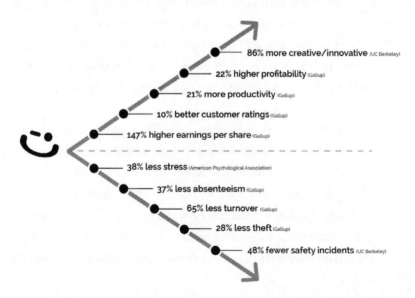

86% more creative/innovative (UC Berkeley)

22% higher profitability (Gallup)

21% more productivity (Gallup)

10% better customer ratings (Gallup)

147% higher earnings per share (Gallup)

38% less stress (American Psychological Association)

37% less absenteeism (Gallup)

65% less turnover (Gallup)

28% less theft (Gallup)

48% fewer safety incidents (UC Berkeley)

levels. Leadership attests that these increases are largely the result of the company's prioritization of culture and efforts to live up to its brand promise to its employees and customers: "We build happiness."[30, 31]

But frankly, stats can get a little dry until you read the richness in the stories of lives being changed. Throughout the rest of the book, I'll keep sharing stories of people who feel whole and fulfilled because they realized how being true to themselves was closely tied to loving their work. I hope these stats and stories—along with the greenhouse model for how it's done in the next chapter—will spawn ideas in your own life, teams, and company so that the movement of positivity *with* profitability can make everyone excited to get to work.

THE NEW ROI: RIPPLE OF IMPACT

Powers of Ten is a brilliant little nine-minute documentary made in the 1970s by Charles and Ray Eames. Even though it's been fifty years since its release, it's still an elegant piece that shows us how interconnected we really are. The film starts with a couple nonchalantly having a picnic in a park in Chicago. With every ten seconds that pass, the frame of view also expands tenfold until the gradual zoom reveals our planet, then our galaxy, then our entire universe from a hundred million light-years away.

At that point we feel like we're sitting on a rubber band that reverses direction and starts zooming back in, taking us back to the couple in the park, but this time zooming inside one of their bodies, through the skin and capillaries, all the way to the double helix of DNA and a proton.

This is what the ripple of impact is all about. From our individual DNA to our collective universe, we're all interconnected.

It's like tossing a stone in a lake knowing ripples will flow out and eventually ebb back in again. Whether we call this the butterfly effect, chaos theory, or good ol' karma, we know that this hyperconnected world means ripples are simultaneously happening all the time. The choice is ours whether we want the ripples to coexist and build bigger waves of positive impact or for them to clash in conflict, wasting everyone's energy when they zero each other out.

If it feels like you never have enough minutes in the day, the new ROI is a way to know that you're spending your precious and limited time in meaningful ways. By doing the work to know our MEs better, starting with Purpose + Values, we ripple a bigger impact to the WEs (teams and orgs) we touch, and ultimately to our COMMUNITY of customers, partners, and vendors in the ecosystem.

As Annie Richmond, previous director of Innovation + Design Strategy at Starbucks, describes it: "It's about doubling down on your own values, getting super clear on priorities, and creating a ripple effect for other teams to take a step back and say, yeah, we have five hundred ideas, but now we know better where [we can] spend our time on what's really important."

Yuka Shimada (chief human resources officer at Unilever Japan and cofounder of DH Japan) shared a similar revelation: "Everything is interconnected. We are transmitting and expressing knowledge and passion, but we really have to live it all the way through. Beginning with the ME, we expand and ripple the impact from there."

I'll never forget a personal story of seeing how the ripple works. It's still one of my favorite moments of that cross-country bus tour for *Delivering Happiness*. It was toward the end of our four-month road trip, and we decided to stop by Pueblo High School in Arizona.

When the book had launched months prior, we had received an email from one of the school's teachers, Miguel Enriquez. (His daughter Celina was and still is an employee at Zappos.) He loved the book so much, he wanted to make it required reading for his students. The issue was that the school couldn't afford a copy for everyone. We were unaware at the time, but it was one of the poorer high schools in the state. We sent them boxes of books in advance of our visit and thought we could surprise them by adding them as a stop on the tour and doing a Q and A for the class. Little did we know they were going to be the ones who surprised us.

When we hopped off the bus, there was an amazing mariachi band playing to welcome us, and the community had come together to cook one of the most delicious spreads I'd ever had. In hindsight, it was because I could hear and taste that it was all coming from their hearts. Their generosity of spirit, show of gratitude, and optimism for their future blew us all away.

A few months later I received another email from Miguel. A group of students and teachers had realized there wasn't a Spanish translation of *Delivering Happiness* yet, and to thank us for our visit, they offered to crowdsource their efforts to translate the whole book for us. They didn't want anything in return; they just wanted to say thanks for stopping by. Again, I was floored by their abundance of kindness and resourcefulness even though they had so little in funds.

Fast-forward a few more months later, a publisher in Spain emailed me to see if it could obtain the Spanish-language rights for the book. I replied that there was a caveat because the book had already been translated by the students in Arizona. After several rounds of negotiation, we finally agreed on the terms. For every Spanish-language copy of the book sold *in the world*, a percentage of the profits would go back to that school and its students in Arizona. When they offered to translate the book, Miguel and his students couldn't have guessed how much the ripples they were making would come back to them.

This was a highlight in 2010 and forever will be for DH.

A few months ago, I was crushed to hear Miguel passed away after his wife died alone in the hospital, both from complications of COVID. As their daughter Celina described it, "After he made it off the ventilator the first time and lost his 'sweetheart' of fifty-five years, he lost the will to live. At the end of the day, he died of a broken heart." Although Miguel's passing was an immense loss to his family and Pueblo High School, his ripples of impact and legacy live on. His students have been forever inspired and continue to live by their motto: "¡Sí, Se Puede!" In other words: "Yes, it can be done!"

As I share how others get to the point of making and experiencing these ripples throughout the rest of this book, it's a prime time for us to revisit what it means to have clarity in ourselves. That clarity enables us to see and feel the measurable impact we're making instead of just proclaiming and hoping we're somehow changing the world.

To actually make an impact in the world, we double down on people, starting with our MEs first. When we effectively apply the concept of the double ROI, rooted in our authentic selves, we know our personal ripple of impact will help others ripple their impact too.

Origins of the Double ROI: Happiness as a Business Model

Back in 2009, Tony and I headed to Lake Tahoe to work on the book *Delivering Happiness*. We had only five weeks until the manuscript was due, so we decided to lock ourselves up in a cabin for a week. Tony being the half man, half robot, full-on alien that he was, we had 80 percent of the book done by the end.

In hindsight, that was one of my most memorable if not magical weeks of "work" on a project. On one hand we had clarity and focus about what needed to be done. On the other we had pristine weather, a view of one of the deepest cobalt-blue lakes in the world, and huge lenticular clouds that made it feel like UFOs were waiting for us to board whenever we were done writing. We pulled a string of all-nighters, taking an occasional break to eat some of the soup Tony made in a massive pot (that strangely seemed like it never went down in volume no matter how much we ate). We experimented and came to the conclusion that coffee beans in vodka were effective for staying up all night, but not the best way to start the next morning.

Tony and I were inadvertently living out one of the psychological concepts that ended up being in the book. We were in *flow*—which

Hungarian American psychologist Mihaly Csikszentmihalyi (pro-
nounced Mee-high Chick-sent-me-high) defines as a "highly focused
mental state conducive to productivity."[32] It happens when you're so
engrossed in something, it feels like minutes have passed by when in
actuality hours have. I couldn't think of a better person to come up
with the concept, because it really does seem like you're on a natural
(Csikszentmi-)high.

Before we started working on the book, we were inspired by (and
geeking out on) concepts like flow and the fact that happiness even existed
as a scientific concept. Life questions that we were contemplating—from
the everyday to the existential—were already being examined. Academ-
ics and positive psychologists like Martin Seligman (aka the godfather of
positive psychology), Tal Ben-Shahar, Barbara Fredrickson, and Jona-
than Haidt had pioneered happiness research. Unlike with traditional
psychology, we realized the focus needn't just be on what's wrong with us;
we could make our lives happier by understanding what's right with us
too. Their studies became an epiphany. Our curiosity grew about how we
could synthesize and test these scientific findings in practical ways, both
in companies and in life.

As we know, science is an ongoing work of questioning, testing, and
drawing new conclusions. Things we all learned in school that were
"scientifically proven" might not be considered true anymore because
the more we apply the scientific method, the more evidence and new
hypotheses we gain. Now we know bats can actually see...dinosaurs
had feathers...Mars has water...Pluto is no longer a planet[33] (I cried
myself to sleep when I first learned of that one). But it just reminds us
that science will always be an adaptive process.

What I appreciate about the science of happiness is that it's actively
going through its evolutionary phases as well...from a universally
human point of view. The original definitions of happiness go back to
philosophers like Socrates, Plato, and Aristotle, when they considered
the meaning of life. These days we hear terms like *positive psychology*,
subjective well-being, and *flourishing* being used interchangeably with

the word *happiness*. In the end I think *subjective* is the most operative word. Depending on who we are and where we live in the world, happiness means different things to different people. But regardless of what we call it, the current definitions and research on happiness are derived from two perspectives: the hedonic (which focuses on pleasure and pain) and Aristotle's eudaemonistic (which focuses on meaning and self-realization).[34]

On the hedonic side, happiness is associated with positive emotions like pleasure, comfort, hope, and inspiration. From this perspective, happiness comes from the presence of positive emotions and the absence of negative ones.

The eudaemonistic side aligns more with Maslow's hierarchy in that happiness is associated with self-actualization.

As Tony and I learned in Martin Seligman's book *Authentic Happiness*, there are a few different types of happiness that speak to the hedonic and eudaemonistic sides. This is how we shared them in *Delivering Happiness*, based on how sustainable each type is:

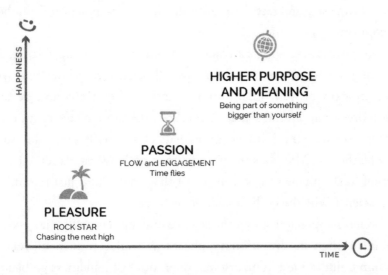

Pleasure is the most short-lived type of happiness. Once the stimulus is gone, our happiness level quickly returns to where it was before—as with watching a funny YouTube video or having a glass of wine (or better yet, both). It's fun in the moment but fleeting. The next type—passion—is more desirable because it lasts longer than pleasure. We see it when athletes are "in the zone" or when we're engrossed in an activity we love so much, we lose sense of time. The last, most sustainable form of happiness is purpose. It's what grounds us and lights our North Star at the same time. Living purposefully is the most enduring form of happiness, and I'll be weaving the idea in extensively throughout the rest of the book.

To sum up, sustainable happiness comes from (1) being aware of how you were born (inherited disposition), (2) your hedonic (utilitarian) circumstances, and (3) your eudaemonistic (self-actualization) aspect. Put another way, happiness comes from being authentically true to yourself, feeling your pleasures, flow, and passion, and living your purpose.

Older studies told us that we were born at a "set point" of happiness that we inherited and couldn't change. Newer studies tell us we can improve our levels of sustainable happiness by "investing" in (or working on) ourselves and the community around us.[35]

But putting the science aside for a moment, I believe there's an art to happiness too. That's where your own subjective definition of happiness gets defined by you, for you. Mixing the art of your authentic self with science gives the most important definition of them all...because it's yours and only yours.

For me, happiness is when I don't overthink, so I can feel. It circulates through my body as it naturally calls out for both the kid and the wiser soul in me to come out and play. Happiness is being present while I grow and learn in the highs and the lows. It's when I'm fully opti-realistic—aware of all sides of a situation—with the freedom to make choices with intention, positivity, some grace and fun, and ultimately love. It's waking up knowing that I surround myself with people I love and that I'm doing the work to make the day's moments count. I'm happiest when I can absorb the scene I'm in—whether it's one of endless stars and sky, lush greens and changing seas, or the tap of a raindrop or rays of sun on my skin—and feel the immensity of being one with it all.

In this moment, how would you define happiness for yourself? There's no right or wrong. The beauty of defining your own happiness is that it's as distinctive as your own fingerprint. Only you can imprint it, and no one can take it away.

As I mentioned earlier, this book starts where *Delivering Happiness* left off. Unbeknownst to both me and Tony when we launched the book in June 2010, a company was going to be birthed from it too. We joked about how I really hadn't known I was going to end up leading it as the CEO. "I never really asked you if you wanted to do it, did I?" Tony randomly realized a few months into it.

"No," I said, lost in the memory of where the journey had begun. I'd had little idea of what a company based on happiness was going to look like. But we had a higher purpose in mind—to scale meaningful happiness to the world—and I couldn't have imagined something more aligned with my personal purpose.

After the success of happiness as a business model at Zappos and its $1.2 billion acquisition by Amazon in 2009, DH set out to create a more universal model so other orgs could apply it to their own companies. I saw Zappos as the petri dish that had successfully tested the concept, and then DH became the international lab of culture experts (or as we say, coach|sultants®—part coach, part consultant) to help others create and test their own company cultures in petri dishes unique to their organizational DNA.

Folks on the DH team like James Key Lim, Ron Mandel, and Sunny Grosso helped create and test the original model, based on the book *Delivering Happiness*—blending the science and lessons learned from Zappos. The original DH model was born and became the basis for our greenhouse model—the *how* that helps you achieve the *why* of the double ROI.

The Greenhouse Model

We've used the original DH model to help build and inspire the sustainable cultures of over four hundred companies around the world, in countries like Japan, Mexico, the Republic of Seattle, Curaçao, Dubai, Vietnam, Turkey, Egypt, Spain, Kuwait, and Kazakhstan. (As much as I'd love to make a Borat reference here, the country and its people are the furthest thing from the movies. But if you're looking for a place of beautiful landscapes and model-esque people of Eurasian descent, you know what to add to your travel list.)

But like everything in our Adaptive Age, I began to see that the original DH model needed to adapt. We couldn't just rest on our laurels, assuming that what we'd been doing successfully in the past would carry its value for the next year, let alone five or ten. Otherwise it'd be easy for others to call out that we weren't practicing what we preach or drinking our own champagne. (The latter being the last thing I'd ever want to be accused of in life. Ever.)

We were seeing how the science of happiness could create purpose and profits for our clients, but how was it going to evolve from there? Our team knew happiness was something we all want in our lives, but we also noticed there were other growing needs we wanted to meet. With the world getting more complex, it was impossible to ignore. We saw the need for people to feel not just happy but real, resilient, and whole too. To go beyond happiness.

With the gestalt belief that the whole is greater than the sum of its parts, we at DH apply the concept of wholeness to every system we're a part of—whether it's within an organization, a community, or (most importantly) our own selves. The original DH model has adapted with the times to write the next chapter of our vision. The greenhouse model is rooted in the core of what it means to be scientifically happy and authentically whole, with org design elements to build sustainable companies that will make an impact. There are things in it that are naturally intuitive, but they might be hard to implement if you don't commit. It's like wanting to be healthier without eating better and exercising. It can't be willed to happen. We don't become happier and healthier until we actually start doing something about it.

By keeping the models simple, we've increased the odds the actions will be done. You don't have to rely on hitting up the prefrontal cortex and thinking about what you need to do every time. As we've seen more people and companies living the model, we've seen how our everyday actions can beautifully ladder up to our purpose and profits. Purpose then makes an impact... within ourselves, our companies, and the world.

But getting there takes work. Not the work you get a paycheck for, but the work you intentionally do on yourself, for yourself. If the ultimate incentive is waking up knowing the rest of your day is going to be fulfilling and purposeful, in tune with what matters most to you, will you commit? Will the payoff make working on yourself worth it?

If so, let's start building.

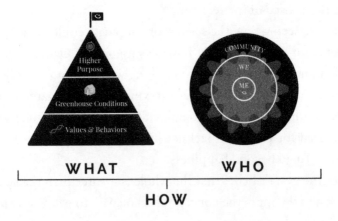

The greenhouse model consists of a pyramid that represents *what* to do. The concentric circles represent *who* does it. Together they form the *how*—as in how we create purposeful cultures, companies, and communities that make an impact on the world.

It's a promising sign that companies are becoming more vocal about being purposeful and mission driven. Tesla wants to "accelerate the world's transition to sustainable energy." TED Conferences is a platform for "ideas worth spreading." Patagonia exists to "build the best product, cause no unnecessary harm, use business to inspire and implement solutions to the environmental crisis."

But what hasn't been explicit across brands is (1) whether their people and practices are actually *living* out their purpose every day, (2) the way that purpose connects to the *most important unit* of every organization (individuals, e.g., *you*), and (3) how purpose works to help sustain and scale organizations for an even bigger ripple of impact in the world.

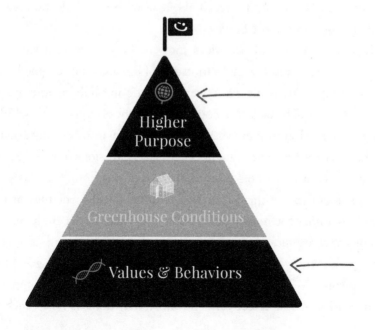

THE GREENHOUSE MODEL: WHAT

Higher Purpose, Values, and Behaviors

To help bring purpose and mission statements to life, we start with the *what* pyramid, with "Higher Purpose" at the top.

Higher purpose is simply the reason we exist (whether "we" is defined as an individual, a team, or a company). It's about being part of something bigger than ourselves as individuals, and doing something more meaningful than just making money as companies. As I explained before, purpose is the most sustainable form of happiness, which is why it's at the top.

Values and behaviors are the way we live out that purpose. They're the beliefs and daily actions we take toward reaching it. We need to define specific behaviors for each value in order to put words into action. They help take mission statements beyond meaningless words on a wall. This helps give clarity about how we actually live out our values in the form of *measurable* behaviors and *systems* that hold us accountable. (We'll go into detail about how to establish these values and behaviors later in the book.)

Together, values and behaviors show us how to enact a value like integrity so we don't follow in the footsteps of Enron, which claimed integrity was a top value while execs were squandering billions in employee pension benefits. The lack of accountable behaviors explains how Volkswagen convinced customers they were selling environmentally friendly cars though they were later caught cheating on emissions tests—a lie that cost the company at least 6.5 billion euros to recover from.[36]

This is not to say these brands are automatically enemies or evil. If you look under the hood of every company, there are people making decisions that are more wrong than right, doing more harm than good in the world. And vice versa. Of course we know there were good people at Enron and Volkswagen. But the difference between companies that prioritize people effectively and those that don't is how much the leaders are committed to rooting their purpose in *accountable* values and behaviors.

That connection means that you get top-down, bottom-up, inside-out alignment across the company and ensure people are accountable for what they say *and do*. That cultivates an environment of people doing the right things for each other and the business, not doing the things they can get away with. It creates trust and assurance that everyone is making decisions not just for more profit but in service of the organization's purpose too.

That's the organizational side of things, but again, the critical part often ignored or dismissed is connecting the org to each of our individual selves. The core of who we are as human beings, the values we hold dear, and the purposeful life we all want to be present in the work we do every day.

When they're all lived together, purpose, values, and behaviors (PVB) become the source of light you're striving toward and the roots in your greenhouse. They're what guides your decisions and defines your character because they include anything that means everything to you. When something in the world doesn't make sense anymore, your PVBs ensure that your own moral compass is guiding and grounding you at the same time. Other compasses may and will differ, but that's OK, because you're staying true to your authentic self.

By establishing what matters to you most, you make it much simpler to let the chaos of the world keep swirling outside and focus on what's within your control. When you have a life decision you're torn about—such as one regarding your career, relationships, or living situation—PVBs help make those seemingly impossible decisions easier. Choices are simplified when you know you're making them from the heart of who you are, not what others want of you.

Most importantly, this is how you see the way your existence ripples an impact from you through your work to the community. It enables you to establish how the team or company should be aligned. As your

PVBs grow within you, you'll naturally start showing your intrinsic self to the world just by being you. You'll feel meaningfully happy and human, grounded and whole, no matter how messy and mad the world can be.

Being fully human at work means knowing your strengths and weaknesses, hopes and fears, tasks and dreams—and embracing them all. It's worth being aware that our prefrontal cortex controls our ability to be analytical so we can make sensible, logical decisions, while our midbrain stores primal impulses to help us survive. When emotion takes over, we want to fight, take flight, freeze, feel shame, or cry for help. We all have a primal "monkey mind" (aka inner voice or critic) and subconscious that are liable to rile our emotions, make us question our worth, or lead us into imposter syndrome because we look or feel different from everyone else in the department or conference room. They can distract or scare us from truly adapting to thrive by pulling us back to what feels familiar and safe.

But it's OK. Our reactions are real, and they're there for a reason. Maybe we burned our hand on an iron when we were six years old, so we get anxious when we feel hot. Or a crocodile tried to kill our ancestors in prehistoric times, so we instinctively stay away from the fence at the zoo. Or we watched Pee-wee Herman as an infant and remain suspicious of red beach cruisers. Who knows, but everyone has their own traumas—some more serious than others—and part of our life's journey is to understand what sets off our alarm bells and make conscious (prefrontal) decisions to quiet those monkey voices down.

Feeling human at work involves what Chip Conley calls being "emotionally fluent," as he says in his book *Emotional Equations*. As he describes it, "Our emotions are like the weather. The torrential rainstorm will end and possibly be followed by a rainbow. But, when we're in the midst of despair, we feel like we're stuck, and nothing will change. Learning the recipe for the influences for anxiety, disappointment, or envy has helped me to better moderate what's happening."[37]

As humans, we're made up of genes that were embedded generations before we existed (our *nature*) and influences from our environment since we were born (our *nurture*). Then, ultimately, there's one last variable: our individual ability to live in this Adaptive Age and make decisions, to exercise your right to make our *choice* no matter what nature and nurture we've been a part of.

If you're already asking questions about who your authentic self is and building a curiosity about becoming more self-aware, you're probably sensing this is more than an exercise in naming your skills. Skill-based assessments are useful in a functional way, for recognizing things like "I'm good at organizing and setting goals for my team" or "I suck at sounding sincere in emails and Slack." (Pro tip: Pretend you're talking to them face-to-face. Make it personal. Add a wine or taco emoji if that's what you wish you were having.)

But deeper dives into self-awareness—exploring your consciousness, subconsciousness, and faith or spirituality—show that our greatest gifts are often hidden in the things we tend to avoid. As Francis Weller showed me in his book *The Wild Edge of Sorrow*, there are lessons to be learned and new heights of happiness to feel when we accept—instead of avoid—pain and loss. And it's important to remember that grief comes in more forms than the loss of people we love, such as traumas accumulated in our lifetimes, the ongoing destruction of our planet, and the emptiness of not having a sense of belonging and community. Weller highlights the bond between grief and gratitude, sorrow and intimacy, that gives us space to live and love more fully.

When I bring up the importance of getting to know your strengths and weaknesses, I mean going beyond the cookie-cutter answers you may be used to sharing. By exploring our darkest shadows and brightest lights, honest self-inquiry unlocks what we truly are and what we're capable of as real and vulnerable leaders within the workplace.

The leaders who are aware of their own greenhouses—and can adapt to the conditions around them—are the ones who are resilient and thrive.

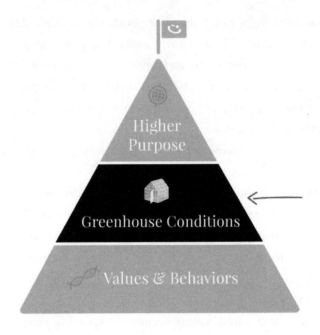

The Greenhouse Conditions

The middle of the pyramid contains the universal greenhouse conditions needed to keep higher purpose rooted with values and behaviors. They're the conditions that keep a person or an organization alive and growing—no matter what the current environment might be. These conditions ensure that happiness and adaptiveness are embedded in our systems so that we're not just getting by, we're also being sustainably nourished.

Scientific Happiness

Implanted in the greenhouse conditions are the scientific levers of happiness. Across all the research that's been done on happiness and positive psychology, three consistent ways—or, as we say, levers—emerged to increase happiness levels within yourself and your org.

These levers are our perceived senses of *control*, *progress*, and *connectedness*. Company cultures that embed these levers systemically are

 CONTROL

 PROGRESS

CONNECTEDNESS

better equipped to assess their current state, evaluate what levers can be used to improve the greenhouse, then adapt to thrive.

- **Control** means giving people autonomy and agency over their work, empowering people with trust, and allowing them to make their own decisions—because they know their roles and responsibilities the best. Control can come in many forms: from choosing when to work (scheduling) and where to work (remotely or in the office) to creating your own job title (like the receptionist who was the director of first impressions) and deciding on the functions you fill.

- **Progress** removes a common stress by taking you from working toward unachievable goals to setting achievable ones. Especially in demanding corporate, remote, and start-up environments, one of the most common complaints is burnout, which is exacerbated by finish lines seeming so far in the distance. Now that more of us are working remotely and the lines between work and life are blurred, burnout rates are even higher. But if you celebrate milestones along the way and reward progress (not perfection), people feel more productive and engaged. The more progress we perceive and the greater the sense of accomplishment we feel in our work, the more sustainably happy we can be.[38]

- **Connectedness** and meaningful relationships are also sustainable levers of happiness. People work harder for their friends than for people who are just their coworkers. Especially with the spike in working remotely, we need to reframe how we build real relationships in the workplace, using practices like kicking off meetings with quick and personal pulse checks or ending meetings with a round of gratitude. Instead of relying on the usual happy hours or annual holiday party, relationships deepen when we launch programs to share personal goals, including the purposes and values we hope to live up to (even when they're unrelated to work), while incentivizing people to support each other in living up to them.

ADAPTIVE ORGANIZATIONS

The scientific levers of happiness are excellent for the ME and WE, but they're not enough to ensure optimal greenhouse conditions at all three levels—ME, WE, and COMMUNITY. This is what we've learned at DH over the last several years. There are four additional conditions organizations need to endure in the Adaptive Age: *alignment, belonging, accountability,* and *commitment.*

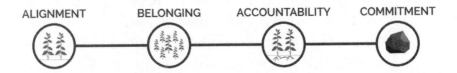

ALIGNMENT   BELONGING   ACCOUNTABILITY   COMMITMENT

- **Alignment** happens when everyone is able to answer the questions "What's in it for me?" and "What's in it for all?" When a company's collective purpose, values, and behaviors (PVBs) are codified and clearly articulated for the entire org, people and teams can align their own PVBs to them. This happens when people are playing to their strengths and mapping them to the goals and needs of the org as a whole. When we create a transparent and adaptable system for working together, orgs are better set up to innovate and test new ideas that will fail fast and fail forward (without feeling fear when doing so). Given the accelerated pace of change, companies need to maintain transparent communication to keep alignment going.

- **Belonging** happens in cultures where everyone feels welcomed, trust is high, and people feel free to be curious without judgment. These are workplaces that provide a sense of security, inclusivity, and equity and where people feel like they're valued, connected, and true to their authentic selves. Cultures of belonging celebrate differences instead of conformity and build cohesion that doesn't rely on similarity. These cultures actually embrace tensions and talk about the elephant in the room arising from people's differences, because they know that they still share PVBs.

    Even prior to the unprecedented isolation of the pandemic, the *Harvard Business Review* said the following in 2019: "Exclusion is a growing issue. We found that more than 40% of those we surveyed are feeling physically and emotionally isolated in the workplace. This group spanned generations, genders, and ethnicities." But there was a silver lining: "When people feel like they belong at work, they are more productive, motivated, engaged and 3.5 times more likely to contribute to their fullest potential."[39] In addition, according to BetterUp's report on *The Value of Belonging at Work*, high belonging has been linked to a 50 percent drop in turnover risk and a 75 percent reduction in sick days. For a ten-thousand-person company, this could result in annual savings of more than $52 million. Employees who reported higher workplace belonging also showed a 167 percent increase in their employer promoter score (their willingness to recommend their company to others). They also received double the raises and 18 times more promotions.[40]

- **Accountability** happens in cultures where people are held to their shared and codified PVBs. This is most important at the executive level given their ability to set the tone for the whole company. In the most accountable cultures, there's a sense of individual *and* shared ownership of what's best for the org. Leaders are responsible for taking care of people; people are responsible for doing the job they were brought on to do. When mistakes happen—as we know they will—leaders assure everyone there's space to learn and grow from them. At the same time, there's a common understanding that people will *do* what they *say*. And if they don't, everyone feels psychologically safe to respectfully call out bullshit in meetings and 360-degree reviews. People all have a fair shot at getting incentivized, rewarded, and recognized, and they will choose to leave before they're asked to, especially if the alignment of performance with (personal and company) PVBs isn't there.

- **Commitment** happens when leaders are invested in long-term growth, not just short-term gains. When a CEO commits to investing in culture because she believes people are an asset that brings more profits, she's doing it because she wants people to be whole and happier too. When leaders realize systemic change in diversity and inclusion (D&I) doesn't happen in a press release or a tweet, they chip away at surface issues daily while getting to the root causes with difficult but real talk. When salespeople commit to meeting their sales goals while also committing to work with (not against) other salespeople on their team, they all know they're building a better sales force for the future growth of the company. These things all demonstrate commitment to real, sustainable change.

  Modern org design in the future of work requires commitment too. The term *self-organization* (or *self-management*) has a bad rap because it conjures up images of people doing whatever they want, whenever they want. But *commitment* is what makes these concepts work. We know that command-and-control structures have to evolve into decentralized, flatter orgs if they are to keep up with the pace of exponential change. What does it mean to have a decentralized, flatter org? According to *Forbes*, "Unlike the traditional hierarchy which typically sees one-way communication and everyone at the top with all the information and power; a 'flatter' structure seeks to open up the lines of communication and collaboration while removing layers within the organization. For larger organizations this is the most practical, scalable, and logical approach to deploy across an entire company. This is the model that most large (and many midsize) organizations around the world are moving towards."[41] With commitment across leaders, orgs are more able to adapt to achieve bigger, more global goals for a long-term gain for all.

THE GREENHOUSE MODEL: WHO

The circular *who* model is best described by the quote: "You are not a drop in the ocean; you are the entire ocean in a drop."

It starts with you—the ME—in the middle. No matter who you are or where you come from, the *who* model makes you the star of your own show. The hero of your own journey. ME is the basic unit, the individual, the leader of your life and work, your whole and authentic self.

From there the impact of your existence, value, and contribution ripple out to the WE. This could be your team, department, functional area, or ultimately your entire org.

From there, your impact ripples out to your COMMUNITY— your company's customers, clients, partners, vendors. Essentially, the entire ecosystem of people and entities you directly touch because of what you do at work. The reason I define COMMUNITY this way, and not as your friends, family, and neighborhood, is that this is what it means to have meaningful relationships in the workplace—to make all these people part of your community.

THE GREENHOUSE MODEL: HOW

THE GREENHOUSE MODEL

The greenhouse model (in the matrix form above) breaks down everything I just shared to show *how* it all works. It becomes a handy tool to help you apply the model across your life, your teams, and your workplace. Looking at the "ME" column, you can see how each layer of the pyramid applies to your ME—your personal Purpose + Values and your greenhouse conditions.

Throughout the rest of this book, you'll see how each of the layers in the pyramid can be applied to your ME, WE, and COMMUNITY. As examples:

- Do you feel like you're living your Purpose + Values every day?
- Do you feel senses of control, progress, and connectedness at work?
- Do you feel that there's alignment, belonging, accountability, and commitment in your workplace?
- What are the things that are going well that you can celebrate?
- What are the hot spots or challenge areas that aren't going well—in ways that you'd like to work on (if it's within your control) or let go of (if it's outside your control)?

The first time you use the matrix, it becomes a snapshot of where you are in your work/life. The next time you use it, it enables you to see the things you've moved the needle on. This makes it easier to tell when things important to you feel stagnant.

It's also important to note that you don't have to have an answer for everything every time you use it. There's no need to fill out every box in the matrix; it's meant as a mental model to spark thought and discussion within yourself, within your teams, and with other leaders as you ripple your impact out.

So how do you ripple it? We just move that shaded column over to the right to denote the WE. Using the same questions and concepts, we can ask ourselves how each layer of our pyramid can be applied to the WE—our teams and orgs—as well. In other words, on the WE level, we can look at the greenhouse conditions to see what's going well, what can be celebrated, and what we need to work on.

We also start seeing the relationship between the ME and the WE in our lives. Do our ME and WE purposes align? Do any of our values align?

THE GREENHOUSE MODEL

Sometimes they're directly connected and sometimes they're not. Regardless, it's worth asking if any gaps can be addressed or need to be accepted. In that way at least you can acknowledge that there's a disconnect instead of ignoring what might be amiss. After doing this with your WE, you can do the same thing with your COMMUNITY. Once you've completed the full matrix, you can see the big picture emerge in the relationships between your ME, your WE (your teams and org), and your COMMUNITY.

START WITH THE ME

The hardest thing is to be true to yourself, especially
when everybody is watching.

—DAVE CHAPELLE

Do the Most Important Work in Your Life

Now that the value of company culture is widely recognized in workplaces, it's time to take people strategies to the next level. The next metamorphosis we need is to *value individuals as their authentic, whole, and purposeful selves*. You may choose to use different terms to mean the same thing, such as *well-being, psychological safety, mental health, self-care, ikigai* in Japanese, and *hygge* in Danish. In the end, it all comes back to doing the most important work in our lives—nurturing our own greenhouse.

Basically, we need to keep two questions top of mind:

- What's in it for ME?
- What's in it for all (WE/COMMUNITY)?

By starting with ME, you know you're taking care of your greenhouse.

By responding to them both, you ensure that everyone's greenhouse is benefiting in coexisting and symbiotic ways.

By following the greenhouse model outlined in Part I, you can answer "What's in it for ME?" You'll need to define your Purpose + Values and monitor whether your greenhouse conditions are being met. This way you'll know which conditions are at their peak and which ones need help improving.

Many of us forget to tend our own greenhouses because we feel the need to tend everyone else's greenhouse first. We wake up exhausted because one of the kids has a cold, which means we forgot to feed the pets, which reminds us that we forgot to do that important favor for our best friend last week, as we can hear the chimes of texts and emails already going off (even if that's just in our heads). And that's all happened before we get to the bathroom to brush our teeth. Who has time for a quick stretch, meditation, or workout when it feels like hell's about to have a party in the house if we don't start getting shit done?

Tending your own greenhouse is where happiness and humanity happen—and there's much more to it than making time for a daily meditation or workout.

The repercussions of not doing it are heartbreaking. Here are just a few things that describe the state of our MEs in the world and our workplaces:

- Depression and suicide are increasing at staggering rates. The World Economic Forum (WEF) says depression is the number one cause of ill health and disability worldwide: "More than 300 million people worldwide suffer from depression, an increase of more than 18% between 2005 and 2015." Much of the blame for depression and poor mental health falls on the experiences employees have in US workplaces.[42] In 2019, for the first time, our mental health crisis was on the agenda at the WEF's annual meeting in Davos, Switzerland (note that this was even before the pandemic).
- Higher levels of economic hardship have increased relationship violence and psychological distress.[43]
- Employed workers are three times as likely to report poor mental health now than before the pandemic.[44]
- Burnout and turnover increase and productivity decreases when basic physical and emotional needs aren't acknowledged and

addressed. A recent Gallup study showed that nearly eight in ten people experience burnout on the job. When we do, we're 63 percent more likely to take a sick day, 23 percent more likely to visit the emergency room, and 2.6 times more likely to be actively seeking a different job.[45]

- Income disparity is growing between the haves and have-nots. America's top 10 percent average more than nine times the income of the bottom 90 percent. The top 1 percent average 39 times more.[46]

At the same time, I've been witnessing how leaders are placing a greater value on holistically bringing our heads, hearts, and consciousnesses into our world's workplaces across all levels and spectrums of life. Ten or twenty years ago, hearing words like *vulnerability, resilience, compassion, mindfulness*, and *love* at work was a huge rarity. If someone—heaven forbid—accidentally uttered one of those in a meeting, it'd be like the needle scratched off the record, and all eyes would be on them, everyone wondering what was wrong with this person. The sentiment was to save that for outside the office, at the watercooler, or on lunch break. Anywhere else—just not where people were trying to work.

When a certain type of CXOs (meaning leaders in the C-suite, not chief experience officers) hired DH in the past, they'd come off as just "checking the box" of culture. Over time I could see them come to realize that it wasn't about giving their employees the impression they cared; it was about actually caring. Walking the talk has never been more important, and they saw how it comes from being real and vulnerable with others. To get the most out of others, they understood the need to give the most of themselves first. Now *vulnerability* and *love* are in our everyday vocabularies and no one blinks if those ideas are discussed by senior leaders, in meetings, or in corporate communication emails. On the receiving end, that's often embraced and respected. The key is for everyone to feel comfortable in being their authentic ME, and oftentimes leaders achieve that by living the example themselves. Living your own truth and not that of others means stepping toward work/life integration.

I've also been inspired by those who aren't in senior management positions who do the work on themselves to make hard choices—like seeking a different role in another department or even leaving the company altogether because their current position isn't aligned with who they are or doesn't enable them to live by their Purpose + Values. And I'm equally inspired by those who feel they can't leave their jobs because of financial or social obligations but have found ways to control what they can, adapt, and contribute to stay aligned with their Purpose + Values.

As I've seen more people lead by advocating for their own ME, I've seen a greater acknowledgment that if things aren't fair, it's our responsibility to right them. Because we know our ME wants to see more opportunities and have more positive experiences, we recognize other MEs in the world naturally want those things too.

Even though 2020 shone the spotlight on our differences and disparities, it also became a casting call for those who wanted to make a change for the better. Those who banded together to affect the complex external world in a different way had usually reached that point because they'd spent intentional time understanding their internal world first.

Part of understanding our individual world begins with revisiting what *success* means and defining it for ourselves.

JUST WHEN YOU THOUGHT YOU'D FIGURED IT OUT

I've seen too many people who believed they had it all figured out because they were successful in a traditional sense—highly ranked, highly paid—and whose burning desire was simply to get to the next stage of this sense of success. Some go the rest of their lives without thinking critically about their definition of success for themselves. But those who recognize a deeper sense of success can seek it out with courage and self-awareness. They strive for purpose and inspire others to do the same.

David Kidder is an experienced entrepreneur, an angel investor in over forty start-ups, and a two-time *New York Times* best-selling author of books like *The Startup Playbook* and, most recently, *New to Big*. Even though these seem like forms of success, he had to face moments of brokenness and fear to get there. In the middle of his journey in life and career, he saw that the only way forward was to start over, by being an archaeologist within himself and rediscovering who he truly was.

He recalled to me a profound intervention in the middle of a peak-stress, blink-you-die moment for one of his start-ups. Late one evening, his CRO (chief revenue officer) called him to ask a brazenly candid question: "The company's failing—why are you accelerating the company's failure?"

David was in disbelief. How could a company with $34 million raised, one that had quickly grown to 180 employees, be failing? How could that be possible if he was giving his whole self to this company? His CRO courageously shared what everyone else in the office was already thinking but not saying: "The company is accelerating to failure because the company is *you*. It's only about your vision and your determination and your will to make it true."

The company was ultimately not about the employees, not about the customers, not about the larger ripple of impact—it was only about David building a successful business (in traditional terms) with strong financial outcomes. The truth stung hard. Despite how much he'd thought he was making sacrifices for the company—at the expense of quality time with family and quality of life for his teams—the business was merely there to provide success for the investors and him.

In that moment, as David put it, "I felt like Hemingway's character Mike in *The Sun Also Rises*, when he described how he went bankrupt." He recalled the writer's narrative of how failure arises: "Two ways...Gradually and then suddenly." David was not necessarily thinking about financial failure but about the failure of living true to his mind, heart, and spirit.

That night was a life-changing moment for David. Depleted, empty, and broken from the weight of a self-imposed problem, he realized he had to "give it over" and ask for help—from his leadership team, his employees, his form of God, and the universe. He had to accept all the outcomes, even outright failure (financial or otherwise), by letting go of his company. David lay down alone on the floor of his attic and cried. It was in this brokenness that he learned he was more than the identity of a company. He was more than any implicit and explicit failure or success, public or private. After he released his emotions, he slept in peace for the first time in a long time.

David stopped white-knuckling his way to a false form of success. He started asking more questions, trusting and empowering others, and accepting the outcomes. Through journaling and meditation, he realized he needed to start over. As he shared with me: "I [saw myself] running brutally hard down this road, and the harder I ran, the thicker the bushes became, and with the thickness came the thorns." The longer David ran with his own path and will, the more he bled and knew he needed a clean road—in his mind and in his life.

It brought him back to what he'd felt as a college graduate. It was time to believe again in a world that was new, open, and full of opportunity and learning. Since then he's made his company Bionic very different, giving it a purpose to ignite growth in large enterprises as if they're start-ups.

Bionic was not spared a tumultuous 2020 as it navigated the uncontrollable conditions of the markets, his team, and the needs of the customers. Months of work, seven days a week, were brutal, but eventually resulted in major pivots and resets. The difference between this test and those of the past was that David tended his greenhouse first. He leaned into his own truth, which gave him an energy that rippled out to the team, Bionic's partners, and the universe. It resulted in a record year, but more important for David was that he believed in himself more than ever before.

Almost three years after Bionic's founding, David's mentor and uncle, Dr. Roger Fransecky, died of a stage IV glioblastoma. It was a staggering loss, but as with most of Roger's life and impact, there was a gift. "My uncle imparted some powerful wisdom in the hours before his passing. He said when you get to the top, whether it's success, money, or even being a person, you realize there is very little there. Life is lived in the valley, in the great tests that grind and shape you."

Forehead to forehead, his uncle said, "Do not focus on who you are to the world. Focus on who you are becoming. Fall in love with the test."

The Hero's Journey at Work

If the structure of David's story sounds vaguely familiar, it's because it's the story of the hero's journey, with David as the hero in his own journey. As Joseph Campbell laid out for us in his book *The Hero with a Thousand Faces* in 1949:

> A hero ventures forth from the world of common day into a region of supernatural wonder: fabulous forces are there encountered and a decisive victory is won: the hero comes back from this mysterious adventure with the power to bestow boons on his fellow man.[47]

What's interesting is that Campbell laid out the hero's journey based on Indigenous teachings and similarities in stories from around the world. The way he brought heroes together, with every human being a hero, rejected any potential boundaries that race, religion, and ethnicity could bring. This is the same mindset we need for more diversity, equity, inclusion, and belonging (DEIB) in the world.

Seventy years later, Campbell's structure is still a cheat sheet for novelists and screenwriters (and now businesses because of Don Miller's book *Building a StoryBrand* and his company, StoryBrand). Whether it's *Star Wars* or *The Matrix* or any other epic movie you've ever loved, we can see what roles Princess Leia, Obi-Wan, Luke, Neo, Morpheus, and Trinity play in the hero's journey framework.

The point is that your ME starts with you, in your own epic film, with you as the hero. And it's not just one blockbuster, it's a series of them that lasts your entire lifetime. (And perhaps beyond.) It's the day-to-day decisions you make that chart your own hero's journey and determine whether you'll look back at it as epic or as a disappointing remake of someone else's story. The difference between the two is whether you shape your journey through your sense of purpose, values, and the true core of who you are.

Miki Agrawal and her twin sister, Radha, had their own hero's journeys too. Their parents arrived in America with dollars in their pocket and brought a melting pot blend of Indian and Japanese heritage. With English as their second language, their parents did everything they could to build a greenhouse for their two kiddos. The conditions they created helped their girls grow beautifully.

The Agrawal twins both became very successful entrepreneurs. They've written books, built pizza restaurants in New York, and founded companies like Thinx, TUSHY, and Daybreaker—collectively they're valued at over $500 million.

Miki's current brand, TUSHY, upgraded the bathroom experience with a modern, affordable bidet so "butts get into the 21st century, away from dry abrasive toilet paper that is killing 15 million trees a year." Radha is running the company Daybreaker, an early-morning dance and wellness movement in cities and campuses around the world that half a million people enjoy. In addition to performing well, these companies have helped more than a hundred thousand girls in Uganda return to school, supported global reforestation projects, and saved millions of trees.

The sisters were living out the American dream, but even then Miki had a sense that there was more she had to work on . . . within. She realized she was avoiding some major fears. By looking inside herself, she learned that one of her biggest fears was the fear of fear itself. "As an entrepreneur, we are often not allowed to feel fear," she said. "It was buried deep inside. I had to really go into the fear, acknowledge its presence, and let it overcome me in order to move through it. What we resist persists, and I was resisting the feeling of fear until I let go."

What Miki described to me was an intentional way to get real with her internal ME. "I was a tree with a storm thrashing through my branches," she said. "Instead of resisting, I finally surrendered to it and the storm passed." By getting acquainted with her internal resistance and then letting it go, she was able to come to a place of peace. From a newfound, accepting relationship with fear, she went up against external resistance differently.

Whether it was in the form of investors who didn't want to take a risk or a society that doesn't like to talk about "shameful" and taboo things like "periods and poop," she took on the fears. By doing so, she's been able to overcome the uphill battle against the status-quo thinking of not talking about what are, after all, normal bodily functions.

By getting to know her internal resistance, Miki was able to resume cultivating her greenhouse in better ways. Today, inspired by her three-year-old son Hiro (which fittingly means "abundant and generous" in Japanese), she's now taking poop to a whole new level, whizzing up ways to revolutionize diaper use and disposal in a process that will help save the planet.

SIDELINING SHAME FOR YOUR TRUTH TO STAND

Keith Ferrazzi, an entrepreneur and global thought leader who coaches some of the most prestigious executive teams in the world, is the founder of Ferrazzi Greenlight and *New York Times* best-selling author of *Never Eat Alone* and *Who's Got Your Back?* He consults with these executives on their transformations and what it means to run modern orgs, helping teams work together in more humanistic, holistic, and collaborative ways to be ready for the future of work.

I met Keith over ten years ago at a spectrum of events—TED, the Summit conferences, and Burning Man. He always struck me as someone with a strong heart who wanted to do good for the world and who had the grand sense of curiosity needed to follow through on that desire, but I wasn't quite sure where he landed as a person. It seemed like he showed up slightly differently depending on the venue, occasion, and people around. It wasn't until recently that I understood why.

Like Miki, Keith shared without a hint of hesitation (and with complete vulnerability) that he was living in shame. Having grown up poor and being gay were at odds with the image he had to maintain in front of some of his corporate-executive clients. He was adding value to them but not always in a completely soulful way that was true to his authentic self. Up until recently, he wasn't able to express to every team what the disconnect was. It wasn't until he started deep-diving within himself, with coaching support of his own, plant-based therapy, and support from his loved ones, that he identified what was wrong. He realized that he needed to connect his supremely capable, highly intelligent "work-self" to his spectacular and spiritual "life-self." In other words, his true purposeful self.

Now he shows up to meetings as who he truly is, no matter who's in the room—whether it's a conference full of older white male heterosexual execs or the beautifully diverse staff he's intentionally gathered within his own company. That's not to say being his authentic self in all settings necessarily comes easily, but making things easy is not the point—it's hard work to know and actualize who we are at our core. But when we're able to show up in the world aware of what might cause us discomfort, we can be vulnerable enough to be OK with that unease. When we learn the mental and emotional tools to not pick fights with our feelings (like shame and insecurity), our internal selves can just freely *be*.

When I see Keith now, his greenhouse abundance of generosity and energy fills the room—even Zoom rooms, so you know that's saying a lot. Through the eyes of a good friend or complete stranger, this is the Keith he was born to be: fully his authentic self, aligned with his purpose and passions, and living out his truth in his own hero's journey. The inspiration he provides allows him to better build others' greenhouses.

"I am never shaken from my belief that humanity will just keep getting better," Keith says. "And I'm also never shaken in my belief that by being on this planet, I'm making a footprint that will last and a ripple effect that matters. The world's going in the direction that it's going, and our job is to be of service. But you can't be of service alone. You have to be in service collectively as a community. In relationship. In coelevation, going higher together." By tending his greenhouse, Keith was naturally inspired to help others build theirs too.

The Hardest Easy Thing You'll Ever Do

While on one level the stories of the previous chapter seem to be about privileged leaders, I chose to share their journeys because they didn't come from privileged backgrounds. Miki and Radha came from immigrant parents with mere dollars in their pocket and an American dream. Keith grew up poor, searching for a safe space to be true to his gay identity, with a fiery desire to do good for the world.

Our journeys are about the greenhouse conditions we were born into, the experiences that shaped our greenhouse conditions from the time we began to grow, and the present moment of how we choose to recalibrate those conditions. The greenhouse of our own body, heart, mind, and soul needs to be tended, every day. Ultimately, we're made of the stories we live, starting with our personal ME stories first.

When I say to put your ME first, I'm not referring to so-called "me time"—the occasional yoga class, Peloton session, or morning meditation on your Calm app that looks pretty but has to be shoehorned into your day. I'm alluding to feeling the wholeness of every minute you're alive. The consummate time that makes you *completely* you. Not just your tasks and to-do list but your internal lights and shadows. Your senses of trust, curiosity, and faith and the fears that have been collecting within you since the day you took your first breath. Your why in purpose and the values by which you live.

Rosalind (Roz) Brewer, the ex-COO of Starbucks and current

CEO of Walgreens, came to this epiphany during her own hero's journey. As a graduate from Spelman College (a historically Black college) with a degree in chemistry, she entered the business world as a scientist at Kimberly-Clark. Even though her brain was geared toward science, she quietly observed how her ideas could only go so far if she didn't have ownership of a crucial decision maker: money. So she learned how to control and manage budgets to see that her decisions would get implemented. As she climbed the ladder with quiet determination and integrity, she experienced what it took to be a true leader... and to be true to herself.

In 2019, she shared a story about the time she was president of a division at Kimberly-Clark and mom to a young child. She realized that she couldn't separate those two parts of herself and perform her best. There needed to be more harmony and alignment. She had to make sense of her identities, redefine her boundaries, and adapt.

It was then that she made the pivot to show up wholly as Roz, and she's been blazing her true-self trails ever since. Becoming the CEO of Walgreens makes her the only Black woman to (currently) be at the helm of a Fortune 500 company. But the most inspiring piece of her backstory isn't that headline, but rather the fact that she doubled down on herself.

If you need a quick, light, yet meaningful refresher in being true to yourself, I highly recommend (re)watching Pixar's *Inside Out*. The film dramatizes something adults need to remember as much as kids need to learn. As characterized by little Riley in the movie, we all contain the emotions of Joy, Sadness, Anger, Fear, and Disgust. Of course we know our emotional intelligence has the capacity to take on a much larger set of emotions, but the bottom line is this—there's only one person who can make the choice to listen to your emotions... and only one person who chooses how you'll react.

Of course, this type of work on ourselves is the opposite of spending ninety minutes decompressing with clever entertainment from a Pixar film. It can take you through the wringer and make you question everything you thought to be true. But the journey shouldn't feel like training camp with the navy SEALs (unless that's your passion to begin with). Should you take it on with a beginner's mindset and the willingness to fail forward, your quest to live a whole, fulfilling, and purposeful life will go from mission unknown to mission (so very) possible.

The tools and methods for doing this work that I'm about to introduce have been around in some form for centuries, but what we're constantly doing at DH is refining them to make them relevant and current to the work world we live in today. As Aristotle said around 300 BCE, "Happiness is the purpose of our existence...*and happiness is dependent on ourselves*" [emphasis added]. This is our time to take these couple thousand years of learnings, imagine what they could mean for you, and start looking inward, not just at the brightest lights within you but your darkest shadows too.

EXERCISE 1:
HAPPINESS HEARTBEATS

One of the ways we define core values at DH is with an exercise called Happiness Heartbeats. It helps you identify your values by mining your own experiences.

It's important to note that for some, this exercise may only scratch the surface. It really depends on *you* how deep you want to go. I also recommend looking into your company's resources for mental health and well-being, or hiring professionals like therapists and psychologists, should you want to explore further for yourself. People in my life have also done their personal ME work by harnessing the powers in spirituality, religion, faith, nature, and/or plant-based medicines. The ultimate result doesn't differ based on your chosen method(s). In the end, this exercise is just one of the many tools in the toolbox we can use to nurture our greenhouses.

Take some time to think about your own personal lowest and highest points. The outcomes of this exercise are a direct result of how deep you're willing to dive into those lights and shadows I've been referring to. The times when you were most proud and felt like your best ME (joyful, fulfilled, happy, authentic) and the darkest times, when you couldn't even imagine how you'd get back to a place of normalcy, let alone happiness.

A key question to ask yourself at this point is whether you want to explore your heartbeats (these high and low points) professionally, personally, or both. At DH we believe in the concept of work/life integration, so we suggest both. But there's no right or wrong answer; it's your call as to what feels most true to you. Choose what you think will give you a greater sense of control and agency in being the leader of your life. No matter how you do it, the most important thing is to select the moments that speak the most to you.

Here are some of my heartbeats as an example:

HIGHS	LOWS
Summiting Mount Kilimanjaro with Tony.	Losing my dad to colon cancer. Losing Tony.
Launching DH (the book and company).	Getting laid off from start-up job.
Being one of the fastest-growing private companies in America (2020 Inc. 5000) while being a company based on principles and core beliefs in happiness and humanity.	Deciding to reset and restructure the company knowing employees (and friends) would no longer be in the new org.

Now, looking at a layer deeper, think about why each moment was a high or low and which value(s) were present (or painfully absent) for each event. What value(s) were at play that made the moment meaningful or painful? My deeper layer looks like this:

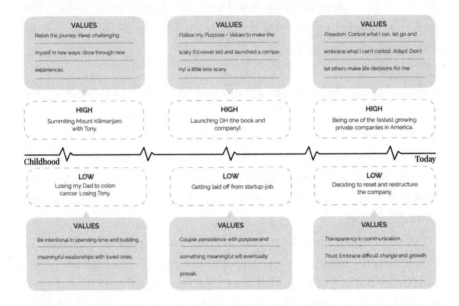

If you're having trouble connecting the moments with values that speak to you, here's a list of common values for reference:

Common Global Values (Use this list for inspiration when filling in your heartbeats)

ambition	exciting life	initiative	love	playfulness	straightforwardness
capability	encouragement	inner peace	loyalty	privacy	self-awareness
courage	family life	harmony	organization - order	pragmatism	trustworthiness
creativity	freedom	innovativeness	optimism	respect	wealth
compassion	friendship	integrity	open mindness	responsibility	wisdom
cooperation	fairness	intellectuality	perseverance	sharing	work - effort
commitment	generosity	influence	personal growth	security	
contribution	gratitude	joy	pleasure	self - worth	
equality	health - well being	leadership	punctuality	spirituality	
effectiveness	independence	logic	positivity	status	

The next step in Happiness Heartbeats is to figure out how to prioritize these experiences for yourself. Do so by asking yourself these questions:

- How did these moments forge the person I am today?
- How were my values lived (or not lived) in my highs and lows?
- Which moments (and therefore values) were the most influential?
- How do I live these values today?

As you reflect on your heartbeats you may start to see a pattern. For me, authenticity, freedom, and relationships crest to the top. The biggest shifts for me after doing this exercise the first time were making greater efforts to stay true to myself and prioritize people I loved as if I might never see them again. Another was deprioritizing things that weren't close to making the list, like ambition and achievements in money, title, and status.

In Japan, Saori Aoki, COO of KAN Corporation and coach|sultant® for DH Japan, shared what she discovered by doing the Happiness Heartbeats exercise:

ME Values Heartbeat

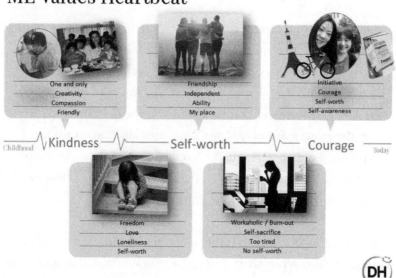

Until I met with DH, I never allowed myself to be happy. The Happiness Heartbeat exercise was very tough for me, but it was a very meaningful opportunity to understand my life and its origins. I couldn't remember any "highs" in my life, even though I had many "lows." I struggled to find my true value and self-worth. I always worked very hard but didn't think about happiness in my life. I was doing my best only to serve people. However, I felt pain from being betrayed and used. I was a selfless giver (referenced from the Adam Grant book *Give & Take*), I realized that I had never given to myself. I believed "happiness" was too bright for me, not suited for me...I was not allowed to be happy. But then I gave myself "permission to be happy." I'm so happy now and I want to make people happy more.

Javier Munoz Mendoza, cofounder of DH Spain, uses the Happiness Heartbeats exercise with clients around the world and has seen its impact. Says Javier:

I learned that no matter the audience, we are yearning to connect authentically, that by exploring these tough moments we honor how they shaped us knowing full well that we would not be who we are if it weren't for them. As you take this perspective you can even feel gratitude and you [begin to] understand how the experience of our shadows provides the awareness to value the light that resulted. People connected to the deeper meaning of happiness from a heightened sense of awareness and connected more with one another.

Saori mentioned Adam Grant in her heartbeats, and I was curious as to how a fellow positivity purveyor takes care of his greenhouse. Says Adam:

I used to say yes to every request that came in. I aspired to be a giver—someone as generous as Tony Hsieh, who helps others with no strings attached. Then the *New York Times Magazine* did a cover story about my philosophy, and I was flooded with requests. I decided that each no was an opportunity to say yes where it mattered more.

My first step was to prioritize who I helped: family first, students second, colleagues third, and everyone else fourth. (I didn't become a professor to help other professors; I wanted to make a difference in students' lives.) My second decision was to set boundaries around when I helped, blocking out a few days a week for my own work and well-being and separate windows to be responsive and available to others. That meant I was spending significant amounts of time in my greenhouse.

My third choice was to be thoughtful about how I helped—instead of being a jack-of-all-trades, I would focus on contributing where I had something unique to offer. As an organizational psychologist, my expertise centers around work and human behavior, and my roles as an author, speaker, and podcast host have meant that my network spans many industries. I realized that I could add value by sharing knowledge in my field and making introductions between two people who could benefit from knowing one another. That allowed me to focus on helping where it was energizing and effective. That's where the light enters.

Identifying and prioritizing your values—then making it a habit to apply them toward everyday and major work/life decisions—has been one of the simplest life-changing practices I've seen people happily adopt. Your life starts aligning with the core of your ME naturally, and you might start wondering how you ever managed spending your time differently.

EXERCISE 2:
WHAT'S YOUR LIVING LEGACY?

> Death is our friend precisely because it brings us into
> absolute and passionate presence with all that is here,
> that is natural, that is love.
>
> —RAINER MARIA RILKE

Thinking about the celebration of your life is another way to think about what you value. I often talk about living legacies and share this concept to our clients, with so much conviction that I have the words, LIVE YOUR LOVING LEGACY on my fireplace mantel at home.

This belief hit home in the most heart-wrenching way in November 2020—the end of a monstrous year for so many of us in the world—when Tony died.

Up until that day, the lowest low on my heartbeat scale was when my dad passed. My dad, Key, was an immigrant whose first job was as a butcher at the local grocery store when he arrived in America at the age of fourteen. He later became a sergeant in the US Army, a restaurateur, a real estate developer, the president of an association to help Chinese immigrants, an entrepreneur in the construction finance industry, and an Asian Frank Sinatra when he sang "My Way" at karaoke.

He wore a lot of hats, which explains why he taught me to believe in the value of everyone's work. We used to hang out in the front yard of our house, and if he'd see garbagemen working their way down the street, he'd always make it a point to remind me, "Everyone has a role in life. And we respect them all."

My mom wasn't the traditional tiger mom; she was tiger mom 2.0. She gave us hugs and kisses, didn't hesitate to use her pink plastic slippers for corporal punishment, and cooked the best comfort food right after grounding me an entire quarter for getting anything less than an A-minus on my report card. On top of working in the role of housewife, she worked at my dad's entrepreneurial endeavors. But no matter how hard she was on us or herself, she always made us feel loved.

Together they lived out Lin-Manuel Miranda's song "Immigrants (We Get the Job Done)."

As with so many immigrants, the reward for all their work was to see their kids succeed. And as with so many immigrants, there were the typical things that qualified as success. For our household it was about getting into a good school, becoming a doctor or a lawyer, and learning a variety of musical instruments. I thought I was on my way to success because I had a couple of boxes checked off the list, with only one left. But I never got to becoming Dr. Lim. I ended up majoring in Asian American studies at UC Berkeley, becoming a consultant at KPMG, and going to work for a start-up—a world that seemed like another planet to my parents.

When I made the call to tell them I'd dropped out of premed to major in Asian American studies, they were stumped. "Asian American...what? Why don't you come home more often and we'll tell you what your Asian study is all about!" When I told them I'd gotten hired as a consultant, my mom continued to ask every week if I had a real job yet. In retrospect, those were some of the hardest things I had to share with parents who were giving their kids their all. But these stands were my first intentional decisions to live my ME, and not by what others expected of me.

For whatever reason, my dad always gave me and my two brothers the benefit of the doubt and said, "I'm proud of you," regardless of our grades. When it comes to Asian parents, it was something unheard of back then. So when I lost him to colon cancer when he was sixty-two, the grief hit me hard. I was twenty-nine, and I thought I'd never get to know him better. With his passing, I thought I'd lost the chance to show how his support had all been worthwhile. I've learned a lot since then, though—most unexpectedly that I could get to know him better by growing into my own ME.

But a whole other wave of thoughts and feelings crushed me after I lost Tony when he was just forty-seven. When Tony died, I felt like I cycled through the five stages of grief a few times in just the first week. I also had never so viscerally felt the word *overwhelmed* before. I couldn't eat, sleep, or respond to all the loving messages from friends who knew us. Everything was surreal—the passing of time, the memories that flooded my head, the lack of separation between reality and what felt like a nightmare. We would've known each other for exactly twenty-one years that year, on his birthday of December 12. And as the news gradually sank in day by day, I felt like a part of me had passed away with him.

I'm sure some will think this was a figment of my imagination, but on the night of his passing, I saw his image in my window. Not in a freaky or haunting way; it was so matter-of-fact and ethereal at the same time. In the book *Delivering Happiness*, he nicknamed me his "back-up brain," and that's what this moment felt like—a lasting impression within me, on top of so many other moments throughout the years. His face and image exactly mirrored mine as I was looking out the window. Both of us had our arms gently crossed, and our eyes met peacefully one last time before our new reality. In one instant it was so distinct, and in the next he was gone. Leaving just my own reflection for me to see.

That experience captured the indescribable feeling that a part of me was forever gone with him.

After he died, messages continued to pour in from all walks of life, from all over the world. He had known and affected so many different tribes of people thanks to his innate nonjudgment. He respected everyone's greenhouse, the purpose and passions they had to bring to the world in their own weird and unique ways. He was inspired to foster these greenhouses, making them as vibrant as they could be.

The outpouring in itself brought another wave of cycling through the stages of grief, as each message re-created another memory and reinforced how far and wide his impact was felt. I mentioned Chip

Conley earlier when talking about emotions, and in addition to being an author and strategic advisor to Airbnb, he pioneered the boutique hotel concept with Joie de Vivre Hospitality and founded the company Fest300 as a good business excuse to attend every festival in the world that he possibly could. He's a dear friend to me and was to Tony as well. As Chip puts it, "In one lifetime, Tony had done what ten high achievers could've."

The irony of Tony's far-reaching impact and living legacy was that he never talked about them. They were never what motivated him to change things in inventive ways with community and humanity at their heart. Just as he helped embed the words *Purpose + Values* in the vocabulary of company culture, he also let them be the guide to his integration of work and life. With Purpose + Values in place, he didn't have to define what his legacy would become because he was actively living it.

I was uplifted when people shared with me how Tony had inspired them to make changes with their work and lives. How he'd taught them that being successful in business doesn't mean you have to be an asshole; you can be human. How he'd led them to take whatever they were thinking and think bigger. How he'd helped them realize the most important thing was chasing the vision, not the paper. So many people had met him only once or twice, and there were a number of people who had never met him at all but still felt touched by his message.

And then there were people who were just at a loss.

They asked good questions in search of ways to process his passing. Why did this happen to someone who obviously believed in happiness and delivering it to the world? Why did a deeply caring, soulful person who had everything have to pass away so young?

Tony had a natural knack for building greenhouses for others while being tenaciously true to himself. In his mind, I believe he was constantly integrating his (weird, authentic) ME, the WE of his companies and friends, and a deeper sense of COMMUNITY. As someone who had known early on what it was like to wake up and not feel like going to work—even when it was his own company (LinkExchange, which he sold to Microsoft in 1998 at the age of twenty-five)—he knew he never wanted to wake up to that feeling again.

I've never known someone who could jump out of bed so laser focused—on building new things, connecting with people, ordering almost everything off the room service menu so he could taste the different flavors to see what he liked most...beginning each day embracing his belief that anything is possible. His passion to create greenhouses for others was palpable in the occasionally brilliant (and oftentimes batshit crazy) ideas he had, the projects he launched, and the communities he created for the people around him. He was a modern-day, more compassionate Pied Piper, but instead of having a pipe, he had a dog named Blizzy and an alpaca named Marley by his side.

Tony was a public figure, so it's hard to fault the hard questions that came out of his death. Was it a psychotic break, as some in the media framed it? Was it the isolation he felt from COVID? Was it depression and other mental health issues? The truth is that there isn't one absolute truth. To oversimplify it from any one perspective would be a dishonor to the complexities of not just who Tony was and his passing but to anyone's passing.

Before attempting to answer any of those questions for ourselves, I want to remind us all of this profoundly simple quote: "Be kind, for every[one] is fighting a hard battle."[48] We all have our internal battles, and most of the time it's not just coming from one source. The complexity of who we are is also the beauty of what we bring to the world. For years now I've been translating what that means within myself, my loved ones, and of course, the workplace. Curiosity led me to new hypotheses and a broadening of what it means to be human—not just happy—at work. I've been anticipating the time I could share what I've learned in what's beyond happiness—and how far and wide our spectrum grows when we vulnerably experience our highs and endure our lows. The irony of this curiosity was laid bare on the night it was confirmed Tony had passed.

As much as I prepare myself that the unpredictable worst can happen at any time in life, I still find myself waking up in disbelief that Tony's not here. But by tending my greenhouse—in all my imperfect ways—I'm reminded that diminishing his loss to just a physical Tony would be ignoring some of the mysterious and wondrous realms of what it means to be human and spiritual, to be living in one realm...with curiosity about how we may transition into the next.

Our legacies are always going to be a mix of the internal decisions we make and what others perceive from their own external points of view. The highs and lows of our heartbeats are a testament to that. Living days to the fullest, with an acceptance of our personal light and shadow sides, is what makes us unabashedly whole and human. Acknowledging that spectrum within all of us dials down the importance of the exact way Tony passed or the months leading up to his death.

What I know is that by living out his tireless desire to be true to his weird self, grounded by a sense of Purpose + Values, Tony has rippled impacts in ways that even he probably couldn't have predicted.

What I also know is that it comes back to starting with the ME. It's up to us to remind ourselves (and each other) just how important it is to nurture our greenhouses first. It's the hardest easy thing we'll ever do.

Motoko Rich of the *New York Times* did a piece on Tony shortly after his book launched in 2011. She wrote something that I thought was insightful at the time: "Mr. Hsieh comes across as an alien who has studied human beings in order to live among them."[49]

It was so on point in some ways, with his constant curiosity to challenge the status quo of the world while keeping space in his brain to think compassionately about others. But what I know now more than ever is that he was a human being too, with the most basic and important needs of humanity that we all share: to feel a sense of belonging within himself and with others and to genuinely experience the most supreme emotion of them all—love—in his heart.

The grief of his loss is allayed only by the legacy he lived and leaves.

The more days pass since the day he died, the more I know Tony's greenhouse lives on. With his uniquely inspired and inspiring ways, he helped build innumerable greenhouses so others could be true to themselves—with purpose and passion—as the architect who had a hand in helping them keep grow.

The question for us now is, What is *your* living legacy going to be?

You may have heard of the social study done by the Australian nurse Bronnie Ware. She wrote a book called *The Top Five Regrets of the Dying*[50] on her personal experiences in palliative care and the words of regret she heard as her patients neared death. Among them were, "I wish that I had let myself be happier" and "I wish I hadn't worked so hard." At the top of the list was, "I wish I'd had the courage to live a life true to myself, not the life others expected of me."

When I first read about this study, it pained me to know what was occupying people's thoughts before their last breath. It's probably because I've had so many experiences of literally watching what happens when the body gives in even though the spirit wants to continue. There was my dad in the years of his battle with colon cancer. But even before then, there was my friend Travis, who tragically died of brain cancer when he was just a teenager. Even though he was smaller in stature than many people, the whole package of his charisma and energy was larger than most.

The memory that remains etched in my mind is of the last time I visited him in the hospital. He had already undergone a series of treatments, so he was bald and skinnier than I had ever seen him. But even though people were visiting to try to cheer him up, he was the one who lit up the room. He effortlessly beamed his legendary smile to everyone who came in. He was the one cracking jokes so others could smile with him. Just by being himself, he was taking away the weight of knowing his end was inevitable and reminding everyone in the room that it was a time to enjoy our last moments together. Writing about it now, I think he was one of the closest things to an angel I've seen in real life.

It made me wonder what it would take for people, no matter how old they were or what condition they were in, to look back without regret and say, "*Wow!* I'm so glad I did that." So glad that they took risks and followed their hearts. I wondered what it would take to live with full awareness that it's not the things we do in life that we end up regretting, it's the things we don't do.

This isn't an easy premise to live by, by any means. Of course, it's simple to look back on our deathbeds and say, "Thank goodness I gambled on that big win!" or "I guess I shouldn't have been sitting on that ledge ten Heinekens in." All is clear in hindsight, but a meaningful life can come from 20/20 foresight as well. If you make decisions today that align with who you are authentically (the core of your ME, your Purpose + Values) and with the actions and behaviors that stem from that, then the chances of achieving 20/20 foresight and living a life without regret are pretty damn good.

As an exercise, consider working on your eulogy instead of your résumé. What values would you want to be memorialized for? What would you want people to say? What words would you want etched in everyone's hearts as if they were on your headstone? These will probably mirror the values you identified in the Happiness Heartbeats exercise, or be deeper, more specific expressions of them.

For Rosa Parks's eulogy, Oprah Winfrey captured her pivotal role in the civil rights movement, her fight for justice, and, most meaningfully, her gentle and beloved heart. She shared:

And in that moment when you resolved to stay in that seat, you reclaimed your humanity and you gave us all back a piece of our own.

I marvel at your will.

I celebrate your strength to this day.

And I am forever grateful, Sister Rosa, for your courage, your conviction.

I owe you—to succeed.

I will not be moved.[51]

What I found so powerful was her repetition of the simple sentence, "We shall not be moved." These lines evoked both the spirit of an African American anthem and Parks's refusal to give up her seat on the bus.

In her eulogy of Steve Jobs, his sister Mona Simpson skipped most of his professional accomplishments to focus on painting the picture of Jobs as a holistic person: his personality, love for family, and unique quirks. In a heartbreaking closing, she shared his final days and ultimately his final words:

> He was saying goodbye and telling me he was sorry, so sorry we wouldn't be able to be old together as we'd always planned, that he was going to a better place.
>
> His breath indicated an arduous journey, some steep path, altitude.
>
> He seemed to be climbing.
>
> But with that will, that work ethic, that strength, there was also sweet Steve's capacity for wonderment, the artist's belief in the ideal, the still more beautiful later.
>
> Steve's final words...were monosyllables, repeated three times.
>
> Before embarking, he'd looked at his sister Patty, then for a long time at his children, then at his life's partner, Laurene, and then over their shoulders past them.
>
> Steve's final words were:
>
> OH WOW. OH WOW. OH WOW.[52]

Everyone, like Rosa Parks, Steve Jobs, and Tony, might be missed for all the gifts their achievements have given the world. But regardless of whether you're an internationally recognized figure or household-renowned best dad, mom, son, daughter, sister, brother, aunt, or uncle, it's not about the titles you have, the money you make, or the multiple statuses you've achieved in life. What will be most missed is the human being that you are and the humanity you showed through compassion, care, and love to others.

So the questions become: "Are you living in a way that centers what you hope to be remembered for? Are your motivations for achievement extrinsic (for some external reward) or intrinsic (because it's meaningful to you)?" "Is your livelihood (the money you make) laddering up to your Purpose + Values?" "Are your decisions culminating in something that's greater than yourself, in service of others and therefore the world?"

YOLO stands for "You Only Live Once."

A close cousin of YOLO is LOYLL. "Live Out Your Living Legacy."

Looking back at your Happiness Heartbeats exercise, think through the words you'd want shared when the time comes for your eulogy to be written. Who would speak at your memorial service? What would they say? What is the legacy you actively live and hope will live on beyond you?

Try not to overthink it—you can keep it simple, recalling the things about which you can say, "*Wow!* I'm so glad I did that!" Reflect on those moments of your Happiness Heartbeats, the highs and lows of your journey that make your ME genuinely you. Write your eulogy in the simplest way that memorializes your ME now. Think of it as the living legacy you want to lead with every waking day, not after the lottery we've all won—being alive—expires.

EXERCISE 3:
WRITE YOUR PURPOSE STATEMENT

Now that you have a better sense of your values and your living legacy, you can see why it's so essential to live in alignment with them every day. Next, by writing a purpose statement, you galvanize how you're a part of something bigger than yourself, and you quiet the questions about whether you're spending your time meaningfully. When it comes to purpose in the workplace, you see how you're making a positive contribution to your ME, WE, and COMMUNITY, no matter what role you're in or the responsibilities your position holds.

There's a classic business school story of President John F. Kennedy asking a custodian what he does for NASA. The custodian responded, "I'm helping put a man on the moon." No one really knows if that's truth or folklore, but from what we've seen at DH, this kind of story is happening every day.

It doesn't matter if you're a customer service rep, a warehouse manager, or the CEO. Everyone is born with a purpose, and each life's journey is about identifying it. Every journey entails experiencing our purpose among our highs and lows, facing that purpose with both courage and fear, and shaping it as we expand ourselves and gain wisdom along the way.

Your personal purpose can be captured as a statement, something you can share with others, reflect on when you're making tough decisions, and rely on when you're feeling lost in the chaos of life. Purpose is what naturally instills the *resilience* to adapt and solve problems we've never encountered and the *motivation* to be productive even in the most challenging of times.

Purpose is what young Mulan sought when she left her home to fight for her ailing father and what Carl, the elderly widower in the movie *Up*, searched for after losing the love of his life. It's the through line of your hero's journey that weaves together the richness of your life experiences and the question you'd walk to the end of the earth to answer. It goes back to the hero's journey every time.

We all need to be guided by our purpose, especially at a time when our world needs ordinary people and everyday leaders to take extraordinary actions and be heroes.

While it may seem daunting to define your purpose, your purpose doesn't have to be static. We can redefine and adjust it along the way. As Frédéric Laloux describes in his book *Reinventing Organizations*,

"Evolutionary purpose...is a much more profound shift in perspective. It asks us to truly see the organization as a living entity...to stop trying to predict and control the future, but instead continuously listen and respond to the organization's purpose. We [then] have a duty to... inquire into our personal calling to see if and how it resonates with the organization's purpose. We try to imbue our roles with our souls, not our egos."[53]

If you've already drafted your eulogy, your ever-evolving purpose statement should be a relative walk in the park, with the two hand in hand.

At DH, we say the best elements of a purpose statement are light, talent, and impact. The same question you asked yourself before the Happiness Heartbeats exercise applies here as well—it's your choice as to whether you're drafting a purpose statement for you at work, outside work, or both. (Note: We're big believers in the buddy or truddy [three-person buddy] systems of doing this exercise with your friends or coworkers. If appropriate, a glass of wine or whiskey to open up possibilities can be included.)

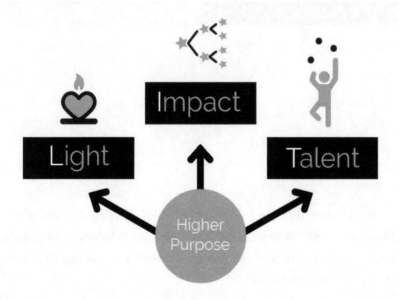

Let's walk through each of these elements so we can draft your own personal purpose statement, starting with light. When it comes to light, think about those moments when you get so fired up by something, you have absolutely no choice but to do something about it. Here are some questions to help identify your light:

- What ignites you in good and bad ways at work, at home, in the world?
- What are your irrepressible urges that no one can stop?
- What triggers you to take action day in and day out?

You might consider things like abuse of power and taking advantage of the underdog; mental shortsightedness, narrow-mindedness, and judgment; conformity and taking the easy way out. Sometimes the fire comes from the irrepressible need to express yourself, whether it's through dance, designing, writing, coding, or inventing; sometimes it comes from an urge to support people through struggles similar to what you've survived yourself.

Light	Go deeper. Find the energy
Common theme:	

Choose your top three to five lights and then go deeper. What is behind each light? Why do you personally care? Where is the passion coming from? Find the energy and from there zoom out and find a common theme among your lights.

Now move on to your talents. Ask yourself:

- What comes easily and effortlessly to you?
- What do your coworkers, friends, and family ask you to help them out with the most?
- What do people you know or complete strangers compliment you on?

You might say, "I'm analytical; I like to ask questions and break the status quo; I'm good at explaining my position and winning debates; I can pick up an instrument and play songs based on sound alone."

Talent	Go deeper. Find the energy
Common theme:	

Do the same thing here as with your lights. List your top three to five talents and ask deepening questions to find the energy that connects them. Note that sometimes it can be tricky to find a common theme if you have an array of talents. Just find a through line that feels true for you.

Now let's shift to impact.

- If you could apply your lights and talents to make a change in the world, what would it be?
- If you could dedicate yourself to any cause, what would it be?

- What would you like your living legacy to be (almost too easy because you've already done this!)?

Again, list your top three to five desired impacts, then go deeper to find the energy connecting them by asking, "Why do those things matter to me? What would the world look like if I were able to make this impact?"

Impact	Go deeper. Find the energy
Common theme:	

Reflect on all your responses and look for places where you're seeing the highest, most natural hot spots of energy coming from you. Put them all together in a purpose statement.

Put It All Together: Draft 1

My Purpose is to use...

my Talent for: **(T)** _____

and my Light for: **(L)** _____

to do [Impact]: **(I)** _____

Put It All Together: Draft 2

My Purpose is to use...

my Talent for: **(T)** _____

and my Light for: **(L)** _____

to do [Impact]: **(I)** _____

A purpose statement could look something like these:

1. *My purpose is to use my talent of deep analytical thinking and my light to fight against injustice to have an impact by expanding love and consciousness in my community and the world.*
2. *I would like to use my talent of connecting with people to create new teams or subcommunities at work that can help defuse social and racial injustice at and outside of work.*
3. *I create visual storytelling through my work for leaders and managers in my organization so we can keep communication and alignment high while our company goes through pivots and massive changes.*

Don't worry if it's not perfect. It shouldn't be. It's important to make progress, not perfection. No one gets it right the first time, and you have tomorrow and every day thereafter to reflect on it, live it, and see how your words resonate or need to be adjusted. This is the raw form of purpose that represents where you are today, not necessarily forever. Like the first brushstroke on a canvas or a piece of clay being shaped, it'll get refined.

Throughout this book, I mention people who have done this exercise and recognize how simple their purpose can be. We tend to overthink what a purpose statement is because it sounds so big and lofty. Articulating the *why* of your existence doesn't necessarily happen in one exercise, but you can capture at least some version of it. And just writing down what fires you up (light), what your superpowers are (talent), and how you want to see things change (impact)—*all together at the same time*—is the best step to take.

Understanding your Purpose + Values helps do away with distractions and gives clarity to your everyday actions. It provides a sense of control over your decisions and a sense of progress even when you have a lifetime of experiences and learning ahead of you. Your Purpose + Values become a barometer that helps you make decisions. Should I find a new role or new job? Should I say yes to this project? Should I go home to visit the family? Should I stay in this relationship?

Then there are the day-to-day decisions you have to make too. Imagine not having to question whether you're spending your valuable minutes in life wisely, because you've already invested the time to align your Purpose + Values with your everyday actions.

But what happens when you follow a paycheck instead of purpose? And how do you get back on track when your purpose is misaligned?

Jorge Rosas Torres spent eleven years working as a labor lawyer and principal partner at a prestigious law firm, checking the boxes of traditional success—money, title, and status—along the way.

On what started as an otherwise unremarkable day, he ran into an old friend and fellow labor attorney, Noemi Zozaya. They commiserated about their jobs and came to a mutual admission that they weren't following their purpose. They had originally become labor lawyers to help people and ended up doing the opposite, debilitating people. Every interaction was the opposite of a triple win, and Jorge made the cringing calculation that he had been in charge of firing at least thirty thousand people.

"I felt like I owed thirty thousand souls in my life," Jorge lamented. "In order to catch up and be all right with my life and my karma," he knew he had to make a change.

What happens in the afterlife is unknowable, but karma was going to be a bitch if Jorge had thirty thousand souls waiting for him on the other side of fate's door. So he decided to transform his career. He started making amends by being a hirer instead of a firer. He went into HR to return to his focus on helping people (his light) by using his leadership skills (his talent) to change lives for the better (his impact), which was the very reason he had become a lawyer in the first place.

He began a new position as an HR executive at Cinépolis, the largest cineplex chain in Mexico. Stopping at a bookstore before catching a flight, he picked up a copy of *Delivering Happiness* and read it on the plane. By the time his flight landed, he knew his company (and the world) needed happiness at work. Ninety-five percent of Cinépolis's workforce was comprised of millennials, and he knew they didn't care much about being "successful"; their priority was to be happy.

Within a year and a half, he hired the first chief happiness officer in Latin America, and together they improved employee engagement by 25 percent and reduced turnover from 100 percent to 60 percent. Cinépolis emphasized the importance of culture and service, gained 25 percent of the region's market share, and was named the best HR team in Mexico by AMEDIRH (Asociación Mexicana de Directores de Recursos Humanos, aka Mexican Association of Human Resources Directors).

Soon afterward, Jorge was hired by Disney as its global head of diversity, inclusion and wellness in New York. It was around that time, fourteen years since their first meeting, that he reached out to his old labor law friend Noemi again. While Jorge had been making amends for the thirty thousand souls he had fired, Noemi had been on her own journey of growth and transformation. She had gone back to school, gotten a master's degree in labor law and human resources and one in positive psychology, and was the head of diversity and inclusion at Citigroup.

When Jorge invited her for coffee, Noemi told him all about DH and her dream of bringing it to their home country, Mexico. Jorge asked, "Why haven't you started it yet?" Noemi said, "I am not sure if Mexico is ready." He said, "Yes, trust me on this one, and if you'd like, I'd love to start this project with you!" After twenty minutes they decided to take the purpose plunge. They quit their jobs, aligned their lights, talents, and impact, and partnered up to form the first DH satellite in Latin America, DH Mexico.

Noemi shared, "It's been pure magic. I used to think that I am a lucky girl, but I realized it's not luck, when you are aligned with your Purpose + Values, you are aligned with life itself."

EXERCISE 4:
THE WHEEL OF WHOLENESS

Before 2020, the trend for companies was to manage the employee experience. But the personal and professional struggles everyone has endured since then have made it obvious that the employee experience isn't progressive—or human—enough anymore. Now it's about being supportive of people's *life* experiences too. Mentally, emotionally, physically, financially, and spiritually. But the onus of defining and prioritizing what this means doesn't fall on the employers 100 percent; it's also up to everyone to decide for themselves what's important in their long-term view of work/life integration. Leaders can then listen and do what's in their abilities to support their employees.

This is the right way to elevate humanity in the workplace, and as we've seen from culture transformations over the years, taking care of people just makes business sense too. People live better lives while performing at elevated levels and making customers happier as well. A 2020 study from Gallup on employee well-being showed that employees thriving in the areas of career, social, physical, financial, and community well-being are more than twice as likely to say they adapt well to change, 81 percent less likely to seek out a new employer in the next year, 41 percent less likely to miss work due to poor health, 36 percent more likely to recover fully after illness, injury, or hardship, and 27 percent less likely to have changed jobs in the previous twelve months. The message was clear: take care of your people and they'll take care of your business.[54] A triple win again.

Wholeness at work is about embracing people's entire lives, not just the time they spend when they're on the clock. Knowing what we feel proud and passionate about is one thing; knowing what we suck at is important too. Empowering employees' wholeness looks like providing a space of psychological safety for employees to admit when they're wrong, to address tensions as they come, and to accept it when people express anger, shame, and disappointment...especially when those emotions are directed at themselves.

The more people feel safe not hiding who they are by putting on a "work mask," the more they can feel like they belong. Trust goes up and fears of being exposed or called out go down. We create more meaningful connections and have a collective purpose for the team (which we'll get into in the next chapter) that has everyone's own ME Purpose + Values completely aligned with it.

The Wheel of Wholeness is a tool you can use to capture what's most important in each individual life and what we as leaders can do to support people through their integrated work/life journeys. It's called a wheel rather than a circle because you can imagine it turning—and immediately see how smooth or bumpy that life is going to be. Someone can be happy because they're feeling high in purpose and spirituality, but at the same time recognize that their basic need for sufficient income isn't being met and needs to be realized in a more sustainable way. The wheel captures the full spectrum of a person, not just a slice.

For every piece of the pie, the individual defines their level of satisfaction. Everyone's wheel can be defined differently, but here are the most common categories:

Wheel of Wholeness

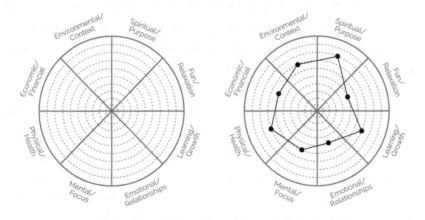

- Spiritual/Purpose
- Fun/Relaxation
- Learning/Growth
- Emotional/Relationships
- Mental/Focus
- Physical/Health
- Economic/Financial
- Environmental/Context

After identifying the eight aspects of work/life experience, people can rank their level of satisfaction in each with a dot in each category and connect the dots to see what their Wheel of Wholeness looks like.

Questions to ask ourselves once we get that "snapshot" of our lives:

- How bumpy (or smooth) is my wheel?
- What makes the high scores so high?
- What makes the low scores so low?
- What are the areas to shift, change, and improve?
- What are the actions that can be taken to make that happen?

By revisiting our wheels every month or quarter, we get to see what's worth celebrating because of the progress made and what needs to be focused on next. Not only does this help with self-evaluation for the ME, leaders and employees can check in with one another for accountability.

Having an honest answer about where you think you land in each category also doesn't mean it's up to someone else to fix your low scores. The activity is about looking into a mirror, not relying on a mechanic. If you're scoring yourself low in the "Economic/Financial" category, it's a good thing to share transparently, but that doesn't automatically mean something can or will be done about it.

What the wheel provides is a way to reflect and have more meaningful check-ins with yourself and the people you work with. The wheel lets people feel valued holistically, not just for the skills they're getting paid for. It can also show potential candidates and new recruits how companies work differently.

In the end, the Wheel of Wholeness is just another effective tool that lets everyone in a company—no matter their role or level in the org—take regular snapshots of their fulfillment, feel supported and seen, and stay on top of living their best ME.

In the earlier chapter "Do the Most Important Work in Your Life," I shared how David Kidder, Miki Agrawal, and Keith Ferrazzi adapted when they faced their blind spots and fears. When they were vulnerable, curious, and courageous enough to face their shadow sides, they spotted a brighter light within themselves and for the leadership of others.

Knowledge of one's own Purpose + Values can also be seen in Tony and his aspiration to build greenhouses for others while fulfilling a living legacy every day before he passed.

There are so many other stories of people who inspire me by the honesty of their actions, who ripple a purposeful impact without expectation of recognition. One I'd like to share is about Manuel.

Manuel was a seventy-two-year-old bathroom attendant for Cinépolis, the same cineplex chain that employed Jorge. Among forty thousand employees, he was runner-up for an award celebrating living out the brand's purpose. But the best part of Manuel's story wasn't about the award itself, it was the way he lived out the company's purpose by living out his own first.

When asked why he is so happy at his job, Manuel said, "I have two salaries. The salary I live on is the salary Cinépolis pays me. The salary *for me* to live is a notebook. I clean restrooms, sometimes twenty-six per hour. After I finish cleaning the restroom, I wait outside welcoming all the guests as if they were entering the Four Seasons Hotel. As guests use the facility, I listen and I write all the comments in this notebook. I hear things like, '*Wow!* This restroom is cleaner than my home!' "

He carried that notebook with him every day, capturing everyone's responses as they experienced the immaculate space that he took so much pride in providing. "*This* is the salary that I live for."

Manuel became a reminder that we can wake up for work every day with purpose, with a smile on our face for ourselves, knowing that smile is contagious. Most of us might not think that being a bathroom attendant is living a purpose. But as American poet and civil rights activist Maya Angelou said, "If you don't like something, change it. If you can't change it, change your attitude."

Manuel's attitude is the epitome of living a purpose and tending one's greenhouse. Being true to that might be the hardest easy work you'll do. But at least you'll know it's the most worthwhile.

Part III

RIPPLE THE ME TO THE WE

It's one thing to know your own Purpose + Values and your living legacy, but leaving it at that doesn't initiate the ripple. That's asking, "What's in it for me?" without asking, "What's in it for all?"

In Part I we talked about Maslow's hierarchy of human needs. I find it fascinating that Maslow had a revelation about twenty years after coming up with his framework. Self-actualization, he realized, wasn't quite the peak after all. If we really want to level up in life, the real top of the pyramid is transcendence. It's interesting how we rarely see this edit, but to me it's probably the most profound part of Maslow's work.

Maslow describes transcendence as "the very highest and most inclusive or holistic levels of human consciousness."

We know that people successfully climb the ladder and entrepreneurs sell off companies all the time, and for a while they think they've

"made it." But inevitably, sometimes very late in their lives, there will be a little voice in their heads whispering, "Pssst. This isn't it."

And I know—because part of my job is about helping people recognize this emptiness in themselves—that this is a gut-wrenching moment. I've seen CEOs who break down when they let their egos go for a vulnerable minute and experience the emptiness of working so hard for so long with nothing to show for it except an uptick in their bank accounts; entrepreneurs who earned a place in start-up lore but at the cost of downticks in their relationships, oftentimes with depression, divorce, and lost time with their kids; and CFOs who apologize for their past callousness in treating people like dollar signs instead of human beings.

I started thinking about people who have been able to separate ego from success, especially those from humble beginnings who became "successful" in public ways. Ashton Kutcher came to mind, so I pinged him to see if he had anything new to share about where he is in life. We met at South by Southwest in Austin during the first book tour for *Delivering Happiness*. Tony and I had rented a school bus to promote the book, give people rides around town, and offer up a charging station for their cell phones. Ashton hopped on board, and we got to chatting.

He struck me as someone who wanted to leverage his fame for good. He had, for example, cofounded the nonprofit Thorn with Demi Moore to leverage technology to curb human trafficking and child exploitation. He also often went back to visit his alma mater, the University of Iowa, and his old professor, David Gould, to inspire students to pursue their passions. He was also curious about how entrepreneurship could be applied toward positivity.

Our subsequent conversations would get to Maslow-level shit pretty quick, so I was curious to see where his ME was. I was heartened to hear how he'd realized that his personal growth meant being his most authentic, vulnerable ME for the ultimate purpose of serving the WE.

Says Ashton:

> I've found . . . that I have a tendency to cast myself in who I once was. My identity as a child was that of a twin brother. Then a good student. Then a child of a broken household. Then the brother of a heart transplant survivor. Then an outsider. When I was eighteen I broke into my high school and was charged with third-degree burglary. I then cast myself as a criminal. At every event of life I cast myself in the role that my personal history had given me and played the victim of those circumstances. The moment I shifted my perspective to that of the [beneficiary] of those experiences and recognized that my identity was choice as opposed to an effect of my past, this allowed me to own my qualities. All of them. [Then] work on the ones

that were working against my goals. It gave me the space to laugh at myself because I know that I can change. It gave me the courage to simply be who I am and pursue the best me possible. *My definition of the best me possible is one that is of maximum contribution to others.*

The disconnect between purpose, values, and success happened to my own brother, James. He's a husband, father of two girls, an established entrepreneur, and an executive coach. He prided himself on the fact that his top value was family. He wanted to work hard because he was providing for the people he loved. What more noble cause is there? But when he noticed his five-year-old daughter was calling him Daddy Work instead of Daddy, he wondered where she got that from. It was because every time she asked where he was, his wife would say, "Daddy's working."

In that moment he was heartbroken. He realized that the way he spent his time was at odds with what he thought he was doing— prioritizing his family. James worked his butt off to make sure they were taken care of, but what good was that when he wasn't around to spend meaningful moments with them? He realized the compass of his purpose said one thing, but his time on the clock was spent in a contradictory way. As selfless as he was being, he was too absorbed in trying to provide the best financial support for his family, forgetting how much that took away from the most important thing—actually being present for them.

But James was self-aware enough to hold up a mirror and look deeply within. He looked at his own lights and shadows, at his true Purpose + Values, and most importantly at the behaviors that were supporting them (or not). He took it upon himself to do a 180 in his life and commit to reprioritizing what he truly valued. He took a long break from work to reestablish his role in the family and commit to his values. They went on RV trips to national parks, he taught them recipes our grandparents used to make, and he attended every one of their basketball games. James earned the right not to be Daddy Work anymore; he was Daddy once again.

What Maslow came to see is that we can self-actualize all day in a vacuum if we choose. But if we don't transcend to the next plateau of caring about others self-actualizing too, we haven't truly reached a place of meaning. Our sense of purpose might feel solid for ourselves, but without identifying how we're serving others, we're not making the most of our MEs.

In other words, as we nurture our own greenhouse, we need to help others tend theirs in order to become our whole, best selves.

I recently spoke with Shawn Achor, fellow happiness junkie and author of *The Happiness Advantage* and *Big Potential*, about this idea. He described what he calls one of his favorite psychology studies: "Two researchers in Virginia found that if you are looking at a hill you need to climb in front of you . . . if you look at that hill by yourself, your brain shows you a picture of a hill that is 20 percent steeper than when you view that hill standing next to someone who is going to climb it with you. This is crucial."

Shawn explained what this study means for businesses. "Happiness is not an individual sport inside our organizations. Instead, we need an interconnected approach to happiness and success."

Amen, Achor!

The study he cites is another way of seeing the never-ending, dynamic balance of the questions: "What's in it for me?" and "What's in it for all?" In the end we're all connected, and we all find that transcendence comes from rippling out from the ME to the WE.

Build a People Ecosystem

To show how much impact WE greenhouses can have on an organization, let's gamify for a moment. Imagine you're playing Monopoly 2.0, an alternate version that prioritizes people and the planet. Instead of the goal being to make the most money, it's to build the most sustainable people ecosystem—a global society made up of collections of purpose-led greenhouses around the world, including those of everyone within each organization *and* everyone the organization interacts with (i.e., COMMUNITY). These greenhouse collections are designed to grow *and* do good for people and the planet. The more greenhouses you have, the more green you have too...in the form of money. In other words, if you do good for people and the planet, you'll be more profitable and sustainable. A triple win.

▶ PEOPLE ECOSYSTEM

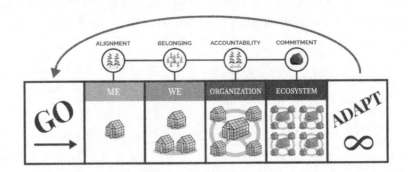

Here's what the Monopoly pieces represent:

- A house is your own greenhouse.
- A collection of houses is your team in the organization.
- A hotel is the organization.
- Everything on the game board is the people ecosystem.

We're not concerned about building too many greenhouses because as long as investments are made to ensure they're sustainable and conditions are maintained inside, they can stay on the board. Everyone tends their (ME) greenhouses so they can work together (WE) and multiply their impact, helping the entire people ecosystem (the collective COMMUNITYs). Profits become the fuel for a more virtuous circle for everyone.

In this game everyone is incentivized to do the same thing—build more greenhouses than the other players—but not at the expense of the others playing. The competition is about how well you build greenhouses, group them together into teams and companies, and keep the people ecosystem growing. All the players succeed by keeping the people ecosystem thriving, even if they don't "win."

I wouldn't be surprised if this board game exists already (if it doesn't...feel free to build on it ☺) because it represents how many companies are beginning to look at the business world as a positive-sum game. It's time for the old-school Monopoly mentality of winner takes all to evolve. In this new game, even the technical "losers" with the fewest greenhouses aren't really losers at all, because our collective MEs, WEs, and COMMUNITYs are growing and increasing their impact on our shared people ecosystem of the world.

When we build greenhouses the right way, we'll have companies and communities that are:

- Self-organized, so people initiate solutions instead of waiting to do what they're told.

- Made up of individual, distributed leaders to optimize the minds of all, not just one or a few.
- Adaptive to new strategies, projects, and goals that will be constantly changing.
- Creative, so they can think through challenges and reimagine how things can get done in a disrupted world.

And we'll have people who are:

- Actively learning and growing, failing fast but failing forward, as technology continues to exponentially evolve and new skills need to be learned.
- Resilient within themselves so they can be resilient for the company.
- Genuinely happier, more productive, and fully engaged to do whatever it takes to contribute in meaningful ways.

If any of this sounds familiar, it's because a healthy people ecosystem is designed to thrive in the Adaptive Age, to quickly address any VUCA or FUD that comes its way.

The Greenhouse Conditions to Adapt and Thrive

As we know, greenhouses help stabilize ideal conditions so plants can grow. They help protect against extreme weather and provide a better climate for plants that would struggle outside. As I mentioned in Part I, we can create conditions within orgs that let people grow and thrive.

These conditions can be found at companies large and small, public and private, in cultures and countries all over the world. You'll notice that the conditions are all inspired by nature. That's partly because I'm a huge fan of living legend Sir David Attenborough, the 94-year-old British nature adventurer, historian, and narrator of pretty much every amazing animal documentary you've ever seen in your life. When I was a kid, my parents wouldn't let us watch *Welcome Back, Kotter* or *All in the Family*, but *Three's Company* and documentaries with Sir David? Absolutely. After hearing the first few notes of "Come and knock on our door..." or the *Mutual of Omaha's Wild Kingdom* theme song, my brothers and I would make a beeline for the living room to see what Jack Tripper or Sir David had in store for us that week.

The systems of nature got into my head, and they've become a place of refuge and inspiration as I reconnect to it. I love hearing footsteps on soft soil when hiking among the redwoods and watching the leaves of trees tremble in the wind, as my dad sang Sinatra, with sentimental ease. But the other reason the greenhouse conditions reference nature is that *nature always wins*. Plants and animal life return after a natural disaster (like a fire) or even a man-made one (like Chernobyl). No matter where humans take this planet, nature adapts and revives to thrive.

Humans? Not so much. Modern org design has a lot to learn when it comes to this. New technologies and statistical methods are giving us more insight than ever into the differences between habitats that just survive and those that thrive. Scientists have discovered that behaviors across all kinds of animal species share very similar foundations. Which implies that whatever animals are doing right, humans should be able to mimic or replicate.

The Darwin-inspired observation that animals "most responsive to change" will outlast the others can now be applied to ensure people ecosystems will thrive too—but only if certain greenhouse conditions exist. Let's do a deep dive into the four greenhouse conditions one at a time.

GREENHOUSE CONDITION 1: ALIGNMENT

Animal behavior at the collective (group) level is more similar than scientists once believed. In one study they looked at the movements of several different species. First bees in their honeycomb doing their job of making honey (yet seemingly butting heads). Then blue jack mackerel swarming in the sea to protect themselves from predators (but never really going anywhere other than literally in circles). Finally they observed how starlings moved in flight. You may have seen videos of them online, appearing as if they had choreographed beautiful dances of synchronized flying. What they were really doing was coordinating their speed and direction based on each other's movements, influenced by the actions of a predator. (Sorry to deflate the romantic notion that they're choreographing a show for you, but maybe you should start paying them more.)

What researchers discovered is that the algorithms of movement in all of these animals were exactly the same except for one variable:

alignment. Technically, they were all getting their job done, but bees had the least alignment, whereas starlings had the most.

The takeaway in the context of org design is that if we want our teams to keep from butting heads or swimming in circles, we need a set of rules in place to get them aligned. That's where individual purpose, values, and behaviors (PVBs) come into play. Purpose provides the destination, or goal, to which the team and company need to go. Values and behaviors act as the rules.

By getting Purpose + Values aligned from the ME of individuals to the WE of teams and the org, we ensure that there's no room for micromanaging seagull managers (those who fly in, make a lot of noise, crap on everything, suffocate creativity and productivity, and then leave).

By clearly stating the PVBs for people to align with, people ecosystems are able to let employees be themselves, with their hands on the scientific levers of happiness—control to make their own decisions, progress knowing they're all in flight, and connectedness because they're heading toward the same goal together.

But what happens when there isn't alignment between a person and an org?

Even when someone believes in the Purpose + Values of a company and has skills that an org needs, the initial fit can still end up in misalignment. With the rate of change in this Adaptive Age, it's not surprising. It should be expected. The needs of both employers and employees are rapidly changing, which is why alignment should be seen as an ongoing process. If someone isn't living according to the company's Purpose + Values or not performing as they are expected to, the hard-line point of view is that it's a detriment to the rest of the company and evidence of a bad fit. We've all been in meetings or on teams where one person seems oblivious to how much they're negatively affecting everyone else in productivity, efficiency, and, ultimately, happiness. If you haven't noticed these people exist, you might want to consider whether that person is you (wink).

But since it's a process, if the organization has done its part by clearly articulating its culture and expectations in the role, then it becomes a dialogue with the potential for coaching, learning, and growth. In adaptive orgs, we systemically embed a growth mindset by providing opportunities for people to keep developing. We encourage them to explore new things, especially when there's an enthusiasm to learn them. At DH we've had folks like Angela Ice, who went from HR to operations to culture to eventually land where she's most passionate—accounting and numbers. When she first started, she wouldn't have dreamed that would become her passion, but her curiosity led her to try new things, and our greenhouse model (or, in her case, igloo) allowed her to grow and land in the right role.

As Carol Dweck, author and TED speaker, describes the growth mindset: "This view creates a love of learning and a resilience that is essential for great accomplishment."[55] Just the qualities adaptive orgs need.

With the growth mindset, there's a fear of missteps and inefficiencies, but if it's about failing forward to innovate, it becomes a no-brainer. When there's accountability (greenhouse condition 3), people ecosystems and orgs can adapt quickly. With open and honest communication, there should be no surprises if culture or skills contribution are no longer aligned. Both employee and org should make it abundantly clear when there's misalignment, to the point where there's usually mutual agreement when it's best for someone to find another role or company. You'd be surprised how many people actually select themselves out when they realize their Purpose + Values aren't aligned with those of others at work. Most of the time, they'd rather find work somewhere they can be their authentic selves.

In the most adaptive orgs, alignment can be seen as social contracts being constantly revised and reviewed together, with every employee having equal rights to express and figure out what collective best next steps could be.

Says Matt Mullenweg (cofounder of WordPress and CEO and founder of Automattic), "We try to make our purpose clear so the world at large, potential hires, and current employees all have the same sense of who we are and what we're doing. I would say that it's rare that alignment on purpose would be the proximate cause for letting someone go; much more important is keeping clear accountability and expectations for a role, and it will usually show up there if someone isn't fully aligned."

The more specific you can be on what alignment means for your org, the more effective it will be. Doing the ME exercises is foundational for understanding how you align with the WE of your teams and orgs. The Happiness Heartbeats and Wheel of Wholeness serve as snapshots of a person to show where they are, and at the same time, they're a gift to leaders to show them how they can best support each person's life (beyond just work). The more people feel supported, the longer they'll stay, the better they'll serve customers, and the more the business will succeed. The triple win.

After DH worked with Toyota in Spain, Toyota shifted from a product-focused to a customer- and employee-focused structure. Improving the holistic employee experience became a priority, so the Experience Toyota program was born. Following a model the company had developed for the customer experience, it designed a program to address every touchpoint the employees had over their time with the company. Verónica Fernández, shareholder and executive coach|sultant® at DH Spain, explains: "The employee experience included all of the interactive moments from hiring, onboarding, change management, and meeting with management. Even to the extent of making sure people being laid off or fired were aligned with their core values."

Mapping out the employee experience helps companies understand the direct one-to-one relationship it has with the customer experience. If the employee lifetime value (the estimated financial value that an employee brings to an org over the lifetime of working at the company) increases, the odds are that the customer lifetime value (the estimated profit from the entire relationship with a customer) will too. When we start reframing employees like customers—both assets to the company instead of liabilities—it makes our finance function happy too. How?

It makes each plot point of the employee experience—hiring and firing, training and development—a metric that matters and needs to be measured. And once you have the elements of culture in place, like Purpose + Values (exercise 2, later in this section, shares how to establish this with alignment in mind), finance will see how any "expense" of culture is actually an investment toward saving money and making more.

Alignment also means systemically creating teams that recognize and help people naturally play to their strengths. Using assessments like CliftonStrengths (previously known as StrengthsFinders, an evaluation tool to assess what people naturally do best) is a decent start, but it doesn't do much long-term good unless it becomes a constant dialogue from there. Having monthly or quarterly check-ins on employees' Wheels of Wholeness also lets you monitor what's going well and what's going awry. What are the projects and tasks that people felt a sense of autonomy, flow, and progress in? Which felt draining and unproductive? What other project paths in or out of people's current roles might they be interested in? How are the team dynamics between coworkers and leads? Would people prefer vegan instead of pepperoni pizza for the late-night sprints next time?

As I mentioned previously, the term *self-management* is tainted with the idea that people do whatever they want, whenever they want. To be clear, asking people for their input within self-managed structures doesn't mean they get to drop every boring task and lounge at the café or clubhouse until an interesting project pops up. Dialogue helps balance what people have to do and what they want to do.

Assuming the heavy lifting (and upfront financial investment) to vet for skills and culture contribution were done diligently in the hiring process, it makes sense to spend the extra effort to see how alignment can continue. Otherwise, we know the cost of turnover can add up really quickly (depending on role and salary, it can range from 150 percent of an employee's salary to 213 percent in the C-suite).[56] And to make matters worse, misalignment erodes into a triple loss because everyone ends up unhappy.

But employees and leaders having open, honest conversations create transparent and adaptable structures for an ongoing, healthier alignment.

Across all our clients, one of the sessions that has the lowest lift for the biggest impact happens when we get executive leadership alignment. If there's eight execs in the room, it's not surprising if there are eight interpretations of their Purpose + Values. By the end of the session, the goal is to unify them on one.

We help remind them of their personal and collective whys in being at the company. We revisit whether their stated values are still the right ones, advise on how the whole company can stay accountable for its behaviors, and help identify their roles so everyone is walking the talk.

We hold up mirrors to see if they're authentically living their values or just expecting others to. We've seen execs voluntarily leave a company because they don't believe accountability applies to them. Other times we've seen leaders step up because they recognize the insincerity in not holding themselves to the same standards as the people they oversee, so they adjust to truly live out their stated values and behaviors. Such a session becomes a time of reckoning not just for the company but for individuals as well.

At an alignment session we had with execs at a financial services company, you could tell tensions were high when the subject of accountability came up. The point of the discussion was for them to see that investing time and money was essentially a waste if they couldn't be positive examples of living their values and embrace the 360 feedback they were getting. One of our coach|sultants®, Ron (aka "the wise owl"), explained they'd be abdicating their responsibility as leaders and hurting their credibility if they didn't. The room got so heated that Ron (who's usually calm and collected, hence the nickname) just called out the elephant in the room. Shaking his head in utter disbelief, he said, "If you don't step up . . . well, the shame is on you."

It startled everyone. Consultants weren't supposed to be the ones doing the reprimanding in the room. But the message landed, and major shifts happened because the CEO chose to evolve to be a more conscious leader. And those who refused to align? They saw themselves to the exit. Those who stayed stepped up to their new responsibilities, and the company grew faster than it ever had before.

When it comes to alignment, I love Chip Conley's metaphor of a rowing team:

> There's a rowing term, *swing*, that has helped me to see that in the most challenging times, you need to create alignment and magical things can happen. For a crew of eight with a coxswain (the person navigating the boat) directing the team, this means finding a way for everyone to row in unison and feel connected. If you do that well, the boat miraculously elevates in the water so that the friction of the water isn't holding them back. This way they can glide faster and more effortlessly. The metaphor has worked with my leadership teams for the last major downturns: 9/11 and the dot-com crash, the Great Recession, and the pandemic.

If you're going to put time, money, and energy into building teams ready for the future of work, it's worth sussing out whether everyone is aligned to be positive examples of values and behaviors so *everyone* in the org—top down, bottom up—will be gliding with less friction together.

GREENHOUSE CONDITION 2: BELONGING

People are three and a half times more likely to perform at their fullest potential when they feel a sense of belonging at work.[57] When we're not only embracing but *creating* greater (bio)diversity in our workplaces, we're building conditions that let people feel that they belong so that they're at their best.

If you're a fan of Sir David Attenborough too, you know biodiversity is what determines why certain ecosystems thrive whereas others die off. When there's an abundance of species and varieties in plants, animals, and microorganisms, it keeps ecosystems sustainable. They're more productive because every species has a specific role to play. Their habitats are more stable and recover more quickly in the event of natural disaster. It's no coincidence that the equivalent of biodiversity in a business creates the same results: sustainability, productivity, resourcefulness, resilience, and adaptability.

Applying the notion of biodiversity to people ecosystems couldn't be more timely and appropriate for the future of work. What we've learned is that all species, including humans, are adversely affected when they suffer a loss of diversity.

Creating a greenhouse of belonging starts with a conscious effort to establish a safe space for interaction and learning. This isn't about operational characteristics or leadership styles. It's about making sure every person feels like they're in a place where they can speak freely and be heard.

Our desire to interact with one another is actually physiologically hardwired in our brains in a primal way, to help us survive. In his book *Social: Why Our Brains Are Wired to Connect* by Matthew D. Lieberman, he shares evidence of how social connections are directly tied to health outcomes.[58] As a stark example, we now know that feeling lonely is worse for overall wellness than smoking fifteen cigarettes a day, making it even more dangerous than obesity according to Douglas Nemecek, MD, chief medical officer for behavioral health at Cigna.[59] But even though it has been scientifically proven that we're social creatures who thrive through contact with our peers, these days we often struggle to have a clear sense of our social needs—especially when it seems most of us would rather binge on Netflix alone than go on a hike with a friend.

A Gallup survey of more than 150 countries found that employees who say they have a best friend at work are seven times more likely to be engaged in their work.[60] When we bond with each other in teams with shared goals, we develop deeper emotional connections that pump out oxytocin, which naturally generates more empathy, more creativity, and a sense of flow in our work. All things we'd opt for over the cortisol that is raised in our bodies when the typical workplace causes us stress and anxiety.

It's important to note that belonging is related to the scientific lever of connectedness but that they're *not interchangeable.* You can have workplaces that are conducive to meaningful connections yet do not have the greenhouse condition of belonging. An "old boy network" of guys practicing nepotism (power that favors relatives or friends) can experience strong connectedness with the adverse effect of others not feeling that they're accepted, that they're treated fairly, or that they belong. These days, it's good to remember Groucho Marx's advice and question whether we want to belong to a club (or a company) just because it accepts us as a member.

This, of course, is where diversity, equity, inclusion, and belonging (DEIB) come in. Recently, more companies have been jumping on the DEIB bandwagon because they fear a loss in sales and customer loyalty. But systemic change in DEIB is not about Instagramming an image of a black square or an inspiring quote by Martin Luther King Jr. on his birthday and calling it a day. What really counts is all the days in between these high-visibility moments.

DEIB is about creating a more just, unbiased, and antiracist society. The pandemic uncovered systemic truths about where we are and how far we need to go. Minority workers saw the highest levels of unemployment because of COVID.[61] Women were more vulnerable to COVID-related economic effects because of existing gender inequalities. McKinsey & Company estimated female job loss rates were 1.8 times higher than male job loss rates globally.[62] And according to the

US Bureau of Labor Statistics, Black and Latina women experienced job loss at higher levels than their white counterparts.[63]

Studies show that diverse organizations are 35 percent more likely to outperform their peers.[64] But despite the evidence that more diverse companies tend to be more profitable and innovative, workplaces still fall short when it comes to including minority groups, especially women and people of color, in leadership roles. Google, for example, has a workplace that is only 3 percent Latinx and 2 percent Black.[65] Intel is only slightly higher with 8.05 percent and 3.67 percent, respectively.[66]

So *how* do we address this? I'll share specific methods in Part V, but the conclusion we can glean from nature is that people ecosystems are more likely to sustainably flourish if they embrace (bio)diversity.

When it comes to belonging, sometimes it's not enough to just acknowledge the elephant in the room. Sometimes we have to agitate it too, in a way that we know will allow tensions to come out. The goal is to create a space of safety, compassion, and empathy so everyone feels *heard* and *understood*. Looking back, we know we've made progress, and we know the work has just begun.

DEIB isn't just about antiracism and equity, it's about inclusion as well. It's about making sure voices can be heard equally regardless of race, gender, sexuality, personality type, rank, or title. Back in the day, leaders faced with difficult decisions believed that they alone had the "burden" of figuring things out. Now we include every voice at the table, knowing it's better to ask for input from many than to assume the input of one is the answer.

Keith Ferrazzi was consulting for one of the largest consumer packaged goods companies in the world, talking to its CEO about the coming year's strategic and financial success. "Why don't we go to your thousand top leaders and present your strategic initiatives and ask all of them to host meetings with their teams to reflect on just three questions? What are the areas of growth? What are the risks we're not seeing? What are the things that we could be doing that'd help fulfill our purpose?"

You can imagine the empowerment of an entire company cocreating implementation of purpose, risks, and growth. It was the opposite of a traditional hierarchical organization. Keith brought tools from his book, *Leading without Authority*, and used the quickest way of collecting the data: via Google Docs. It didn't take months to do; it took just weeks to collect and synthesize everyone's input. The process also spotlighted those who were impassioned to lead and make change happen.

Says Keith, "Imagine how people in an organization feel when leadership is doing things with them rather than to them or for them, right? Coming up with things for you is so different from when leadership is doing this with you." Furthermore, "It makes a huge difference in the overall of how people feel."

This goes to show that creating the condition of belonging has to start from the top. When leaders walk the talk, it trickles down to everyone in the company. "DH taught us everything starts from *you*," Aman Omarov, the CEO of BI Group, a construction company in Kazakhstan, shared after realizing culture was not just about his employees but started with his own ME too. "We are not the only company working in tough conditions, but we became one company that really cares about their people. Who really want to motivate and give people more to increase their loyalty, happiness, and all things that make our company people-centric." We saw Aman evolve from an unconvinced investor of people into a leader who became their biggest champion.

"People are changing. They are transforming by themselves!" Sofiya Akmesheva was at one time an event manager, then directed her passions to become the head of happiness for BI Group. "Our overall turnover rate decreased by 16.6 percent in 2019 and by 14 percent in 2020, Net Promotor Scores increased by 12 percent in three quarters, 2020 sales hit a record high with an increase of more than 20 percent in comparison to previous years, and profit increased 1.5 times from

2019 to 2020. In *Forbes*, Kazakhstan students chose us as a top-three employer for several positions. We took care of our people through COVID to keep productivity and engagement up in this crisis, which made a huge difference. Our internal happiness index has been rising from 7.5 out of 10 in 2019 to 7.7 in 2020. All of this has affected our brand attractiveness to external candidates and job seekers, and between the first and last quarters of 2020, the number of responses per vacancy increased by 162 percent!"

Especially for Gen Z and millennials, a culture of belonging comes from the creation of spaces where people feel safe, supported, and able to be themselves. Most importantly, from the creation of a place that nurtures their MEs and WEs so they can live out their higher purpose.

As the employee happiness index kept rising, Sofiya reflected, "We believe it's because they feel supported to do something bigger than themselves. It comes back to meaningful work and a sense of belonging."

GREENHOUSE CONDITION 3: ACCOUNTABILITY

The word *accountability* is one of the most abused (and least responsibly used) these days. Compared to words like *nature* and *humanity*, it also feels bureaucratic, dogmatic, and political.

Some people tend to expect accountability from others but somehow feel exempt when it comes to their own responsibilities. We see it happen in everyday society, across every level of government, and in law enforcement, military, and school systems. Someone else is always to blame, and, sadly, the fault often settles on someone who had little to do with the problem. Once in a while we see justice being served, but oftentimes it feels like a lost cause to fight for accountability.

But within orgs, we have an amazing opportunity to lead and act with accountability and structure in place. People across all levels should feel that there's fairness in who's being hired, fired, promoted, and censured. By creating accountability at work, in a system that's more reliable than what we see in broader society, we can restore a sense of equity and humanity in life.

Some leaders expect everyone else in their company to take responsibility for their choices, but it's a shame how many of those leaders don't want to be accountable themselves. This is where leaders can step up by being vigilant in walking the talk. If we're expecting everyone to walk in step together, we need to establish a precedent for accountability.

One way to reframe accountability is to think about it from a more human perspective. Instead of being overseen by Big Brother (or Sister), think of it as connecting and banding together. A term for this is *co-owned accountability*. When it's just about accountability, there's a sense that managers are "making" people accountable. The motivation is extrinsic because it's about expectations, rewards, and consequences. But when there's also co-ownership, people are claiming their responsibilities. People are more engaged because they're exercising the scientific levers of control, progress, and connectedness with one another. Adaptive orgs need these levers to embed co-owned accountability.

Humans are better able to survive and adapt when they work together. We used to band together as tribes to hunt or live together in villages to leverage our resources and increase our odds of survival. We were instinctively accountable to each other, because we weren't very useful when we've been eaten by a lion. But unfortunately, we've lost sight of that, and it's time we put that accountability back into our orgs. Within companies, we need to build a firm social contract around having each other's back, because we are working toward the same goals—we believe in the purpose our company has established.

When thinking of accountability in this way, I often think of my grandfather. When I was growing up he showed us how accountability is about everyone doing their part in the greater system, contributing with their own roles, and respecting the work of others. But beyond that, he had a sense of appreciation for those who pioneered before him, and he felt accountable to the generations that would survive him.

He grew up in a tiny village in the county of Toisan, Guangdong, in Southern China. His hero's journey of realizing his American dream started out with a clerkship at a grocery store and eventually led to his becoming one of the most successful real estate moguls in Sacramento. He never forgot where he came from, though, and he knew he was standing on the shoulders of every Toisan immigrant who came before him. As his Happiness Heartbeats would have it, his high swung to a low after JFK got assassinated and he lost most of his wealth in 1963. But not before he was able to give back. For years he sent money back to the village and ran the local Lim Association in Sacramento to help new immigrants get on their feet. His sense of accountability was shared across both communities—he felt a responsibility to pay forward his own success. He was a man of few words and let his actions speak for themselves.

I had an unforgettable opportunity to visit Toisan in 1995 with my entire family. It was one of those once-in-a-lifetime cross-generational experiences—stepping onto the soil of where we all came from, in the presence of the people who were born there. Watching the little kids run around in tattered T-shirts and worn flip-flops made me realize that could've been me too, and even though our lives were oceans apart, we smiled at each other with a sense of connection. A connection most strongly felt when I looked over at my grandpa, who had recognized a childhood friend he hadn't seen in about sixty years.

They shook hands and took a picture together. My grandpa was double his friend's girth. It made me think of the difference between the stout cows we see in the States and the skinny ones in Toisan. What a difference our environment can make to our bodies, but their toothy smiles in the picture were the same, as if they were little boys again. The silent respect they exchanged with their eyes made it feel as if the friendship of their youth had happened just yesterday.

This is why accountability should be reframed in a more humanistic way. Accountability isn't about blame or guilt—it's a nod to everyone who came before us and to what they fought, lived, and died for.

Nowadays we scientifically know we work better together in teams—our modern-day version of villages—bound by Purpose + Values. My dad used to point out the importance of the garbageman's role to me as a little girl, and *every* role in society and orgs is needed for us to collectively survive, let alone thrive. Reflecting on our people ecosystems gives us the opportunity to embrace our accountability to each other as humans again. With this in mind, we can see accountability as a two-way street between teams and teams of teams:

- **Leaders** are accountable to the people they lead not because they want to squeeze work and productivity out of people, but because they care about helping them grow and achieve their goals, inside and outside of work. Leaders recognize and incentivize both culture contribution and performance, not just one or the other. (As a result, leaders reap the economic rewards of people being more productive and engaged.)
- **Individuals and teams**, as well as their leaders, are accountable for their pact within their teams and company once they sign on. They live by the company's Purpose + Values (through specific behaviors), and the pact helps them perform and provide the value they were hired to do. (It's part of the pact that our life *and* work goals are supported by our leader.)

The kind of accountability I'm talking about isn't about finger-pointing or blame. It's a shared sense of respect and responsibility, built from what it means to be human to each other. Everyone is rewarded (from high-fives and "Hell yeah"s to bonuses and raises based on contribution and outcomes). Everyone owns their shortcomings or mistakes and shows their commitment to grow and improve.

Of course, we can't just pinky promise each other, then hope humanity will magically happen. Accountability also means there needs to be consequences that apply to every level of the org (including senior leadership). If any of these things aren't consistently being lived up to over time—purpose, values and behaviors, roles and responsibilities, skills and performance—from either side, it's a breach of a social contract that makes it abundantly clear there's no longer a good fit.

As I shared when I listed greenhouse condition 1, alignment, if the dialogue has been open and honest, and attempts to coach haven't created progress over time, it's time for realignment to happen.

We all know it just takes one person—in a meeting, a department, or the entire company—to hurt others' productivity (and therefore happiness). Accountability requires a hard line to be drawn with consequences in place. Otherwise people will doubt the company values have any weight because others get away with not living by them. It just takes one or two weeds to wipe out the conditions that greenhouse needs to grow.

When done right, tying rewards and repercussions to how well people live by purpose, values, and behaviors can (unsurprisingly) lead to amazing cultures. Especially when leaders walk their talk, people contribute not just for job security, promotions, or a paycheck. They contribute also because they're emotionally invested, feel like they belong, and are living their personal Purpose + Values.

If you're wondering about the most common fail factor I've seen in implementing the greenhouse condition of accountability, it boils down to one thing: lack of clearly defined *desired* behaviors. They're critical in closing the gap between good intentions and good practice. Values without behaviors are like trees without leaves. Clearly identified behaviors are the leaves (every single action and interaction) that bring values to life. People typically don't come to work with an intention to violate values. Yet every day, people behave in ways that show they don't know what their company's values are.

By providing clarity through defining behaviors, leaders can give people feedback, internal coaching, and the opportunity to improve on living the values. When we define behaviors, we live values with clarity and create a clear path to measuring, recognizing, and rewarding one another for living those values. A good example of clearly stated values and behaviors comes from Netflix, a company known for a culture that prioritizes people and values their values. Here's its example of how specific behaviors (and therefore accountability) can get:[67]

Judgement
- You make wise decisions despite ambiguity
- You identify root causes, and get beyond treating symptoms
- You think strategically, and can articulate what you are, and are not, trying to do
- You are good at using data to inform your intuition
- You make decisions based on the long term, not near term

Communication
- You are concise and articulate in speech and writing
- You listen well and seek to understand before reacting
- You maintain calm poise in stressful situations to draw out the clearest thinking
- You adapt your communication style to work well with people from around the world who may not share your native language
- You provide candid, helpful, timely feedback to colleagues

Innovation
- You create new ideas that prove useful
- You re-conceptualize issues to discover solutions to hard problems
- You challenge prevailing assumptions, and suggest better approaches
- You keep us nimble by minimizing complexity and finding time to simplify
- You thrive on change

Inclusion
- You collaborate effectively with people of diverse backgrounds and cultures
- You nurture and embrace differing perspectives to make better decisions
- You recognize we all have biases, and work to grow past them
- You intervene if someone else is being marginalized
- You are curious about how our different backgrounds affect us at work, rather than pretending they don't affect us

Curiosity
- You learn rapidly and eagerly
- You contribute effectively outside of your specialty
- You make connections that others miss
- You seek to understand our members around the world, and how we entertain them
- You seek alternate perspectives

Courage
- You say what you think, when it's in the best interest of Netflix, even if it is uncomfortable
- You make tough decisions without agonizing
- You take smart risks and are open to possible failure
- You question actions inconsistent with our values
- You are able to be vulnerable, in search of truth

Integrity
- You are known for candor, authenticity, transparency, and being non-political
- You only say things about fellow employees that you say to their face
- You admit mistakes freely and openly
- You treat people with respect regardless of their status or disagreement with you
- You always share relevant information, even when worrisome to do so

Impact
- You accomplish amazing amounts of important work
- You demonstrate consistently strong performance so colleagues can rely upon you
- You make your colleagues better
- You focus on results over process

Passion
- You inspire others with your thirst for excellence
- You care intensely about our members and Netflix's success
- You are tenacious and optimistic
- You are quietly confident and openly humble

Selflessness
- You seek what is best for Netflix, rather than what is best for yourself or your group
- You are open-minded in search of great ideas
- You make time to help colleagues

Netflix 2021 (jobs.netflix.com/culture)

GREENHOUSE CONDITION 4: COMMITMENT

As scientists have known for a while, animals and humans both live in complex systems. Trying to survive out in the wild isn't too far a cry from trying to survive in a workplace. (Sadly, I think most of us can attest to that.)

But an added finding of research on complex systems is that groups of animals in the wild act from a set of internal behavioral rules that every individual member is totally committed to. Even if groups don't have a leader, those internal rules will guide the individuals' actions. The rules themselves are largely based on how adjacent animals are behaving. If one animal starts moving right or left, the likelihood is that others will follow. As an example, that's how the flock of starlings

I mentioned earlier will self-organize, even without a single designated leader. Every starling is moving based on the multiple starlings adjacent to them until a new, temporary "leader" emerges (which could be any one of them).

So what makes certain teams highly effective at their common goal? Why are pods of dolphins or killer whales so extremely competent when they're hunting for food? Their success comes back to their commitment to each other—on the levels of what they're individually supposed to do (the ME), what's good for the pod (the WE), and to their collective *long-term* survival together. There's no reliance on one single leader to make all the decisions. They're all in it for success. They trust and leverage each other's senses, movement, and brains to capture their prey in smart, efficient ways.

But trust and instincts don't necessarily guarantee results. Whale and dolphin pods actively apply their intelligence, maintain high levels of communication, cooperate while hunting, and constantly learn and teach each other new skills and fishing methods. Within every pod, members have specific roles—from bubble blowers who form organic nets to cluster their prey to deep-divers who drive fish up toward the surface. Pods are the epitome of teamwork and adaptability, whose fishing methods are unique to the specific habitat they're living in.[68] We even call our departments "pods" and teams within them "sub-pods" at DH, to remind everyone of the organic, dynamic nature of how we're organized.

But when humans are left to their own devices, researchers have found that we can be as impressionable as a flock of sheep. Just one person walking in one direction can get the whole group to move in the same direction. If you've watched an episode of *The Walking Dead* or *The Office* or stepped into the typical office in corporate America (or the world), this is far from shocking.

What we've learned is that people ecosystems still need structure but can no longer be based on the archaic org charts of the past. The rigidity of the one-leader, top-down command-and-control structure no longer works in the future of work. The pace of change and the necessity to adapt have made traditional org charts obsolete. When org charts stay rigid, the leader doesn't dynamically shift according to the ever-changing needs of a sustainable org. The commitment is to one leader, not to all.

Taking the place of those org charts are the principles of self-organization and self-management that allow for choosing from a rotating set of leads depending on what the project is; the leader becomes the person who's best not just in qualification and skill set but in purpose alignment too. The complex system of an org becomes a network of individuals acting independently but performing the same set of behaviors, like orcas in a pod or birds in a flock. Rather than a set of teams listening to the one commander at the top, there's a team of teams (as retired US Army general Stanley McChrystal describes in his book—wait for it—*Team of Teams*) that makes decisions at all levels. All the critical information is being shared and disseminated to empower everyone—regardless of "rank"—to make informed decisions. When we modify org charts into growth maps instead, people have roving roles in projects driven by purpose and skills alignment, dynamically changing with the needs of the business.

The key here is taking the taboo from the four-letter word *self*—*self-management, self-care, self-entitlement*...and of course *selfish*. If everyone is truly committed to a common purpose, we have no need to fear people being self-guided in day-to-day work. We know we need to keep updating to new versions of an organizational operating system. But unless long-term commitment is a foundational feature of the system, we might as well be the poor folks falling into a *Walking Dead* pit of zombies waiting for lunch.

My friend Matt Mullenweg, who built WordPress when he was nineteen and is currently the CEO of Automattic, a company worth $6 billion, lives out these greenhouse conditions in his businesses not because they're cool but because they work in a world that's moving fast—and they're the only things that work at scale.

He explains the greenhouse of his more recent venture, Automattic, the company behind WordPress. Its mission is to democratize content on the web: "We built Automattic [so it would] be easy for anyone no matter where they were geographically located to be able to participate in building our products. We describe this not as remote work, but as distributed work, because there is no 'central' to be remote from. Every node on the network, every person in the company, is equally connected to each other [and] has an equal opportunity to contribute."

He also recognizes that the real power of self-organization is adaptability.

"As a side effect," Matt says, "this also made the company quite resilient to crises or challenges that only impact one geographic area, because 99 percent of the company is probably someplace else, and also to a global challenge like the pandemic since people could already work from home and weren't required to travel. We're still vulnerable in other ways; for example, if the internet were down it would be difficult to do our work or serve our customers, but when we rely on something like that we try to rely on systems like the internet that are themselves distributed, have robust failover mechanisms, and aren't reliant on a single company or organization to keep going."

Just as we can't be reliant on one company or org, we can't rely on a single person or team. As we test new versions of operating systems in this future of work, we see how self-organized, distributed companies and teams are becoming more of a norm than an exception. Every node on the network, every person in the company, is not only connected and can contribute but must commit to their role to keep the OS running.

Nature helps us understand how complex systems work through self-organization. As humans we can learn and mimic what's valuable for us. By applying the conditions of alignment, belonging, accountability, and commitment to our greenhouses, we're creating people ecosystems that foster control, progress, and connectedness (the levers of happiness). In effect, we're building environments in which people can self-elect and commit to (or self-select out of) the long-term view of adapting and thriving together.

EXERCISE 1:
CULTURE PACT

A Culture Pact is an easy go-to tool that incorporates the four greenhouse conditions: alignment, belonging, accountability, and commitment. We incorporate this activity into the start of all our workshops to set the tone and establish trust. The goal of a Culture Pact is to cocreate the conditions for folks in the room to feel seen, heard, and comfortable sharing, as well as to cocreate a safe space in which to learn and grow together. This exercise can be used to kick off projects, important meetings, or a new team. The larger org has a set of core values, but that doesn't mean you can't have your own subculture and agreed-upon values too (ideally inspired by the umbrella values of the greater org!).

1. Ask the team to think about great, high-performing teams they've been in or seen in action. Ones where the members felt truly supported and able to share ideas freely.
2. Ask them to identify specific qualities these successful teams have (e.g., caring, compassion, courage, innovation, support).
3. From there, turn these qualities into specific observable behaviors (e.g., support could translate to "Check in with how you're feeling before diving into work" or "Use language like 'yes and' rather than 'no but' when building on each other's ideas"). Have the group align on the qualities and behaviors that would most support this project/session/team and ensure there's a sense of belonging.
4. Have the team answer the question, "What do we do when things get tough or uncomfortable?" Have them determine a way anyone can keep the group accountable if the Culture Pact isn't being lived up to. It can be a safe word like *bacon*,

snaps in the air, or balling up a piece of paper and tossing it in the middle of the room. When there's a sense of trust in the room, just one of these acts can diffuse the tension to open the way for conversation.

5. Have each person agree to the Culture Pact showing they're in. From there the tone is set and you can proceed accordingly. Keep in mind that the Culture Pact can be edited by the group should new needs arise.

What qualities do we want?

Our Culture Pact	
QUALITIES OF OUR CULTURE	WHEN IT GETS TOUGH
☐ I Agree	
Signature	

Do we commit?

Establishing Culture Pacts with trust and honesty will oftentimes shed a light on the elephant(s) in the room. When we did this exercise with one of our clients, the atmosphere was thick with tension because new leadership had come in, but the previous CEO had practiced a command-and-control style that showed in the look of PTSD on most employees in the room.

When the exercise started, people brought in the usual first qualities that come to mind: "teamwork," "respect," "open mind." But then someone slowly raised their hand—it was the last person in the room anyone expected to say something. He was a young man who always seemed to be a bit distant and stoic. He suggested the quality of "being vulnerable." Everyone was shocked to hear from him as he shared that it was a quality he'd always wanted but hadn't felt safe to explore because of the top-down leadership the company had before. He said, "If we all really knew what the others here were going through, perhaps we could have more empathy and give each other the benefit of the doubt."

He shared how it used to feel like they lived in a "world of no" where ideas were consistently shot down. But now that things were changing, it was time to create a workplace where people could begin to feel safer sharing ideas. It was like the saying, "When you speak from the heart, everyone listens." By speaking his truth, he broke the lingering ice from previous leadership, and the tense feeling in the room melted into a new reality.

Others began chiming in, people who hardly ever spoke up, and they shared innovative ideas. By the end of day one, the CEO was in tears at the impact the workshop had had on him and his team. The human connection and group sharing that the team had experienced were things he had never felt in any workplace. With the new skills it had gained, he knew that the team was firmly on a path of delivering happiness both to external clients and to its own members.

He was touched and proud of his team. The experience was more than he could've ever hoped for, and he felt the healing in the room. All of this had originated from one brave soul who had taken a moment during the Culture Pact exercise to get real and address the things no one else had dared to say, which in turn made everyone feel comfortable enough to express their truths.

The power of that moment showed that the impact of the activity was less about the exercise itself and more about creating a space where people felt safe to unlock their energy and heal, with a desire to flow in a more positive direction.

The key to a Culture Pact is not to underestimate the power of what belonging can do. We've seen CEOs who had felt like they didn't belong in the company they were running finally feel connected because they realized it wasn't about one person's journey, it was about their collective journey. We've seen Type A naysayers sarcastically respond with answers like, "World peace and happiness!" when asked what kind of Culture Pact they were looking for, but by the end of the day's session, the same naysayers have the sincerest epiphanies and say things like, *If there's anyone who can actually influence happiness in the world it's the people. It dawned on me: my higher purpose is aligned with this.*

Example of a Culture Pact

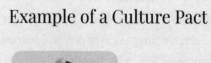

Diverse Voices

Listen fully

Encourage, Empower, Play!

Innovate & experiment

- Bring in diverse voices to encourage creative conflict and collaboration
- Listen without interrupting and give pause before responding
- Inject interaction, humor and playfulness
- Encourage, empower, and support everyone to be their best
- Innovate and experiment to positively impact the future
- RESULT ORIENTED = Strive for action :)

EXERCISE 2:
PURPOSE (OR VALUES) ALIGNMENT

We do this exercise to make people aware of how the purpose (or values) of every individual person aligns with that of every other on a team, and then ladders up to that of the company—from the ME to the WE.

From a macro perspective, this alignment is one of the linchpins in running culture-driven orgs of any size, in any country in the world. It takes people in your ecosystems from showing up for a paycheck into showing up for their own personal purpose too. No longer will they feel they're living the values on the wall because their company is telling them to; they're doing so because they've found the overlap with their own personal values, connecting what's valued by the company to what's most meaningful to their ME.

I'll walk you through what a Purpose Alignment looks like, but you can change it when you want to align your team and organizational values too. Both are important, so we recommend doing one alignment session for purpose and one for values. This is where you'll put to use the exercises you did in the ME section (such as Happiness Heartbeats and Write Your Purpose Statement) to align it with others.

1. Prepare a "canvas" on the surface of a wall with paper large enough for everyone to paste their ME purpose on it. Ask everyone to write their personal purpose statement on a piece of paper.

2. In the center of the canvas, draw a circle and write (or print) out the WE purpose as defined by the company (e.g., Red Bull's is "Uplift mind and body").

3. Ask people to stand up and, one at a time, read their personal higher purpose to the rest of the room and then stick it on the canvas around the company purpose. As they do this, ask, "Do you see alignment between your purpose and the company purpose?"

4. When the answer is yes, draw a line that connects them and perhaps write a few words about that connection. It's actually rare that it doesn't connect to the higher purpose in some way, but if it doesn't, that's okay too. It may be an indicator that there isn't alignment, or perhaps that person will be invited to reflect and find a connection in step six.

5. As more people start sharing their purposes, invite everyone to start noticing not only the alignment between their purpose and the company purpose but also interconnections between one another's purposes. For example, if one participant talks about building community and ending social injustice, and someone else's purpose is about creating a more inclusive, compassionate world, draw a line between the two. Drawing these lines helps folks more clearly visualize how everyone's purposes are actually more connected to one another than they think.

6. Pause so everyone can look at the canvas. Ask for people's thoughts, feelings, and insights, and remember to bring in the people from step four who might not have found an obvious connection. If they struggle, see if others can help think of connections for those who haven't yet articulated how they relate to the org's higher purpose. Eventually, after you brainstorm together, everyone's purpose should connect in at least one way.

In 2017 we helped Sallie Mae undergo a large-scale culture transformation starting with a values refresh. It found itself in a place where it needed to increase employee engagement, customer experience, and brand loyalty. Over the course of eighteen months, we helped it redefine its company values. While this work was spearheaded by the values leadership team, a cross-functional group of strategic leaders at every level of the organization was involved. From executives to folks in the call centers, each person had a voice and was invited to give their input. Once this was completed, we designed a four-hour all-employee session, fittingly titled "Our Values, Our Voice," which was rolled out to all 1,800 employees. In the program, the first exercise we did was helping people find their ME values, and then we did an exercise to dig deeper into those values. We ended with the activity where we aligned with the company values on the wall.

This approach sent a message that leadership sincerely cared about what everyone's personal ME values were and wanted its people to have an experiential connection to each value (rather than just reading an email informing them of the values they were expected to follow). It also gave employees a sense of ownership and control; they weren't instructed that they needed to live by the values execs had come up with at an offsite meeting, but were asked to align with the values in a way that made the values meaningful to them personally.

As an example, during the Values Alignment exercise at the end, if someone's ME value was love, they might choose to map it to Sallie Mae's value of connect. If their ME value was freedom, they could map it to dare to do. If their value was harmony, it could connect to thrive. Identifying what was important to them personally showed that they didn't have to go out of their way to live by Sallie Mae's values; all they were really doing was being true to their authentic selves.

Here's a visual example of what we did:

Values Alignment

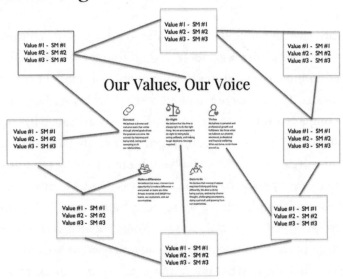

Your Name: *Monica V*

Personal Value #1: LOVE   ⟵⟶   Sallie Mae's Value #1: CONNECT

Personal Value #2: FREEDOM ⟵⟶ Sallie Mae's Value #2: DARE TO DO

Personal Value #3: HARMONY ⟵⟶ Sallie Mae's Value #3: THRIVE

There's more to knowing your colleagues than knowing how many kids they have, their favorite sports team, or their preference between almond and oat milk. When you get to share—with trust and acceptance—your Purpose + Values with the people you interact with every day, your relationships instantaneously go from surface level to a deeper connection. A connection that isn't reliant on being coworkers on a team but tied to being human with one another.

At Canpa, our client in Turkey, the leadership team made the effort to align everyone's ME values to the company's WE values. To underscore that effort, the team redesigned everyone's business cards to highlight each person's favorite company core value. Beyond showing Canpa's commitment to honoring their personal values, this gave people a sense of pride when they handed the cards out. Salespeople would report back to say how much their prospects and customers loved the new cards. Some said it made the sales process much easier because people instantly knew Canpa wasn't there just to make profits but also because of its belief in people. Others said their customers asked if Canpa was hiring so they could join the team!

Imagine what your team and company would be like if every single person identified their personal higher purpose and aligned it with their work. Think about the major changes you'd see and how you, as a leader, might take steps to empower them to live their higher purposes at work.

EXERCISE 3:
GROWTH PERFORMANCE

At DH we've long believed that it's not enough to evaluate someone just by the skills they bring to the table. Equally important are the ways in which they contribute to the company, for their colleagues, through their culture. The more clarity (and accountability) you set around expectations, the more likely it is that they'll be met.

Here's how we make values and behaviors more relevant to people's growth and performance: by tying them to their reviews and bonuses. The goal is to shift the focus from weighting someone's performance based purely on what they did (performance of task) to evaluating *how* they did it (living the values). In other words, you look to see not only if a lead or manager is providing consistent feedback (or as DH says, to make it more of an action for the future, "feedforward") to their teams but also if they did it in a way that reflected the value of "communicate with honesty and respect."

Evaluating value-based performance is where specific behaviors are extremely handy. Being granular on what all your values mean when it comes to everyday behaviors helps make them measurable. Expressions like *Bring in diverse voices to encourage creative conflict and collaboration in projects and meetings* are more effective than *Be diverse and inclusive*. Other examples of specific behaviors:

- Give credit and constructive feedforward by being SMART (specific, meaningful, authentic, real, timely) beyond "Thank you" or "You can do better."
- Check in to understand and appreciate where every person is coming from.
- Actively support each other's professional and personal goals.
- Follow through with what you say you're going to do.
- Only say things about others that you would say directly to them.
- Help other team members without being asked.

A good place to start is to weigh feedforward and evaluations 80/20. This can mean 80 percent performance and 20 percent culture contribution. It can also mean 80 percent is allocated to the responsibilities themselves (the what) and 20 percent goes to how the values were lived as they were performed (the how). Getting to 50/50 is the goal.

At times, specific evaluations can use different weights, such as 60/40, if you want to emphasize how a particular person should be living the company's values. Weights can shift depending on the areas in which a person needs to grow. Different people excel at (and need to work on) different values, so it's important to create a growth and development plan that's customized to each employee and how they can best contribute to the company!

Adding in 360 feedforward from everyone in the company can help in both qualitative and quantitative ways. But for it to be most effective, everyone should be giving and receiving it—execs and senior leaders included. Even if that means everyone needs to add a layer of Teflon on their skin. (This is one of the reasons the ME work in Part II is essential, so people at every level of the org feel the psychological safety to share the good, bad, and perceived ugly sides of themselves. We're all nuanced and need to embody all these elements.)

Surveys such as 360 feedback and tools from companies like Culture Amp can help you customize questions for your organization's specific values. This helps ensure that the 360 review is not just inviting people's disgruntled or subjective opinions but operating within a framework of integrity and objectivity. Framing these exercises for employees by setting the intention that they're for personal growth and development (not a means to indict others with a bad review) gets you the most honest and constructive responses for progress—for both ME and WE.

ME to WE Alignment: The Starbucks Story

In Part I we last saw Starbucks as it was facing one of the biggest decisions in its fifty-year history. Beyond the competition from "cooler" coffee cultures like Philz, Blue Bottle, and locally owned, community-supported cafés across the street, it had been confronted with the pandemic, the recession, and the need to respond to the Black Lives Matter movement. Danny Brooks had laid out the stakes in the most unambiguous terms: "It's in times of crisis when you see [what a company stands for]. What are you—what are *we*—going to cling to? Which boat are we going to cling to? The money boat? The people boat? The purpose boat?"

The answer soon became clear: "This has been a purpose exercise for us."

What Danny was referring to as a "purpose exercise" was a reboot of what the company had been doing for many years: living up to its mission statement. It was wrestling with what the reimagined strategy, brand, culture, and operations needed to look like. Like all companies in 2020, it had to rethink its near-term actions to address COVID safety issues for its partners and customers. But it also didn't want to ditch its pre-COVID plans of mapping out the future so Starbucks could endure another fifty years. Was it going to be able to juggle both?

Annie Richmond, Danny's coleader on the team, expressed a similar sentiment. "People have always been a part of our mission and our values," she said. "But when put to the test, are we actually going to live mission and values instead of just stating them as words on the wall?"

At that point, even though revenues took a huge beating, Starbucks made urgent and meaningful decisions, such as the decision to offer store partners the choice of coming to work or staying home—and to pay them regardless. This instilled their brand pillar of comfort (and a sense of control) in a time when things felt psychologically and physically unsafe for everyone. The company was determined to show its commitment and clearly articulated its number one priority: the health and safety of every partner at Starbucks.

The pandemic seemed like the catalyst for change, pushing leadership to honestly reflect on its own purpose and consider the entire company's mission as well. Whatever the reasons were, its choices made clear it wanted to do things differently.

But 2020's unpredictable events kept on coming, as did the punches that came with them. After a series of unjust and inhumane deaths of Black Americans culminated with the killing of George Floyd, the Black Lives Matter (BLM) movement was reignited. These deaths were a blatant reminder that systemic racism still existed within law enforcement and the legal system in America, but protestors weren't filling only the streets of our country—they were filling the streets of the world too. It was the largest movement in US history, and one of the largest the world has ever seen.

Every corporation in the world was under scrutiny for its actions, but Starbucks was under a microscope, in large part because it's such a globally recognized brand and mission led. At the emotional height of BLM, an internal Starbucks memo was leaked to the public, one that barred partners from wearing anything that showed support for BLM. It didn't take long for the hashtag #BoycottStarbucks to trend on Twitter. People pointed out the insincerity of the company in showing social media support of BLM on one hand (saying it was "committed to being a part of change") and sending a completely inconsistent message to its partners internally.

In a couple of days, the decision was reversed, and Starbucks once again iterated its support of BLM. "Our partners (employees) told us that they need a way to express themselves at work and we heard them," Starbucks tweeted. "They may now wear Black Lives Matter T-shirts, pins and name tags."

Starbucks was in unchartered waters, and not just with the short-term triage but also with the long-term hope of enduring. It knew the question had to be answered: How was it going to adapt to the whirlwind of change?

It was the ultimate test to see what the company would set as its priorities and, most importantly, whether it would actually prioritize them in its decisions and behaviors. At a time when revenues and stock prices were getting pummeled because of a global crisis, with the internal politics that are always a problem in large corporations, these questions loomed large. With everyone in Starbucks's global ecosystem—partners, customers, farmers, and communities—suffering in unprecedented ways, would the leadership team agree on how to move forward and what the company was going to stand for?

What happened next was an extraordinarily bold move for Starbucks. Prior to 2021, social impact was a department in the company— a smaller part of a large universe. It was doing good things here and there, but not scaling for good in the ways it could.

In 2021 Starbucks leadership put a major stake in the ground for the kind of company it wanted to be. Starbucks put big money where its mouth (and most importantly, mission) was by announcing it was going to be a people-positive (PP) company, redefining how it cared for its people. It committed to making seismic shifts in the way it operated, putting people first. A new chief social impact officer was put in place to ensure that all stakeholders in the Starbucks ecosystem—partners, customers, farmers, communities—would be heard.

Listing all its PP initiatives would require a mini presentation, but some of the highlights were:

- Programs to further its efforts in I&D (inclusion and diversity) in the forms of accountability to add mentorship programs between BIPOC (Black, Indigenous, and people of color) partners and senior leaders.
- Continued commitment to providing partners with access to undergraduate education so they can advance their personal journeys.
- Doubling its support of coffee farmers to a $100 million Global Farmer Fund so farming families can access capital to strengthen their farms and improve the quality and yield of coffee around the world.
- Planting 100 million trees by 2025.
- A 50 percent reduction in carbon emissions in Starbucks direct operations and supply chain by 2030.[69]

With all the difficult choices the company had to make about what to invest in and what to prioritize, it chose people and the planet.

It was its way of clearly stating how it was going to live the words on the wall. But even more inspiring were the teams of people collaborating behind the scenes—not just the top leaders who announced the changes. These teams both came up with the big ideas and actually put them into practice. Starbucks essentially reignited its mission with relevance for the After COVID world.

How did Starbucks do it?

It takes a village to make transformation happen. Most of the successes I've seen come from curious people with a desire to grow and be their authentic MEs. They're living a purpose, scared and unafraid to fail at the same time, and aware they need others for great things to happen. Danny and Annie made their ME choices and eventually carved out roles that helped transform a company. But they would never have been able to do it without the right conditions—without the supportive WE of Starbucks leadership and the team of teams—that made them feel empowered.

The two of them came from different backgrounds. Ex-chef and IDEO consultant Danny was now the VP of innovation culture and methodologies at Starbucks, and Annie—the super-sharp analyst and strategist with a background in planning and development, change management, and love of the St. Louis Cardinals—had been promoted to director in 2019.

That they were two clever peas in a pod *and* their names rhymed were just added bonuses.

The two of them assembled an eclectic team of internal Starbucks folks and people with external experience from Airbnb, Pinterest, Proctor & Gamble, and DH (yours truly). Shortly after I joined the team, DH facilitated some sessions on Purpose + Values (like the Happiness Heartbeats you did for your ME), and I could tell Danny and Annie were not interested only in bringing innovation to Starbucks; they also wanted to learn and become better leaders.

When we did the exercises as a team, Danny and Annie had no idea what was in store for them at Starbucks, but what was obvious was that they were ready to do the work. "Discovering my own purpose impacted how I woke up and how I showed up at work... how my team supported me, how I supported my team, and how we collectively tried to achieve [our] brand promise," Annie shared. "Seeing others find their purpose was so inspiring. We [dove] in to get all the depth of the moment."

They knew it was mission critical to make sure their personal MEs were aligned with the WE: "[As a team] it helped us remember who we are and what really matters. What we value. What's important to me and you. It helped us get clearer on how to make [hard] decisions. It reminded us that this is what it looks like when we're at our best."

CREATING THEIR OWN GREENHOUSE CONDITIONS

Having their foundation of Purpose + Values in place within themselves and the team, Danny and Annie saw how they could take their ME to the WE in approaching the ambitious goals they wanted to accomplish. They were trusted so much that they were invited to help define how Starbucks will equitably care for every stakeholder for the next fifty years. They worked to support the long-term vision of Starbucks to be a triple bottom line company—People, Planet, and Profit positive with social impact at its core.

There's no doubt it took people in the C-suite—like CEO Kevin and (now former) COO Roz—to make the pivot toward reprioritization. Then it took a village—the rest of Starbucks—to execute it. Danny and Annie are just two people who keep nurturing the greenhouse conditions within themselves and care deeply about their work and about growing others on their team. Within a place like Starbucks, they were fortunate enough to be given the greenhouse elements to thrive. Here's a look at Danny and Annie's work through the lens of the greenhouse conditions:

Alignment—Danny and Annie's WE team purpose evolved over the years to "Design a prosperous future where our brand comes to life at every moment of the Starbucks experience." It was an aspirational statement that people on the team could align with and find personal meaning in, knowing Danny and Annie would get shit done and make it happen. Essentially, it was a team purpose statement that could help answer the questions "What's in it for me?" and "What's in it for all?" Even in the most chaotic times and pressurized situations the team rallied because, in Annie's words, "We were able to see how each of our individual purposes connect to our brand and our mission. With more awareness and understanding of what each individual's life purpose is, we were helping each other articulate it and make it happen."

Belonging—Every team (even a "dream team") is inevitably going to have its share of conflict. But when teams get tested and are able to overcome challenges with perseverance and purpose, they usually end up deepening relationships and performing their best. This greenhouse condition was one of those challenges for Starbucks.

Danny and Annie were amazing at bringing the right people on in order to accomplish what they wanted to do. Even better, they did it with inclusion and diversity in mind. But with such different working styles and personalities, tensions flared up from time to time. When the external stakes felt so high between a pandemic, income inequality, and social injustice—let alone all the personal ME feelings everyone was trying to process internally—the elevated sense of purpose was bound to bring fraught times.

Team members would sometimes ping me to express their ME concerns about all that was going on in the world, with the team, and within themselves. While these sidebar conversations are to be expected, if they're not addressed openly, they can infect and spread like a virus. Tensions aren't easy to air out, so the responsibility is on us, as leaders, to codify values that acknowledge tensions are inevitable and to provide a safe space for anyone to voice them.

The sense of belonging—feeling trusted, safe to be curious and ask questions without judgment—was being tested, but one thing would remain true: differences were being honored as much as they could be, as shown by the fact that honest conversations continued to take place.

Accountability—According to a Gallup study, only 27 percent of employees strongly believe in their organization's values, and less than half even know what they are. That's why self-organization, rigor, and team of team structures are so important. There's no way twenty people in a boardroom or C-suite can police all the people in an org—nor would they want to. And there's no way people can do their jobs well if they're not feeling a sense of control.

That's what accountability is for. To safely and respectfully question the current structure and clarify who the team is and what it values. As Danny laid it out: "Are those really our values? Do we live by them? Have they changed? Did we miss something? Starbucks partners, like a lot of great companies, have an incredible pride by working here. One of the shadow sides is not questioning the structure that you work in. Now we question ourselves with the tone of curiosity and desire to grow and evolve."

When reflecting on our team's dynamics, Annie shared a similar sentiment. "My word is *accountability*," Annie said. "[There can be a] gap between stated and lived values, [but] really putting a mirror up to your face I think is just something you don't really do, it's not common in the workplace. We stayed accountable to their Purpose + Values with each other, knowing someone on the team would call bullshit if someone wasn't."

Full disclosure: that someone calling bullshit was sometimes me. One of my values is authenticity, and I felt that my purpose on the team—especially because of the openness to be real that I felt from Danny, Annie, and Roz—was to hold up the mirror and not just be the friendly mechanic in the form of a consultant. It was worth it to me to risk bringing up hard questions and calling out tensions because I wanted to adhere to my own Purpose + Values; otherwise I wouldn't be living my ME.

Commitment—Because of the high sense of control (autonomy) Danny and Annie had, they took it upon themselves to lead by example—for both their immediate team and executive leadership. With their hit series of successful projects in such a short time, they ended up systematizing and scaling a distributed leadership model by cocreating guidelines *with* (not for) people in every function in the entire org globally, to create a truly cross-functional way of working.

As we all know, systemic change is painstaking, time-consuming work that most strategists and designers would not want to spend more than the blink of an eye on. A typical reaction to hearing the O-word (*operationalize*) is to put an index finger gun to the temple and pull the pretend trigger (wink). But the more Danny and Annie worked together, the more they oiled the machine by practicing forms of self-organization in order to figure out who was best suited to do what. Through trial and error, they determined who was committed to their ME responsibilities and wanted to do what was best for the WE across the org.

"We know how important rigor is [in our culture], and we learned the ability to articulate that to other people, both in show and tell. It has had a real impact on the way that we communicate with people, their expectations of our communications, and then the way they communicate back to the organization," Annie shared. "Our team is [now] looked at as a model for new ways of working in a way that it ripples out. The way that we have worked throughout this time of crisis is really just getting super clear on our priorities and our values and doubling down on those. And with that kind of ripple effect, I think a lot of teams are taking a step back and saying, yeah, we have five hundred ideas. We could go after what we could resource in the hopper, but right now, how do we focus on what's really important?"

Commitment to the org, ourselves, and each other is still the number one challenge of every org. What Danny and Annie helped do with Starbucks wasn't an easy feat. They thought about the more than four thousand partners at the SSC (Starbucks Support Center, their global headquarters), four hundred thousand "green apron" partners globally, an international customer base, and an ecosystem of communities and farmers. It didn't faze anyone to occasionally see Danny lying on the floor for spontaneous meditations in between meetings (or perhaps he was crying inside, sometimes it was hard to tell) or Annie ordering up another round of French 75's (which I truly appreciated), her petite body somehow taking in all the stress and champagne with a smile.

But the results prove it was well worth the commitment and effort. These days, Starbucks can confidently back it up when it states, "[We're] redefining the role and responsibility of a for-profit company—creating long-term value for our shareholders while enhancing the lives of our partners and people in the communities where we live and work."[70]

In some ways, I know I'm getting ahead of myself by sharing this story. It's obvious that Starbucks's ripple went way beyond its ME and

WE to the COMMUNITY, as well as our society and the planet. But in this story, the point is that we're oftentimes unaware how much the ME can ripple to the WE. Behind the scenes, that's what it takes to kick-start the major changes we see in the headlines of our news feeds—one person like Roz staying tuned to her inner compass, staying the course of her path built on her vision (not others'), and saying, "This needs to happen, and it needs to happen now."

When I first met Danny and Annie, I had no idea that they would end up playing such a big role in nudging the world, at scale, by leveraging one of the biggest brands in the world. I'm sure they didn't either. Their elevated curiosity to learn and take on new challenges was one thing, but they also embraced their strengths while staying humble and aware of what they didn't know. Some days we felt like we were all Formula One drivers on an endless track. On other days we were in anticipation of what it'd feel like to land on a new moon.

Regardless, with their resolve to be true to their ME Purpose + Values, Danny and Annie built a WE team that could align with the work that needed to happen, scaling Starbucks's mission for global good, and making their indelible mark on the world.

So many people tell me that they worry every day about climate change, racial inequality, and political divisiveness, among other global issues. They talk about reacting to the news, wringing their hands about what to do. But when you're doing mission-led work, aligned with your personal purpose, you don't have to wring your hands anymore. "I don't [wake up in the morning and] read the news," Danny shared with me recently. "I'm working on climate change and social justice...every day."

Starbucks is living its mission and scaling for good in the world, but the latest plot twist is my favorite part of the story. If you caught the earlier footnote that Danny and Annie are no longer at Starbucks, it's because they've started their own consulting company. Leaving a successful, stable, globally recognized company to charter the unknown waters of entrepreneurship is never an easy choice but they did it anyway.

Why? Because of their passion to focus on the work they love—helping clients scale their impact and purpose through brand, strategy, and systemic change. Because they want to keep evolving—personally and professionally—in their own ways. Because they want to keep making positive changes for people and the planet.

As I see it, Danny and Annie were driven by living their authentic MEs of Purpose + Values to build their own greenhouse. And I'm sitting on a lawn chair outside it with a huge Koozie of anticipation of how much they'll ripple their impact to their WE, COMMUNITY, and the world.

Part IV

RIPPLE TO YOUR COMMUNITY

Now that we have your WE aligned between your team(s) and the company, it's time to think about your COMMUNITY. In our model, COMMUNITY is the ecosystem of people your company *directly* touches: your customers, partners, and vendors. COMMUNITY includes everyone you have a transactional and relational interaction with. These relationships go from transactional to meaningful when you can answer those two important questions: "What's in it for me?" and "What's in it for all?"—where "all" is the MEs, WEs, and COMMUNITYs that coexist in these ecosystems.

THE GREENHOUSE MODEL

Triple win thinking is what's most beneficial for everyone in the relationship, in the long-term view. There are always short-term gains, like the gain from charging customers more without the service to back it up. Or treating vendors as potential competitors instead of the long-term partners they have the potential of being. In both cases, the probability is high that the relationship won't last because you'll lose the customer or vendor to a company that can provide a transaction with a better product, service, or price.

The old adage is that the customer is always right.

The newer one is that customers are right...unless they mess with your ME and WE. Then the customer deserves to be "fired."

One of our clients in the financial services industry went through its entire book of business to "fire" a subset of customers because, after reestablishing their internal Purpose + Values, they recognized a fundamental misalignment between what they wanted for their company culture and the way their employees were being treated by those customers. To leadership, it wasn't worth the millions of dollars in revenue they were making if those customers weren't aligned with the culture and were making their employees unhappy.

The old adage is to pick the right vendor based on price or the prestige of its brand.

The new one is to pick the vendor that aligns with the ecosystem you're creating from your foundational ME and WE.

Back in the day at Zappos, the company openly shared its proprietary data with vendors—even if they were competitors—to enable them to make better choices. Vendors were shocked at the generosity and the reality that they could technically use this data against Zappos, but Zappos didn't see that possibility as a threat; they saw sharing data as a way to help grow the businesses (and relationships) together. As a result, vendors knew which styles to manufacture more of, Zappos was able to keep its customers happier by keeping up with their demand and perks like overnight shipping, and everyone in the COMMUNITY was able to sell more shoes. The triple win.

We're now seeing this alignment happen on the ME, WE, and COMMUNITY levels across companies in even more meaningful ways. In Part III I shared the great lengths that Starbucks went to in order to rethink and create new ways to provide long-term value for its community stakeholders and shareholders. As you think of your own community of stakeholders, here are a couple ways I've seen our ripples of community work recently.

Like most of the world, employees of our client Toyota in Spain started working from home when COVID hit. As an alternative to feeling helpless amid uncertainty, they decided to create a program to loan their personal vehicles to help transport the sick and elderly as a contribution to their community. Toyota dealerships took the biggest hit from the pandemic, but mechanics stayed around to prioritize repairs for vehicles that provided essential services. You can imagine the sense of purpose this gave people.

When Airbnb readied for its IPO in 2020, the company held back more than nine million shares of stock to fund a host endowment that it hoped would grow to over $1 billion. The intention was to set the money aside to represent "the host community's voice and make sure that hosts' ideas are heard" as to how that money would be spent. It would help hosts weather tough times like they saw after COVID hit. In better economic times, it could be used toward grants, investments, or education for hosts who most advanced the Airbnb mission and purpose to make people—customers and hosts alike—feel like they were living the company's purpose statement of "belong anywhere."

This meant that hosts would stay more loyal to Airbnb than to other companies. The overall quality of the service that the hosts provided would increase and, as a result, so would customer happiness and revenue for Airbnb and the hosts. Triple win.

Rethink Your Stakeholders

The question "What's in it for all?" leads to the question of who is the "all" in your COMMUNITY.

The concept of "stakeholder capitalism" isn't new, but it's been dormant until recently. Even though the term sounds like corporate-speak, the reality is that every stakeholder entity clicks down to a person. Just as we can map out customer or employee life cycles to show every touchpoint we have, we can do the same with partners, suppliers, and everyone in our COMMUNITYs. Some examples I use involve progressive companies that aren't necessarily using the same terminology I am, but they know they're doing the right thing by living their Purpose + Values.

The basic idea of shareholder capitalism has been around even longer. It's long been filling the pockets of shareholders as the primary reason companies and corporations exist. But the tide is finally shifting to the concept that *every stakeholder*—customers, suppliers, employees, shareholders, and local communities—should be given their piece of the pie. If companies continue to adopt this notion, they'll be taking a step in the right direction, moving from short-term gain for shareholders to long-term value creation for everyone who contributes. This reconfiguration can also serve as a way to bridge the widening gap we're seeing in income equality not just in the US but in the world.

But of course, the most operative word is *if*.

In 2019, Business Roundtable, an association of top CEOs in America, released a *Statement on the Purpose of a Corporation* that is finally inclusive of stakeholders. Jamie Dimon, CEO of JPMorgan Chase, said the business community is "pushing for an economy that serves all Americans." Billionaire philanthropist and Salesforce CEO Marc Benioff believes that "capitalism, as we know it, is dead" and thinks that Salesforce's success came from the viewpoint that stakeholders should be treated with equity in mind.

But will Big Corp, international companies, and financial institutions make substantive changes, especially when there's nothing to hold them accountable for their words? Nothing beyond perhaps a social media slap on the wrist for doing the same things they've been doing for decades? This was the question we were asking before a global pandemic and recession. During the pandemic and recession, the question became even more raw, as these exacerbated inequities and divisiveness that had been centuries in the making. These realities were in the news every day, on our streets, in our faces. There was a groundswell of belief that things need to change, or we've really no one to blame for our demise (and the demise of this planet) except ourselves.

Companies such as Apple, Akamai Technologies, and UPS announced renewed commitments to stakeholder capitalism, which includes:

- Paying fair wages.
- Reducing the pay ratio between CEOs and workers.
- Ensuring safety in the workplace.
- Providing good customer service.
- Investing in local communities.[71]

While these are declarations in the right direction, to be completely transparent, when I was writing these examples of commitments, my first thought was, *Are you kidding me? Have we not progressed beyond this?* I may have been spoiled by my experiences in working with purpose-led companies that consider those things table stakes, but that's one of my reasons for writing this book: to show how we can evolve from short-term value for the few into actionable steps that create long-term value for all. Through this, and prioritizing Purpose + Values in our companies, we can nudge the way global capitalism works, one company at a time.

The great news is that once you get your ME and WE alignment down, the ripple of impact you'll have to every stakeholder is that much easier to identify. Your Purpose + Values become a through line that connects actions in a meaningful way. Companies that donate to charities that have no relationship to their business (or worse, donate to charities simply because it's what everyone else is doing, as so many did with the Black Lives Matter movement) just leave a bad taste in people's mouths. But in the equation of a triple win, since you already have two wins figured out between the ME and the WE, all you have to figure out is how the third party will get true value from the relationship too.

It's almost impossible to hide the sincerity (or insincerity) of a company's actions these days because anyone with an internet connection can be a whistleblower. But especially in times of chaos, the true character of individuals and companies will inevitably show. The factor that determines whether a certain action is perceived as genuine or a PR stunt is whether it originates from your Purpose + Values or not.

With companies like TOMS Shoes and charity: water, their purpose is clear and directly related to the way the customers interact with the brand. Buy a pair of shoes, someone in need gets one too. Raise funds for clean water on your birthday, get photos of people smiling from the GPS coordinates of the well you helped build.

What are some ways your team and company can start envisioning how you can play the positive-sum game for every stakeholder in your ecosystem? How can you do that in a way that reinforces your Purpose + Values internally to your teams and broadcasts them with pride externally to your customers and COMMUNITY . . . and makes them feel proud too?

Here's a simple exercise to kick-start the ideation of possibilities.

EXERCISE 1:
THE STAKEHOLDER RIPPLE WITH MOMENTS
THAT MATTER

In the book *Delivering Happiness*, Tony wrote about WOW customer service. The concept was based on the belief that most of the customer experience is driven by emotion. A more recent study by Capgemini showed that 70 percent of customers with high emotional engagement spend twice as much or more on brands they're loyal to.[72] And as Maya Angelou said, "People will forget what you said, people will forget what you did, but people will never forget how you made them feel." (Insert mic drop here.) More than ever, we know that sentiment drives profits, loyalty, and happiness for customers and employees alike.

Now that we've moved into a new era with the future of work, it's time we apply the same principles to *every* stakeholder our business touches, *every* greenhouse in our people ecosystems, and *every* ripple of impact we know we can make, starting with the ME and WE, out to *everyone* in our COMMUNITY.

As you prepare for this exercise, think about those moments in your personal life when you were WOWed. When you were surprised by the hotel that passed out Popsicles on a hot day. Or when your neighbors brought you flowers and pizza the day you moved in. Or when you spoke with a customer service rep and it felt like you were talking to an old friend. These were moments that mattered and had meaning to you—the kind of feelings we want to spark with our customers, partners, and vendors.

For every defining moment in the COMMUNITY life cycle, there are opportunities to create a strong positive (or negative) experience and to make a lasting impression. From a team or company standpoint, what would each of the stakeholders in your ecosystem want or need that goes beyond just the transaction, and beyond just table stakes?

Think through the interactions you have with suppliers every day. With every touchpoint and interaction, brainstorm ways to surprise them, make the moments meaningful, and imbed a personal emotional connection. Think about how you might make an impression by:

- Exercising *empathy.*
- *Listening* actively.
- Giving them a sense of *control.*
- Providing a sense of *progress.*
- Sharing a sense of *purpose.*
- Taking *proactive action* so they know you're tending their greenhouse.

Just remember, this is the ideation stage of taking things from the impersonal to the personal. We're trying to consider decisions through a human lens, not a transactional one. I'm sure finance or your CFO will eventually have a (very important) say in how new processes and interactions are implemented, but with the triple win in mind, together you can create those ripples that differentiate the way you work, with humanity at the heart of it.

VALUES IN SERVICE OF A COMMUNITY IN CRISIS

In Mexico, a company called Estafeta (the equivalent of FedEx) was facing its own set of challenges caused by COVID. But fortunately for the company, it had the foresight to work on its values. Estafeta is a family-owned company with a strong culture and solid values, and in the last few years it has focused its efforts in building a stronger relationship with its customers and strategic partners. When it approached Jorge Rosas Torres and Noemi Zozaya at DH Mexico, Estafeta asked them to help it update its values and define its higher purpose to face the unforeseen challenges of the future.

Those elements were already in place when COVID hit. As delivery companies faced unprecedented demand, Estafeta was ready to adapt.

It asked DH Mexico to help craft a purpose statement suitable for a pandemic. While running that project, DH made it a point to listen to the needs of everyone in the company, especially the delivery drivers. DH discovered that drivers knew how to live one of their existing values, efficiency, very well (in delivering packages as fast as possible) but that safety wasn't discussed. After DH presented these findings to the board, Estafeta agreed to add safety as a value.

Since they were considered essential workers, drivers were slammed after COVID hit. Safety quickly became the company's number one value, not only for drivers but for the community of customers, who wanted to know that the packages they were receiving were not going to bring the virus to their doorstep. With the Purpose + Values reset, there were fewer accidents, workers felt more appreciated, and brand reputation improved. People knew leadership cared about their lives, not just the packages. In this case, there's a pretty good chance living by the company's Purpose + Values literally saved lives.

Integrate Work and Life to Create Wholeness

In 2018 I went to Tokyo to speak at a conference alongside Marty Seligman, the godfather of positive psychology. As Marty and I delivered our talks and held Q and A's, the room was relatively quiet (compared to what we might be used to in the West), but it was clear by the questions they were asking that the audience was attuned and attentive. As curious as they were about happiness in the workplace (and life) I sensed a tension: they were wondering how someone can be intrinsically happy *and* be productive/effective at work *and* prioritize their communities and country all at the same time. In other words, how someone could fulfill their ME/WE/COMMUNITY.

There was an obvious conflict between what I was presenting and what they were hearing that wasn't computing in the equation. It dawned on me that everything the country has gone through—from World War II and the bombs in Hiroshima and Nagasaki to cycles of booming (global) economic growth and recession in a country the size of California—had had a lasting impact on how everyone at that conference was showing up to work (and life) every day.

The notion of our ME/WE/COMMUNITY ripples wasn't making sense to this audience. Self at home and self at work in the Japanese culture tend to be separate personas from self in the community. Most people working in Japan (though perhaps not the kids chilling on the streets of Shibuya) have a deep-seated reverence for their country—to the point that love of country can take precedence over love of self and love of others. While the audience understood and embraced what people, meaningful connections, and purpose meant to them, it was at odds with the cultural values they believed they should prioritize first.

But as we got deeper into the discussion, there was a revelation in the room. Times have been changing drastically, and it felt as if the audience began to realize how ME, WE, and COMMUNITY could coexist in harmony. The love of their country *could* coincide with their love of their own personal well-being *and* sense of wholeness.

Having been born in the US, I sometimes forget how "the pursuit of happiness" is entrenched in our culture as one of the most popular inscriptions from our Declaration of Independence. I forget how our interpretation of those words comes from a place of individualism and meritocracy specific to our country. But in so many other countries, like Japan, people don't prioritize individual happiness. That philosophy couldn't be more obvious when natural disasters or chaos blindside us. When the tsunamis hit in Japan, people would wait in orderly lines to take their share of the food and supplies left on the shelves. When earthquakes or other crises like COVID hit in the US, it becomes a race to see who can stockpile the most toilet paper for themselves (or worse, when inequities have been especially magnified, people loot and steal from Big Corp stores, small businesses, and each other). Our established right to pursue our own happiness becomes an every-man-for-himself mentality.

But the cultural changes and psychological mindset shifts I was observing in Tokyo—the ones that brought ME, WE, and COMMU-NITY together in harmony—weren't happening only in Japan. They were also happening in companies all over the world (even in companies here in the US, where people were learning that individual happiness was not the only thing worth focusing on). The stereotype that Westernized companies would be the only ones pursuing happiness (because personal happiness isn't as central to Eastern mindsets) wasn't true at all. Our list of clients spanning the entire world was a testament to that. The companies that were prioritizing happiness, humanity, and wholeness were *any*—regardless of geography, nationality, or culture—that knew they had to commit to operating differently, not to make more money, but because there had to be something more to work and life. And they were determined to start living ME/WE/COMMUNITY in coexistence.

I connected with Yuka Shimada, the head of HR and people at Unilever Japan, at that conference in Tokyo. Unilever is one of the more culture- and purpose-led multinational companies, so when Yuka got in touch with me after COVID hit to say she'd had a revelation, I had to take note.

"The concept of wholeness is expressing what's exactly happening in the situation," she said. "Most people are working from home now, and people are enjoying it. The mindset of the leader and employees has changed very much. It's helped people to consciously really think about 'What's important to me? What's the meaning of life? What's the meaning of work? And why is connection important?' This situation has helped people to feel into 'Who am I?'"

Yuka saw people realizing how connection and wholeness were critical to their lives, including their work. Although this sounds like a ME-to-WE story, the ripple to COMMUNITY came from Yuka's realization that her role wasn't just about working with the brightest stars in her team and org; it was about helping to connect the galaxy of stars throughout her entire community. One that was expanding every day. It dawned on her that she wasn't there to just talk about being whole; her entire team was there to authentically *live* what it means to be whole. It wasn't on the shoulders of one or two people—like an exec or her as head of HR and people. The onus was on everyone to have a shared sense of responsibility because we all have our own roles.

From our whole ME to WE to the Milky Way, her revelation was that we're all interconnected. And we need to start treating each other that way.

EXERCISE 2:
SIX DEGREES OF IMPACT: HOW TO ENVISION
YOUR FUTURE

I'm convinced that the "six degrees of separation" have been reduced to three. Not just because of social media or the internet but also because Kevin Bacon seems like he'll be alive and kicking for a good time to come.

The Six Degrees of Impact exercise is about envisioning your company's future. Earlier I brought up the concept of Joseph Campbell's hero's journey and how almost every epic Hollywood film you've ever loved follows the same path. This time, imagine you're the director of the movie you're about to make, the actor playing the hero's role, and the popcorn-lover who can't wait to see it when it's done.

1. Start with six pieces of paper. On one of them, sketch out where you are today as a team or company. Just write a brief description.
2. Now imagine the final scene of the movie—the place where you want your team or company to end up. You're dreaming up your future, with Purpose + Values in hand and no holds barred. Write that final scene on another piece of paper.
3. Next, storyboard what happens in the four scenes between those two. The point is to register what it's going to take to get you there. It's a total of six scenes from the start of the movie to its end.
4. Then brainstorm the specific people (names or roles) that you want to contact or work with to bring your company vision to fruition. It's a visioning exercise, so it can be anyone you can dream of.
5. For each of the scenes, ask yourself:
   ○ How do I personally play a role in the story? How does that create an impact?

- ○ How are my ME and WE Purpose + Values present in each scene?
- ○ How does my team(s) play a role in it too?
- ○ What actions can we take tomorrow so this epic storyline comes true?

Six Degrees of Impact

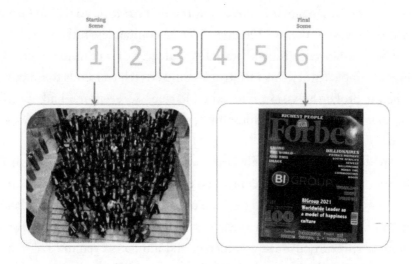

When we did this exercise with the HR leaders at BI Group (a construction company with seventy HR leaders across five companies) we tweaked it a bit and asked them to focus on three things:

1. What BI Group values are in this vision?
2. What are the five or six common key actions you need to take to achieve it?
3. What's your personal role in achieving this impact?

Their purpose was already defined ("We build happiness"), so we elevated the dream of what happiness can mean to include not just the company's employees but the region as a whole.

With this exercise they naturally thought about their relationship with the COMMUNITY as a success factor for their internal program. Even though this was a visioning exercise for what they wanted internally, each degree (or ripple) of impact led them to a greater connection to the community. They wanted to show new graduates that companies don't just stand for profits anymore; they care for people's well-being too.

By the end of it, their sixth degree was the vision of being on the cover of *Forbes* magazine. The ambitious and strategic goal of BI Group was to be one of the top 100 construction companies in the world and the best employer in Kazakhstan. Every degree of separation led to the highest-impact story this HR group could stretch its minds to imagine. Then it broke the vision into tangible steps so everyone had specific actions (with shared accountability), showing how it could actually get done.

About a year and a half later, Sofiya, the head of happiness at BI Group, pinged us with uncontrolled excitement: the company was featured in *Forbes Kazakhstan* as one of the best employers for students. It had been voted number one for students for engineering positions, number three in business commerce, and number seven in IT.[73] It was the first time it had even placed in the category of best employer, which had featured names like Microsoft, Samsung, and KPMG. Soon after, in November 2020, its CEO, Aman, was also featured on the cover of *Forbes Kazakhstan*. The company was living its purpose of building happiness for its employees and new graduates in the community.[74]

It had realized its vision of six degrees into reality.

This exercise creates the seed to make the COMMUNITY greenhouse conditions grow by leveraging everyone's creativity and desire to make an impact with Purpose + Values in the room. One of Tony's fabled mantras was, "Whatever you're thinking, think bigger," and this exercise shows both what that means and how you can actually do it. By storyboarding your six degrees and connecting them with relationships, you manifest what a better future can look like *and* the actions it'll take to get there. With Purpose + Values in tow, you're equipped to make better day-to-day decisions, with you and your team as the heroes in a collective journey to drive an impact bigger than you could've imagined (or made) on your own.

ME/WE to COMMUNITY Alignment: DMG and Automattic

LITERALLY BUILDING HAPPINESS: DMG

Once our client DMG in Egypt realized how alignment of the ME and WE had catapulted its company to another level of success, it knew it wanted to expand that ripple to its customers and local communities as well. Because it's a construction, real estate, and architecture company, its culture transformation inspired it to design and build a headquarters that physically reflected its Purpose + Values, the greenhouse model, and most importantly the culture and people housed within.

When we first had a meeting about the project, I thought it was an awesome idea and an inspiring aspiration. This undertaking showed how greenhouses flourish in their own unique and creative ways when the seeds and conditions are right. As they scrolled through the presentation, I thought I was looking at the architectural vision and early renderings of the new headquarters.

Then they showed me actual photographs. It had already been built.

I was floored (bad pun intended; Tony would either be shaking his head or proud). The company's spirit in adopting our model into its culture was one thing, but seeing the physical manifestation of Purpose + Values come alive with how people work and connect was another. The CEO, Amr Soliman, with his architect hat on, had realized his purpose was about the people, the place, and the physical pathways that connect them. He saw how offices and spaces could reflect the company's culture in interactive, energetic ways. The team's vision was to build an iconic structure in Egypt—not a short order, considering the Egyptian pyramids were not too far down the road in Cairo.

Meeting rooms were designed to physically reflect each of the company's values, to remind everyone entering that space what they were expected to prioritize and embody—e.g., "Hey, everyone, ten minutes, we're meeting in the Gratitude room." Spaces were labeled MIND, BODY, and SOUL in big block letters to give people the choice to work on their own or with each other for their minds, use the exercise workstations in the body zone, or meditate in the soul room. Unlike too many buildings in Silicon Valley, assumptions weren't made that people would always want to collaborate.

When an employee entered a hallway using their personal security

card, the audio system would play one of the employee's favorite songs
or sing them happy birthday, if it happened to be that day of the year.
Outdoor spaces were designed based on local weather patterns so
people were encouraged to get fresh air during breaks or at lunchtime
without being subjected to gusty northern winds or the sunniest hot
spots of the building. Walkways connected various towers to encourage interaction between different teams and make conversations more
cross-functional. In other words, DMG was literally building bridges
for meaningful relationships.

As DMG saw productivity, engagement, and profits rise, it knew
every residential and commercial development it created thereafter
needed to be designed with connectedness, values, and well-being in
mind. The happiness, wholeness, and success felt within its company
couldn't be contained. Each of its multimillion-dollar developments
since has been designed with these learnings in mind. For residential
communities, it designs to balance tenants' need for their own space
with their desire to feel connected to others. For entrepreneurs, it simi-
larly designs for flexibility, creating offices that the entrepreneurs can
call their own while they can also connect to other entrepreneurs in
a shared space of like-minded people. DMG is able to share its new
insights and philosophy with the broader community through the
physical structures it builds.

Even when the country was at its height of instability and uncertainty, during the revolution in 2011, leadership led the company with
humanity. Instead of there being layoffs as with most businesses, everyone agreed to halve their salary to avoid the termination of teammates.
The company survived and in just six months stabilized its revenues,
and the years that followed (prior to COVID) saw some of its largest revenue growth. It was the consistency of the way leadership made
decisions, even in the most volatile times, that built trust and helped
sustain the love and loyalty teams had for DMG.

The ripple effect didn't stop even when the business took a major
hit in 2020. After a series of dilemmas following the spread of COVID,

DMG was able to make "brave decisions" with its Purpose + Values prioritized. Though revenues were suffering, Amr still modeled behaviors from the heart. The company focused on taking care of its WE, its people, first. Living up to its value of safety, leadership stopped all construction to make sure it had enough information to keep its people as secure as possible. To support innovation, another one of its values, the company pioneered new safety protocols called PCF ("people come first") before resuming business. To maintain the value of family spirit during quarantine, it sent kits to employees and residents (their customers) with games to encourage connection and items to help them stay safe and sanitized.

As COVID raged on throughout 2020, it continued to make donations to its external community, including those who were on the front line, like the "White Army" of doctors and nurses, as well as those who had lost their jobs. Even though revenues hadn't bounced back yet, it didn't cancel its partnership with one of the biggest food banks and community institutions in Egypt. It was committed to doing as much as it could.

Given its level of commitment to its internal and external communities, it's no surprise that DMG was the first Egyptian company to be certified by the Top Employers Institute in its entire region. Or that it was able to double its revenues, increase retention by 50 percent in three years, and decrease absenteeism by 40 percent in the years that we were working with it before COVID. Knowing how it adapted and thrived after the revolution, I'm confident it will do so again the next time a crisis hits.

Shereen Eltobgy (DMG project lead, DH coach|sultant®, and our culture experience orchestrator) described how the company's journey was the "pinnacle of a lifelong dream to serve my country of origin with our purpose to measurably ripple happiness to the world. I went to DMG to inspire them with our DH vision, and nearly five years later, they have inspired me in a way that only pillars of light and leaders like DMG can do."

People at every level of the company have experienced what it means to ripple their authentic ME to WE to COMMUNITY. They were inspired to ripple the happiness and humanity they felt in their own offices outward to everyone they touched in their ecosystem. Customers now live in homes designed with scientific happiness integrated into the neighborhood. Wanting to ripple the impact even further in the Middle East, DMG certified itself as an official DH partner, and DH Egypt was born. After seeing its own success, it wanted to scale the programs across the region with the same goals at heart.

COMMUNITY IS IN THE CODE: AUTOMATTIC

When it comes to envisioning the future and rippling impact to community, the most respected leaders and entrepreneurs already have every stakeholder in mind from the day ideas were born. Matt Mullenweg, founder of WordPress and CEO of Automattic, whom I mentioned previously in the WE section, is one such leader.

His roots were his desire to provide a free, open-source tool to help people build websites and share their content with relative ease. He launched with the community in mind—giving everyone he touched in his ecosystem as much freedom and flexibility as he could from day one. Now, twenty-one years later, a mind-blowing 40 percent of the web uses WordPress with an estimated seventy-five million sites. That's seventy-five million greenhouses and growing.

As I shared in the WE section, Matt has since built one of the oldest, most successful fully distributed (aka remote) companies with his crew of 1,300 people. His next level of impact almost naturally ripples for him. Recently he told me:

I believe that freedom is the most fundamental of human rights. As more and more of what we read, how we publish, even who we date is influenced by computers and algorithms, it's more important than ever that we have the ability to take charge of our digital destiny. Open source is a digital Bill of Rights for software, and by making open-source options ... we're increasing the freedom of the internet. I hope I'll be able to work on WordPress the rest of my life, but even if I don't, I will definitely continue to work on open source. It is my life's mission, and I feel very lucky that I get to contribute to it every day.

With the purposes of his ME/WE/COMMUNITY fully aligned every day, his values of freedom and human rights are rippling impact to society in even bigger ways.

Part V

THE NEW RIPPLES: SOCIETY + PLANET

EXPANDING THE RIPPLE OF IMPACT

The more DH worked with different companies in various geographical locations and industries, the more proof we saw that orgs that adopted the ME/WE/COMMUNITY model were flourishing. What I didn't anticipate was a new pattern of opportunity as well. When a company shifted its priorities to Purpose + Values, it had unintended side effects: these orgs were also positively affecting society and the planet.

This ripple of impact surprised me because I had always believed that change is effective only when you have a controlled set of variables in your system. Companies can hire and fire based on alignment with values or performance. This kind of control isn't easy to exercise when it comes to more complex systems like society and the Earth itself.

But it became evident that the impact of our model extended beyond the walls of any org, and even beyond any org's immediate community of clients and other businesses. The first time I observed this was when the seeds of a more human way to work were planted at Zappos about fifteen years ago. Not too long after I started producing their Culture Books—physical books that captured (transparent and unedited) sentiment about what Zappos culture meant to employees—there was an employee who was shopping in a grocery store and noticed that the man in front of him in line couldn't afford all of his groceries. As the employee wrote in one of the Culture Book editions, he literally looked down at the Zappos T-shirt he was wearing and decided to live by the company's values. He offered to pay for the rest of the man's groceries. Because the company had instilled a sense of values in its employees, one of them made a concrete positive impact in society.

That's when it dawned on me: capitalism and companies are often demonized for being profit-driven and soulless, but the new opportunity went against that grain. Responsibility doesn't sit only in the hands of parents, schools, and churches. Businesses can make a conscious choice to actually inspire people to be *better human beings* too. By instilling Purpose + Values, companies can remind us to do good whether at or outside work, then ripple our impact within the neighborhoods we live in, the people we identify with, and the mother of all greenhouses, our planet.

When the greenhouses are set up right—with the ideal conditions fostered and rooted in Purpose + Values—we've seen how ME/WE/COMMUNITY can coexist in a symbiotic way, each ripple positively

amplifying each other. When we see the alignment, everyone involved can confidently answer the questions "What's in it for me?" and "What's in it for all?" We're essentially cultivating an interconnected web of greenhouses that forms the greater people ecosystems of our society and our planet.

This brings up a common question: "How can the greenhouse model ripple out beyond our MEs and WEs?" Within the greenhouse of an individual, the conditions are somewhat controllable. We all make our own choices about the purpose we want to define for ourselves, the values we want to live by, and the passions we want to pursue. The same applies to businesses. The variables are somewhat controllable because there's a structure in place. Some structures are broken, some work better than others, but regardless, there's something in place that shapes the way that business works.

But what happens when you're trying to ripple beyond the controlled conditions of individual and business greenhouses? We can't walk up to someone and tell them they're not a good fit for this street because they're not wearing a mask or practicing social distancing in the middle of a pandemic. We can't ban a manager from our favorite restaurant because he unconsciously mansplains to every woman he interacts with. And we can't fire a customer from a hotel because they're irrationally accusing another person of stealing their iPhone just because of the color of their skin. As much as we want to play Whac-A-Mole and bop people on the head with a sense of awareness, what's left to do if we can't weed out those who aren't aligned with our fundamental values and beliefs?

As annoying or blood-boiling as it is to encounter these things in our daily lives, this is where I've seen the humanity we create at work ripple out to the humanity we hope to see in society. By building our greenhouses intentionally, we're actually enabling ourselves and those we connect with to make an impact on society *through our work and workplaces*. There will always be things beyond our control, and this is where we need our ability to accept and adapt to any unforeseen circumstance to kick into high gear. This is where our commitment to living our Purpose + Values will truly be put to the test.

The role of business in society keeps evolving, and even though we saw some of the worst of times in 2020, we also saw a glimmer of hope for the best of times to come. The world, and therefore businesses' role within it, has forever changed. We saw companies like Proctor & Gamble, IBM, Pfizer, and Moderna pivot, innovate, and help the world with COVID at breakneck speeds. Executives at Starbucks and CEOs like Dan of Gravity put people first. Businesses became more vocal about their stances on social phenomena like Black Lives Matter, #MeToo, and combating hate crimes against Asian Americans. Google and Microsoft upped the ante by publicly committing to do their part with climate change. The world's largest investors, like BlackRock and T. Rowe Price, put their money where their mouth is by focusing on environmental, social, and governance (ESG) portfolios. In a bold (and controversial) move, Twitter took away President Trump's bullhorn to "reduce the risk of further incitement of violence." *Care*, *kind*, and *love* were no longer unspeakable four-letter words at the office.

As volatile as the world has been, it's impossible not to acknowledge that this new abnormal is an opportunity to put our ecosystems of people and our voices, our power and privilege, and our resiliency and resources to better use. The business case for society and humanity has never been stronger, and *the time to do something about it is now.*

Build Greenhouses in Society

In the years since that story of the employee paying for a stranger's groceries was published in the Zappos Culture Book, DH has been helping its clients build happy cultures and greenhouses so we can be true to our (weird) authentic selves at work and seamlessly step into the world as those same selves. Our purpose has become so much more than one-off opportunities to pay it forward in the form of buying groceries or volunteering at a nonprofit; we were inspired by the long-term impact that *every one of us* can have, based on the day-to-day choices we make in living out our Purpose + Values.

We've seen the ripple into society happen time and time again at companies large and small, in various industries and innumerable countries and cultures. We've begun to see precisely how this process can make positive change for equity, inclusion, and belonging for all people and for our whole planet. When the ME, WE, and COMMU-NITY levels are established, the ripples to society can naturally grow, adapt, and take on lives of their own.

EXERCISE 1:
EMPATHY MAP

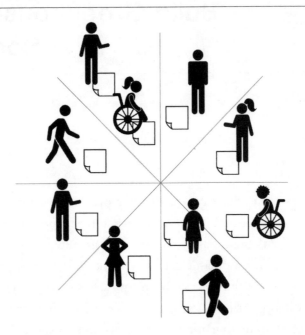

The purpose of the Empathy Map, inspired by our friends at DSIL Global, is for you and your team to expand your ability to understand one another and to widen your collective awareness of various stakeholders in your COMMUNITY and society.

1. Start by creating a "map" by using masking tape to create a pie on the ground.
2. Together with your team, create a list of various stakeholders in your particular ecosystem or greenhouse (e.g., sales, marketing, delivery, customers, partners, local community, members of society, environmental groups). Jot down each stakeholder and place them sporadically on the map.
3. Ask folks to wander around the map silently and have them choose a stakeholder position that is not their personal role in order to "try it on."

4. Encourage folks to drop into that stakeholder's perspective and reflect silently on the following questions as you read them aloud:
   - What is on my mind?
   - What challenges do I have?
   - What are my goals and priorities?
   - What am I feeling?
   - What do I want this group or team to know about me?
5. Next, ask a few people to share any insights they had. Encourage people to practice deep listening (no one is wrong or right, everyone is just exploring together).
6. After a few shares, encourage folks to walk around and find a new role to step into.
7. Repeat.

This exercise can be very powerful for building empathy across a wide range of stakeholders. If people can feel even an ounce of what it's like for their colleagues and recognize the challenges they face, progress can be made. It's often a very heartfelt process. From execs to employees, I've seen people well up in tears as they heard how much they were understood by another person but never knew it; in the end, they just needed the space to listen, share, and be heard. It can also bring out new insights about customers, local community members, and society at large if you take a moment to be fully present as you walk in others' shoes.

Ripple with Diversity, Equity, Inclusion, and Belonging (DEIB)

The topic of diversity, equity, inclusion, and belonging (DEIB) in our orgs, communities, and society has been surfacing recently in urgent ways, making it impossible to ignore.

What exactly do we mean by DEIB?

I'll share the Friday night DEIB club version first. Diversity is being asked to the dance. Inclusion is being asked to dance. Belonging is being able to dance how you want. Equity is having a turn to pick the DJ.

If you'd like a slightly different, still simplified, everyday version, diversity is about representation. It's ensuring that orgs contain people from the various communities that surround them, people who represent different identities in terms of race, gender and gender identity, sexual orientation, age, education, geography, and beliefs (just to name a few). Inclusion involves creating a culture where everyone can actively participate. Equity, which is often the hardest of the concepts to grasp, means ensuring fair treatment, access, and advancement for all people. And belonging, as we now know, is about feeling fully accepted as who you authentically are.

As we've heard from social movements for equity, women are being harassed at work and not believed, queer people feel unable to bring their full selves to work for fear of being fired, Asian Americans are being beaten and killed in hate crimes, and harsh—or deadly—treatment by police is making Black people feel unsafe just going about their lives. We're seeing that there are undeniable differences in our experiences that currently prevent equity. So it's on us to identify and eliminate the barriers that prevent everyone from fully participating. This is what brings hope of justice.

Here's another way to look at it:

As with the ROI (return on investment) of culture and happiness that I shared in Part I, we've seen a similar impact from DEIB on productivity, innovation, and adaptability for the bottom line of all orgs. When you add the social and moral reasons it should be at the forefront of our minds, it's no wonder more companies are prioritizing humanity in the workplace.

I know some companies will hold out and wait for others to keep leading the way. But knowing we'll be living in a world with varying degrees of equity for an unforeseeable time, we really *can't* wait for other people or institutions to start doing something about it. Nor can we wait for a louder signal. We must simply start . . . now. Just as there's no ideal time to bring a baby into the world or to work on leveling up your culture, there's isn't a perfect way or time to start making the world more equitable.

As we do with culture transformation, we can take a snapshot of where we're at with DEIB, analyze what's working and not working, build a plan to test new things for a better outcome, and measure to see what the delta is. Rinse, repeat.

THE INTENTIONAL OUTCOME

I heard one of the most poetic arguments for why DEIB matters at the Summit conference in downtown LA in the winter of 2019. There was a fireside chat between Tracee Ellis Ross (singer, actress, entrepreneur, and daughter of Diana Ross) and Roz Brewer (CEO of Walgreens, COO of Starbucks at the time) in a beautifully restored historic theater, and it was time for the Q and A. The venue was filled with people of all colors (including white), and a woman in a hijab walked down the aisle with a cane, a friend escorting her. She was blind and needed help finding the mic. The woman in the hijab made eloquent comments about her perspective on equity in the world, stating things about her identity and experiences that were obvious given her appearance and other things we never would've guessed because they were internal to her.

Then she said something I'll never forget, a perfect encapsulation of her presence. Her simple and persuasive request was:

Nothing about us without us.

Roz and Tracee looked at each other because they knew the mic had been dropped for them by someone in the Q and A portion of their talk. The woman was referencing a phrase, popularized by disability activists and political movements more recently, that originally dates back to the sixteenth century in Central Europe. What she was saying was that we shouldn't assume we know how to help people without directly involving them, listening to their actual needs, and letting them take the lead. People often assume they're being Good Samaritans by doing what makes them feel good instead of focusing on the person who's receiving what they are offering.

This is a small example of a much larger issue, but one of my friends thought he was doing a good deed by giving a burger to a homeless person in Oakland. The man politely said, "No thanks, man, I'm vegan." The point is that we shouldn't try to "help" without asking if our actions are helpful in the first place.

The woman's words in downtown LA were powerful in that moment, but the way Roz has lived that truth in her career has been just as inspiring. I've watched Roz work as a servant leader, spreading what she believes about women, Black people, and all people—that everyone deserves the chance to become who they must become.

She's been refreshingly honest about the "ingredients" of her success. Hard work led to successful outcomes. Relationships with people in (social/political/institutional) power gave her stretch opportunities. More visibility, more responsibility, and more experience added to her mojo too. But it was the realization when she became a mom that she couldn't separate parts of herself *and* be her best at the same time that led to the greatest change. I imagine it was because changing diapers and cleaning spit-up weren't too different between a nursery and a meeting. She knew she needed to show up true to herself while letting everyone know what she'd come to accomplish . . . which might be different from what others wanted her to accomplish.

In her commencement speech to a graduating class at Spelman College (a historically Black college in Georgia) in 2018, she said:

You are today at an intersection between who you have been and who you must become—full of hope and knowledge, staring down the face of a daunting challenge. Stronger than you have ever been, and also learning with every breath. . . . The generation of Spelman women who came before me were all first-of-a-kinds. The first Black woman to...the first Black leader to...the first Black judge to...the first Black surgeon to...a generation of way makers. My generation is what one might call "Generation P," and that *P* is for *perseverance*— we've had the job of keeping the fires that our grandmothers and mothers fought for, lived for, died for alive.[75]

It's as simple and deeply wise as that. The importance of keeping those fires alive is what I felt as I was standing with my grandparents and parents in our village in Toisan. It's what we all feel when we sit still with gratitude for all that's been done and sacrificed for us...while we receive the sacred baton and look forward to what we'll do for all those who survive us.

"Nothing about us without us" is the most sensible statement to keep us moving forward, hacking away the weeds of history, shining light on what we can do differently to move the needle now. Whether it's an issue of nationality, ethnicity, gender, disability, or membership in any group marginalized from political and socioeconomic opportunities, the way to keep moving toward a brighter, more equitable light is to invite people—all people—to bring their whole selves into the room. That's when we go beyond just speaking our voices; that's when we become a part of change that will endure.

ONE WOMAN'S JOURNEY TOWARD PURPOSEFUL (AND INCLUSIVE) HAPPINESS

As a woman of color who identifies as Black, Jeannine Carter has come to realize she occupies what the poet Gloria E. Anzaldúa called "La Frontera," the vague and indeterminate borderland between two ethnic groups, due to her biracial descent and having been raised both in the US and abroad. As a little girl, she would observe her father, one of the first few Black neurosurgeons in the US, and her mother, a white pediatric nurse. As she sees it now, they were forging their own paths of racial justice and equality while also essentially practicing what we now refer to as "inclusive leadership behaviors"—for example, commitment, courage, humility, vulnerability—as they navigated life as a biracial couple in New York in the sixties. She saw how, by sharing stories, exposing people to differences (in culture, race, ethnicity, geography, gender, work/life/family choices, etc.), and modeling empathy, compassion, and other inclusive behaviors, she could shift people's mindsets, unlocking true cultural and systemic change.

These childhood observations were one of the many experiences that set her on her own hero's journey to rid the world of our archaic corporate systems and -isms. Through her own Happiness Heartbeats of highs and lows, she decided she wanted to guide people in the corporate world through a process of healing, to hold space for people who were underrepresented to be and feel represented, and to have challenging conversations and continue to fight for others.

After graduating from Stanford with a BA in international relations and from the Kellogg School of Management with an MBA, she pursued her passion to do work in the space of diversity and inclusion (D&I) at a time when it was still a relatively unknown field. Her classmates wondered why she had made that decision, as many were pursuing coveted positions at top corporations. Some even said to her, "You didn't go to Kellogg to build an unknown firm and in an unknown field!" The question kept coming up: "Why diversity...and wait... what is it again?"

But she followed her passion and started a business in D&I—a consulting firm that put her on an amazing path of helping orgs with their DEIB efforts. And then she was offered the opportunity of a lifetime— a chance to build diversity engagement efforts at Facebook. Leading up to this time, she had done all the things that are supposed to make you happy. She got married, had a daughter, held other leadership roles, participated and led many important efforts, and traveled the world doing something she believed in. As someone who was always told by her parents, "You can be anything you want to be and do anything you want to do," she thought she was doing and, to a degree, being it. Her passion became her life's work ... and work became her life.

Extrinsically, Jeannine had it all, but intrinsically, something started to nag at her. Incredible growth, pressure, and demands were mounting in the "move fast" culture of one of the most visible social media companies in the world. Despite all the experience she had, she started questioning herself and the work she was doing. The conflict between her ME and WE had begun to feel heavy on her whole being, on many levels—emotional, mental, physical, and spiritual. She started to ask herself (something she had pushed off for a while) if this was "imposter syndrome"—ironically, something she taught people how to overcome—or something else. Was this "superwoman syndrome"— being a woman of color, striving to improve things for communities of color, and coming up against old systems that haven't changed? Or both? Or was this something regarding purpose, values, and the need to do something different? She realized that she'd had this nagging feeling before. She therefore knew deep in her heart this was something she needed to explore and figure out, but she struggled to create the space to do so.

She didn't want to be a quitter; she wanted to continue to be an advocate and do the good work that she and her team were doing. After all, she was at one of the "best companies to work for" and had major opportunities to make a significant impact given what she was working on within the company. And yet she kept bumping up against her intuition that there were other, potentially more meaningful ways for her to do the work.

Jeannine was at an impasse and wasn't sure what to do or what she needed. All she knew was that she had always overcome her challenges and taken the road less traveled. She realized there might be other roads where she could explore ways to implement systemic DEIB change, but that would mean leaving an extraordinary organization and the people she was in service of. It was a lonely time. This period of loneliness brought a level of pain that she hadn't felt in a very long time. In one of her lowest heartbeats, she realized again that there was no playbook for her dilemma. And it hit her that the real support she needed had to come from within herself.

She realized that most of her previous life decisions had been reflections of her purpose, her values, and the alignment between them. She had learned that as long as she remained self-aware and conscious, when either of these intrinsic motivations was in conflict with her job or the work, it was probably time for a move. She decided to focus on her sphere of influence and what was within her control—her behaviors—so she could replenish herself again, which was necessary to create the positive impact she wanted. She knew she had to tend her greenhouse first. She also knew that this would benefit those around her.

So she left.

Some people were shocked that someone would leave a dream job. She had been at Facebook a long time (by tech industry standards), had helped to build the D&I infrastructure and strategies, and had an awesome team and colleagues she still holds in high regard. But those who were close to her, who were aware that it had been one of the most difficult decisions of her life, also knew she hadn't been living her authentic self anymore. So when she broke the news to her friends and family, they congratulated her. Some even cried with joy.

Jeannine wasn't exactly sure what the next phase for her would look like, but she had a general vision in her mind, and she knew she had to return to her Purpose + Values. She had to get back to tending her greenhouse of ME.

As she got back to tending her own greenhouse, she recalled another lesson learned over her lifetime: the importance of community. She thought about the community that had surrounded and supported her when she was doing work she loved, even if the work could tire her out and beat her down at times. Community was essential in recognizing how the work was affecting her. Jeannine had nurtured strong relationships that bolstered and supported her vision and work. It was time to get back to them.

She realized that when she took care of her ME—doing the self-work, "the work before the work" as she says—and held her community close, she was able to make a tremendous impact. Even if at times her goals seemed unattainable and fleeting, when she combined a healthy ME with WE and COMMUNITY, she felt a greenhouse effect of happiness.

Around this time, I reconnected with Jeannine. We had met when she brought me in as a speaker for Facebook's annual Global Women's Summit several months prior, and then we had run into each other at a Saturday afternoon edition of Snoop Dogg deejaying in San Francisco. It's easy to think a serendipitous encounter involving Snoop Dogg is going to lead to something epic, although we weren't sure what it would be. We connected again after she left "the Book" and talked about her decades of experience in D&I and our efforts toward sustainable culture change.

Even though we were coming from slightly different angles, we recognized how similar our approaches were. We both believed in leadership alignment, having a set of agreed-upon values and behaviors, assessing gaps, establishing accountability, measuring the things that matter, and communicating those priorities. We were like two teenagers getting giddy because we had the same favorite band, but the music we loved was diversity, equity, inclusion, belonging, culture, and happiness. Our terminology was slightly different, but where it overlapped was what got us most excited: *systemic change.*

Sustainable change never happened because of a one-off conference, keynote, or workshop. If orgs were really committing to positive change, they had to provide more than a rah-rah one-day training class. They needed to commit to a lifelong journey of embedding DEIB, happiness, and humanity into their culture.

Jeannine returned to her entrepreneurial roots and rebooted the second company she had started after graduating from Kellogg, rebranded it to Incluvations (a portmanteau of Inclusive Innovations, which she'd started in the early 2000s), started collaborating strategically with others in her field, and became a part of the DH family as our chief DEIB innovator and advisor. These days, she helps our clients embed systemic culture change with the most current information about how DEIB can affect organizations.

Since we started collaborating, Jeannine's been inspired to bang on her table during meetings when she gets excited (something we do and highly value at DH), which makes us all want to bang on ours too. On a random Zoom call we had the other day, she just started shaking her head and saying, "Mmhm mmhm mmhm" under her breath.

Initially I was concerned. "Is something wrong?"

But she said with a smile, "I realize we are all going through so much right now, this just makes me happy."

After taking her own leap of faith to get back to her ME and find a WE that she could be better aligned with in this chapter of her life, she transformed into the epitome of someone who adapts to thrive. She is continuing her commitment to systemically making a difference in DEIB and society, and doing it, as her parents had always said, by being anyone she wants to be.

ONE COMPANY'S JOURNEY TO DEIB CULTURE CHANGE ON A GLOBAL SCALE

When it comes to systemic DEIB improvement in a traditional multinational company, change is directly correlated to level of commitment. It's not easy, but through dedication it's possible.

One of the world's leading companies in the energy industry wanted to start their D&I strategic journey. They engaged Jeannine to develop and guide these efforts. She was essentially given a blank sheet of paper and tasked with creating a large-scale diversity program from scratch. As with all massive change-management projects, it was going to take people aligning to accomplish it.

To establish trust and relationships, Jeannine decided to do her initial assessment—discovery and data gathering—via an assessment "road show" in a number of locations the company worked in, including regions such as North America, Europe, Central and South America, and Asia Pacific. The road show was designed to get input while beginning to educate employees about D&I and bring them together to help build stronger connections.

"The work would not have gotten done without the care, concern, passion, and commitment from the people," she says. "There were so many examples of humanity through this process. I'll never forget the time I hopped into a huge truck with one of the workers, a woman in this male-dominated company, to conduct a one-on-one. I can still hear her telling me that she loved her job because she got to be outdoors, and she wanted to help me so that more women and people of color would know that others like her can get and do these jobs as well."

After this phase, Jeannine went back to the US and pulled together a cross-functional team to create the strategy and business case for the org. With continuous input from the leadership team and board of directors, she worked to integrate diversity into the overall company's strategy and values.

This part of the work was most challenging because it required modifying cultural norms and practices that had been around for decades. But by leveraging relationships, education, and data, she moved the needle and started integrating D&I into the org with People, Talent Management, and Learning & Development roadmaps. In just a few months, in collaboration with other brilliant minds and generous souls, they built a strategy across the workforce, workplaces, and communities with board alignment and executive buy-in. The overarching strategy cascaded with a communication strategy throughout the rest of the multinational org.

It was some of the most difficult work Jeannine had ever done, but she started learning lessons very quickly:

- Commitment from all levels—senior leadership, management, and employees—is essential for successful implementation and sustainability.
- Inclusion has to be a part of the equation, and both diversity and inclusion need to be incorporated into the values of the org.
- D&I needs to be treated as a business priority just like other business priorities.
- Employee/business resource groups can provide essential input and help to create even more inclusive workplaces.
- Inclusive behaviors need to be practiced and modeled by all.
- Quantitative and qualitative data are essential to gain buy-in and monitor the success of strategies and programs.
- D&I efforts are ongoing.

"For this work I pulled everything I had in my diversity tool kit. I channeled things that I learned from childhood, college, and grad school, as a consultant at the first firm I cofounded and then later when I had to facilitate tough conversations across racial and/or cross-cultural differences between members." Jeannine also remembered what was most important: "What my mentors taught me about trusting myself and the process and bringing myself to the work."

The D&I space has many opportunities for receiving different forms of recognition such as Best Corporate Citizens List in Diversity, the Human Rights Campaign Foundation's Corporate Equality Index, and Women's Choice Awards. Since embarking on its D&I journey, this company has received numerous recognitions and earned its place on many of the key lists, demonstrating that if you adopt Jeannine's "If not now, when?" philosophy, you can achieve positive outcomes on your D&I effort.

Jeannine brought her best ME to work and made a company in one of the most traditional industries a notable star in D&I practices.

With all the highs and lows Jeannine has seen over the years, this is what she believes: "People can set the pace on racial justice and DEIB through conversation and dialogue, collaboration and innovation. The future of work requires being more intentional...by demonstrating respectful and inclusive behavior and establishing authentic and productive relationships."

To exemplify how it all comes down to people and intention, I want to share one profound example from a challenging conversation Jeannine had in one of the workshops she held. At one point in the session, one of the participants blurted out that he was totally against interracial marriage.

As a biracial woman, Jeannine felt deeply affected by the statement, but regained her composure as she saw the confused faces of the other participants and once again realized this was what she calls a "diversity moment"—something the whole room could learn from, not just the man who had expressed himself so boldly.

The man continued to tell her how he didn't understand how a white person could cross racial lines and "mix" with a Black person. He reached the point of sharing many stereotypes he believed in. This could have been a very unconstructive dialogue, but Jeannine did everything she could to probe and paraphrase for some kind of understanding.

She finally had to ask, "Why are you telling me this, given I am biracial?"

He said, "You seem normal and cool. You know...you seem like me, and I've never had an opportunity to meet anyone like you. I've only seen people like you on TV. And I'm telling you this because my daughter married a Black person and they just had a child. And I want to be a part of the solution and not the problem for them."

Everyone could hear the dead bolt unlocking in the room. He was figuring it out for himself and was willing to lay bare his own prejudices in order to break through them. And instead of letting her anger emerge and drive the conversation, Jeannine tried to model what needed to happen in hard conversations like this. She turned the negative impact into curiosity and wonder to see if the dialogue could go deeper.

The conversation continued with power and impact. Over the

two-day session Jeannine, this man, and the rest of the group were able to dig to deeper levels of even harder conversation, learn from one another, and bond. This process created the greenhouse conditions that they needed to carry them on this journey.

I get inspired by stories like Jeannine's because I know we stand on the shoulders of those who fought and paved the way for us to be in the position we are in today. There are more paths to pave, but we've come so far. No matter how many inequities we encounter in the world, we can have faith that rays will keep feeding all our greenhouses while humanity, inclusion, and love keep our routes lit every day.

WE'RE EITHER COMING TOGETHER OR COMING APART

Stories like Jeannine's are vital to share because they remind us that the need for systemic change happens in the everyday moments of people's lives. We're always either coming together or coming apart, and we're constantly being presented with opportunities to make that choice. When it comes to situations that needle the core of who we are, these decisions are rarely easy.

I had a similar experience to Jeannine's one Fourth of July at idyllic Flathead Lake in Montana. It's a tradition for old friends to gather at Averill's Flathead Lake Lodge (a family-owned dude ranch) every Independence Day. We go boating on the lake, go horseback riding, and eat Maureen's (Averill's mom) famous baked beans at the steak fry/barbeque—just having a good time and making memories.

One of the trip's highlights is hands down the annual parade in the nearby town, Bigfork. It's one of those quintessential small-town Americana experiences. You can always count on an abundance of fire trucks, Coors Light, and every red-white-and-blue decoration imaginable. No matter which way you turn, there's incredible nature in the form of massive mountains and Big Sky. You can practically hear "America the Beautiful" playing in your head.

Bigfork is 90 percent white,[76] but I never felt like I fell in the minority—until 2018. That year, my patience with the inequities in our country and the world was running razor-thin, so on parade day, I decided to make a small act of defiance about how immigrants were being treated. I wore a black T-shirt that read I AM AN IMMIGRANT. I threw on a cowboy hat and a pair of made-in-China sunglasses shaded with the American flag that I'd bought from Amazon for three bucks. (At least I could laugh to myself about the irony of my outfit.)

There was immediately a different vibe in the air, and I no longer felt like I blended in as I walked through a sea of red MAGA (Make America Great Again) hats with matching MFGA (Make Families Great Again) T-shirts. My body felt tense with a need to be vigilant. Every year prior, the chants of "U-S-A" had made me smile with patriotism, but that year, they gave me goose bumps and made my skin crawl. I felt the delta between reading a different opinion online and being physically face-to-face with it. I was still the same proud American, but my pride was clouded by the palpable divisiveness.

Reactions to my T-shirt ranged from disapproving side glances to "I love your shirt!" yelled by someone who looked like Sue Ellen Ewing straight out of the TV show *Dallas*. Another (white) woman told me how glad she was that I wore it because she had her own anxieties about the current cultural climate. Right after the parade, she went back to her room and changed into the shirt she had been unsure about wearing: it read ALL FAMILIES MATTER, a reference to the practice of family separation at our southern border. Because we could stand together, she felt safe to express her dissent about how migrant children were being treated.

When I got back to the ranch, a guy I had gotten to know over the years shouted at me incredulously, "You're not an immigrant! You were born here!" He was wearing a red MAGA hat, and my body was still tense, so I tried to respond in my calmest manner, "Yes, I was born here, like you. Which means you're probably an immigrant too."

He had a confused look on his face, so I shared with him what my

T-shirt meant: that almost none of us are truly Indigenous. The guy went on to explain his point, using phrases like *us vs. them* and saying we have to fight "because of what's ours, not theirs." When he said "us," he meant the people he loved and would do anything to protect. He was making hand gestures to indicate that I was in the "us" bucket with him as a US citizen, as if to convince me that we were in this "us vs. them" fight together.

We ping-ponged a few more of our impassioned thoughts back and forth and came to a point where we both realized we weren't budging in our beliefs. Somehow we found a shared peace and started joking around. A friend came by and snapped a picture of us two sitting together—an older white dude with a MAGA hat and an Asian American gal with a pro-immigrant shirt and a cowboy hat. We were both genuinely smiling.

Walking away, I started to imagine how different our conversation would've been if we hadn't had the years of knowing each other. I tend to want to pull a Mike Tyson and metaphorically punch people in the face when they don't see what it means to be the underdog, but that afternoon, there was a shift in me. We weren't agreeing on much of anything, but I'll always remember how it made me feel to go from anxiety and uneasiness to being at peace. We were both speaking our truths on a symbolic day that celebrated our freedom to do so. I left Montana with a deeper sense that no matter what we each believe, we all just really want to be seen, heard, and understood.

These kinds of encounters don't often end on such a high note. Hate crimes against Asian Americans in US cities rose 150 percent in 2020, even as the number of overall hate crimes fell.[77] UN Secretary-General António Guterres urged governments to "act now to strengthen the immunity of our societies against the virus of hate"[78] because "the pandemic continues to unleash a tsunami of hate and xenophobia, scapegoating and scaremongering."

What exactly does that hate look like? In March, a seventy-five-year-old Chinese woman was violently attacked on a street corner as she waited for a light to turn green in San Francisco, just across the bay from where I live. I felt sick to my stomach as I saw the aftermath: her eyes bloodied by a white thirty-nine-year-old who had punched her in the face. But the elderly woman, Xiao Zhen Xie, fought back with a wooden board she found on the street, and the attacker ended up bloodied on a stretcher while she was the one still standing. I had to shake my head and smile at her fierce resilience. "Immigrants," I thought, "we *still* get the job done."

Xie's grandson set up a GoFundMe to raise $50,000 to cover her medical expenses and therapy treatments for the trauma she'd experienced. Within a week, almost a million dollars had been raised. The campaign brought in donations from 26,000 people from all fifty US states and forty-two countries, shockingly becoming the most-viewed fundraiser on the GoFundMe platform at that time.[79] Despite the impact that a million dollars could have on her life, she told her grandson to donate all the money to the Asian American community to fight racism, insisting that the issue was bigger than her. I imagined all the people she had just boosted on her shoulders.

As I watched the news, I heard Xie speak in the Cantonese dialect of Toisanese, the language my grandparents and ancestors spoke. I was overcome with emotion, knowing that it could've been my parents and grandparents being beaten and killed. It was the same sensation I'd had when George Floyd and Breonna Taylor died or Ahmaud Arbery got chased and shot. That could've been my friend or sister or brother from another mother.

These events make my blood boil, but I'm also reminded of this truth: being human is a given, but keeping humanity alive is our choice. We are always either coming together or coming apart. Everyone wants to fight for justice for the people they love, and no matter how many inequities we still face, we have to constantly look for opportunities to share and speak our truths while actively reaching out to others to listen and be heard.

EXERCISE 2:
START THE DIALOGUE TO SYSTEMICALLY EMBED A DEIB CULTURE

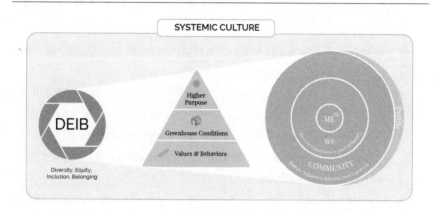

Jeannine believes that the right kind of communication leads to the right kind of trust, which leads to the right kind of action. When people trust each other, they're better able to communicate and collaborate for everyone's well-being. Welcoming teams, communities, and organizations become the antidote to community distrust. But a lot of pieces need to be in place for these things to happen: working agreements, alignment across execs and the organization, equitable systems, and culture shifts that require thoughtfulness, patience, commitment, and leadership.

No, they don't happen overnight.

But at the core of all this is one simple thing: people.

I recommend getting someone as objective as possible (normally that's someone external to your team or org) to facilitate this exercise. Doing it with someone internally is like asking your parent to settle a heated dispute between you and a sibling you're fighting with. How it ends usually depends on how the parent is feeling that day, or the assumptions they've built from previous conflicts.

So instead of a step-by-step approach, here are some things to keep in mind when you're ready to start dialogue about DEIB in a real, sustainable way.

To build a generative and safe environment that encourages different voices and perspectives:

- Create the space for the conversations with the right working agreements and conditions.
- Be clear about what aspect of DEIB you currently want to address and what the takeaways are and are not.
- Establish a group Culture Pact (an exercise in Part III)—a set of working agreements for the conversation, such as how confidentiality will be handled.
- Encourage behaviors such as showing trust, showing respect, and valuing differences.
- Acknowledge that people may be at different stages of awareness and engagement on these topics.
- Acknowledge that people may experience discomfort and that this work is about "becoming comfortable with discomfort" (as Jeannine says).
- Ensure that people leave with a short-term call to action and some way to report back for accountability.

The point of these conversations is exposure to the differences among us—in experiences and perspectives. They should lead to empathy, which ultimately leads to adaptiveness and transformation.

Ripple to SOCIETY

When we apply the model right—with our authentic ME/WE/ COMMUNITY rippling impact in people ecosystems—we don't have to lose as much sleep stressing over some of the biggest issues of our time. Businesses that align with our Purpose + Values can help us do some of the heavy lifting by using profit for good. They can help solve the problems humans have brought on themselves and the planet. *In other words, businesses shouldn't be cast off as always being a part of the problem; they can be the leaders of global, meaningful change with solutions.* And we can align with them.

GBfoods is one such leader. It is a 1.2 billion euro company with a team of 3,300 employees and presence in more than fifty countries throughout Europe and Africa. It was founded in Barcelona in 1937, and some of its brands have been in consumers' kitchens for more than sixty years, to the point where they're now an integral part of the local culture. Think mayo, ketchup, and spaghetti sauce; GBfoods is the Kraft Heinz of our neighbors in the Eastern Hemisphere. Its business touches one billion people annually.

With eighteen factories and products in fifty countries like Italy, Germany, and Nigeria, the company is its own melting pot of global flavors. The challenge (and intrigue) of working with it was both its international presence and its recognition of how much it could strengthen traditions as a global community through the universal love language of food. GBfoods believes that food is a way to remind us of our rituals and remove barriers so we can focus on shared roots, not differences.

Alex Dilme, lead for purpose and culture, spoke with us about the company's culture transformation journey recently: "I like the idea of humanizing companies. How can we be both productive and human? Companies are starting to realize that management transcends the employees. They need to connect a huge amount of stakeholders, NGOs [nongovernmental organizations], and other companies. The world is becoming more complex, [and we need to] change the way we manage ourselves as companies."

Alex, GBfoods, and DH seemed to be cut from the same cloth from the get-go. The culture and brand transformation the company executed proved how far, and deep, the ripples can go.

What Alex made really clear in sharing the GBfoods story is that he is not the hero of the story—the GBfoods leadership team and the company as a whole is. To undergo a change like this requires a company that is first and foremost open and willing to evolve. Alex shared, "I am immensely thankful for the opportunity to change a 'working culture.' Culture is an aligning process where the people who aim to change it need to respect the current culture. From that point of mutual respect and understanding, cultures can evolve."

As always, it takes a village. And what he shared gave a sense of how it can be done.

One of the unique aspects of the organization was that Alex and his small but nimble Purpose + Values team already had the ripple and stakeholder strategy conceptually in mind; they wanted to define the company core values in a way that added value to employees, society, and the planet. "If you do that, then it can be shared across [society] and be universal. It's important to define your core values, but overall the goal is to choose [the ones] that add value to your business and society as a whole."

The team realized that to have a successful rollout it would need (1) proof in the business case for why profits should be reinvested into people and society and (2) executive alignment.

For the business case, the team took a two-pronged approach, demonstrating both the business impact and the social impact and then connecting those with a slow and steady long-term approach. "Each of us have our motivations. You need to make sure when you start this kind of journey that you appeal to the two sides. You appeal to the mind driven by sales, growth, and profit and to others who are motivated by making the world a better place. You must make sure your speech is inclusive for approval."

Then, once your strategy aligns with both priorities, you can drive home the message that "we can't expect to have great talent and efficiency if our people aren't happy. Customers won't stay if they're not eating things that are nutritious, tasty, and joyful." By coupling business impact in profits with social impact for people and the planet, the team was able to push the Purpose + Values agenda forward.

CREATING THEIR OWN GREENHOUSE CONDITIONS

Here's a look at Alex's work through the lens of the greenhouse conditions:

1. **Alignment**—The biggest transformation Alex saw was in the mindset shift of the leaders when the Purpose + Values team got the execs aligned. While GBfoods believed in "living local flavors," it needed broader alignment. Together the team and the execs were able to further codify a vision that was already in the business. The vision was to be a company with both social impact and business growth. With that clarity, their mindsets started evolving. "It was an evolution, not a revolution, that was key to our success," says Alex.

    Keeping with the idea of local cuisine, DH helped GBfoods align the execs and define values for their culture. The next phase was to create company-wide awareness of why Purpose + Values matter and which values were key for the company:

    ○ **GBhood**—We take care of what matters: our team, our customers, and the planet.

    ○ **Proximity**—We practice a local mindset.

    ○ **Joy**—We celebrate and are passionate about what we do.

    ○ **Authenticity**—We offer the best version of ourselves every day.

    ○ **Ownership**—We set the bar very high! We trust in and empower our employees.

    GBfoods formed a dedicated culture team to run "Purpose Days" at nineteen offices around the world, explaining to people in person why particular ME and WE Purpose + Values were chosen (with specific examples of how these values were already benefiting both the business and society). Alex and his team made sure they were bold about communicating what culture meant to the company and its vision.

2. **Belonging**—After alignment came the greenhouse condition of belonging. Alex's challenge was to create a sense of ownership so the rollout of Purpose + Values felt not only top down but genuinely bottom up as well. He tested ways to gamify his approach: "I looked at it like the Sims game with bubbles over everyone's head. I needed to understand each person's ideas that they already had and then light the bulb." Every employee, on their own, then started to connect with the bigger idea. "We couldn't scale by launching a thousand things for people to do a thousand times, with everyone having different ideas in their bulbs. We needed everyone to feel empowered to [take the next steps] themselves!"

    With locations in fifty countries, the team also knew it had to embed the condition of belonging in its values. "One of our values is proximity—staying close to each other, understanding local realities, those are things everyone can connect to...that's love!" Another value is joy, and they saw its cultural distinctions in different contexts. In Africa joy clicked easily, so the team didn't need to put a lot of energy there. In other countries, though: "Work is work, and you're not meant to experience joy at work, so we had to put more energy into that one. But even if there's different cultural contexts, you can find common ground."

3. **Accountability**—Naturally, as in all orgs, the team encountered resistance to change. But it had faith that persistence would pay off in time. "If you strive to change a culture, there will be resistance, but it's good, it protects the culture. Resistance also transforms into understanding because in the end it's a living thing, not fixed. If there is no resistance, there is no change.

That's something we had to realize very early. Sometimes it's frustrating because you want to change people and you can't. It's not that people don't want to [make a social impact], they just feel they have other, more important, things to do. Eventually they navigate their fears, and if you're persistent enough with them, they will get there. Like the Sims example, eventually [the light bulb shines] and it clicks in their head!"

The team found success in both "micro- and macromanagement." They went directly to some of the internal rock stars (the leaders whose opinions others valued) to have more personal conversations (essentially coaching). The team strategically put them on panels and made them publicly accountable. "When a rock star talks about mindfulness and diversity, it sends a strong signal throughout the [rest of the] org."

4. **Commitment**—To empower people and give them a sense of shared ownership of the Purpose + Values, Alex's team approached the rollout with a decentralized mindset, using an ambassador program, open communication, and a playbook full of ideas for leaders to make their own.

"We launched several tools [such as] Workplace from Facebook to open up lines of communication. Not just from the communication team but for anyone to speak up. We also launched programs that gave a lot of freedom, so each local hero or ambassador and their business units felt empowered to do things." Within six months of launching, employees had generated over fifty initiatives on their own. High communication and the decentralized mindset were huge for GBfoods. "We wanted lots of ways to connect to people, but we didn't know what would touch them. This is the third time we've changed our values, so we wanted to show that this time it was real. We're still on this journey, but we're committed."

Since the team realized it couldn't do everything on its own or get true investment in the endeavor by imposing it, it worked to empower people by giving them control over tailoring the new program for their individual teams. Every regional and HR manager was given playbooks and support so they would feel capable of rolling the program out, and the managers continue to create initiatives on their own.

GBFOODS RIPPLES OUTWARD

The next ripple—and in this case the most intentional one—is to society.

While this is an ongoing journey, GBfoods internally started with its HR team to redefine its employee value proposition to inspire and attract like-minded candidates to join the team. The company has also begun to work with consumers and brands to define a purpose for each brand that connects to the larger organizational purpose. As it has started to do this, it has seen how it positively affects customers by creating more intimate and loyal relationships with local markets.

For society and sustainability, GBfoods saw itself as a community of people who *can* and *will* solve social issues while making sure they're not creating additional problems for society to solve. Now social and environmental strategies are a part of the broader company efforts and are focused on four areas: employees, nutrition, communities, and the environment. Those strategies include improving the nutritional quality of the ingredients in GBfoods products, building factories, creating new jobs, reducing the company's carbon emissions, and using less water.

This is only the beginning; the company is now working on a united sustainability strategy to last for the next many years. This commitment speaks to what GBfoods fundamentally believes: "We want to be a company that solves a real social problem and has a bold purpose.

We also want to be a company that minimizes the problems we create and solves other problems along the way."

"An individual has only so much impact, but GBfoods gave me a platform to have such a greater impact." Alex beamed with gratitude. "If I work with our 3,300 employees and [the] one billion consumers every year we touch, it's a gift. I don't know who gave me the opportunity to participate in that, to be a lead coordinator of this whole initiative, but it's amazing. Having this opportunity to drive change at this scale is unbelievable. I had no idea what I was getting into, but it's the biggest gift I've ever received in a professional environment."

Alex is living the life of a giant by standing on the shoulders of a multinational billion-dollar company, deriving purpose in his life from tangibly affecting the world through the work he does every day.

As you reflect on GBfoods and the role Alex has played in its transformation, you may be thinking, "Yeah, but that would never work at my company" or "The rest of my exec team would never go for it." Fortunately, we've heard this less over the years, but if that's still the case for you, leverage both business and social impact as Alex did. The way you appeal to an audience with mixed motivations is by finding a triple (or quadruple!) win for purpose, profits, people, and the planet.

Instead of trying to sell the idea, show how it works. Run smaller prototypes with select teams instead of the whole company. Using data the company already collects (e.g., data on sales or burnout), show the increased productivity of teams that are connecting their work to social issues. Using the new data that's coming out every day, show how positive ESG (environmental, social, and governance) practices can lower expenses in the long term, improve operational efficiencies, and improve stock performance.[80]

Then, as you reflect on your own life, this becomes another opportunity to get real with yourself. If, after you've made your best effort to outline the benefits of becoming more Purpose + Values driven, the company you're working with or running truly still isn't open, willing, and receptive like GBfoods, that company may not be the right fit for you. This applies regardless of your title or tenure because it's *your living legacy*, not theirs. If you can't find alignment on purpose where you are, your talent and impact are better placed elsewhere. As Alex's LinkedIn profile so aptly puts it, "Find something you love, do it every day for the rest of your life, and eventually the world will change."

Ripple to the PLANET

RIPPLE TO A NATION: THE COUNTRY OF GOLD BARS AND HAPPINESS

Before we started our project with the United Arab Emirates (UAE), I used to joke that Dubai was the equivalent of Las Vegas...on steroids. Take a big plot of land made of sand, add a couple hundred billion dollars, invite the most inventive minds in the world to help develop it, bake it in the sun over the course of several years, and see what comes out of the oven. Like Vegas, it seemed like a place where virtually any-thing was in the realm of possibility. Fly a helicopter to the Burj Khal-ifa, the tallest building in the world. Stay in the world's first seven-star hotel, which has a concierge desk on every floor (perhaps six stars just weren't cutting it). Get cash or gold bars from the ATM. Flip a coin between buying water and gas—they cost about the same. But unlike with Vegas, what happens in Dubai doesn't stay there.

When two representatives from the country's National Program for Happiness and Wellbeing approached me after a talk I did in Madi-son, Wisconsin, and explained they'd like to explore the possibilities of our working together, it seemed par for the course (not too different from waking up in a hotel bathroom with a tiger, as in *The Hangover*).

Dubai is a fascinating world of extremes and paradox. It sits in one of the richest countries in the world (the UAE), and, while most assume Dubai's economy is driven by oil like those of its neighbors, revenue from oil is actually eclipsed by revenue from tourism. The cul-tural differences between locals and expats are noticeable as you walk the streets of restaurants and hotels. (A clear indicator of the differ-ence is the alcohol expats consume because it's haram—forbidden for Muslims.) There are also the ethnic extremes of the disproportionately large percentage of Asian and Western expats blended with locals from the UAE and visitors from Arab countries. It's the epitome of a melting pot, with a stock base of Middle Eastern flavors.

I thought to myself, *If we can deliver happiness in a city as diverse and nuanced as this one, we can probably do it anywhere in the world.* My curiosity about the government representatives' purpose was piqued.

In our first interactions, I was heartened to learn that over half of the government was made up of women, a far cry from the stereotypical depiction of Arab countries in Western media. The DH team attended and spoke at elaborate events like the World Government Summit, and we had the honor of serving on the Global Happiness Council and Wellbeing. It felt like the UAE government's intention was to be the global hub of innovation and progressiveness. It had the best-of label for so many tourist attractions in the city (tallest skyscraper, biggest mall, highest tennis court, largest cup of tea) and seemed keen to bring the best-of people, from French monk Matthieu Ricard and British baron Richard Layard to Goldie Hawn and Robert De Niro, to create best-of experiences at its conferences.

Some months into our working together, the UAE government officially announced a ministerial position that is now called the minister of state for happiness and wellbeing. It made international headlines that the UAE was taking happiness pretty seriously and wanted to elevate it to a new level. We worked with the minister, Ohood bint Khalfan Al Roumi, and a group of people who were clearly passionate about what pioneering a happiness initiative could do for their region and perhaps the whole world.

We soon realized the why behind their push for happiness.

Sheikh Mohammed bin Rashid Al Maktoum (vice president and prime minister of the UAE and ruler of the Emirate of Dubai) was clear in his beliefs: "The role of government is to create the environment through which people can achieve their dreams and ambitions and do it for themselves. Our part is to create this environment and not to control it." He published a book in 2017, *Reflections on Happiness & Positivity*, sharing his thoughts on leadership strategies and ways to foster relationships among team members. "Our aim is to make happiness a lifestyle in the UAE community as well as the noble goal and supreme objective of the government."[81]

Because the objective of happiness was coming from the highest leader in the region, everyone wanted to be a part of it. It seemed like the gold rush in California in the 1800s, except the rush was for happiness (and the gold was in the ATMs).

Over the years I spent working in Dubai, I saw a government dedicated to approaching happiness in its own way—it wanted to pioneer with positivity in the public sector, then the private one. It wanted to do it scientifically and measurably, with no expense spared, to bring about a happier nation that would inspire the world.

We started as we always do: with the foundation of purpose, values, and behaviors. From there we helped build a program for sustainable happiness, seen through the lens of the people leading the UAE government. Beyond purpose, values, and behaviors, the framework included growth and development, health and wellness, positive relationships, and the physical environment. These were the pie pieces in the Wheel of Wholeness, which the government referred to as the Happiness and Positivity Framework. Soon after, the rollout began across hundreds of the UAE's agencies to scale that framework across every governmental greenhouse it touched.

Was it successful? As with every groundbreaking endeavor, there were yeses and noes.

In the 2020 World Happiness Report, the UAE was ranked first in its region for the sixth year in a row. We saw a spike in creativity in apps and physical ways to capture and measure what it means to be happy as a nation. The government focused on designing happy experiences for both customers (their citizens) and employees. As an example, in 2015 it launched a Happiness Meter in Dubai to measure various customer touchpoints throughout the city. A few years and 22.5 million votes later, the government scored 90 percent on its happiness index across both public and private sectors.[82]

It has also just launched the National Wellbeing Strategy 2031,[83] a ten-year plan focusing on well-being as a tool for achieving happiness throughout life. It's training chief happiness and well-being officers in all federal government entities to champion the agenda, as well as establishing a Business for Wellbeing Council[84] to create a platform to be used by the government and the private sector to promote well-being at work. (While all of this is impressive, one of my favorites is still how the government redesigned the hallways of one of its offices with faux grass instead of carpet.)

But we also saw the other side of things. The government realized sustainable happiness is not a series of launches of a concept but a lifestyle consisting of choices people make every day as they adapt to the world around them. It saw how people can be initially happy but that levels decrease as things become routine, so programs constantly need upgrading to keep happiness levels high.

The UAE is committed to progress. It continues to make amazing strides to create systemic change in what it believes should be a right—not a privilege—for its people. And time and time again, measurable progress comes back to commitment, intention, and the alignment from ME to WE, no matter where you are in a COMMUNITY, our SOCIETY, or our PLANET.

I wanted to include this story because it's such an ambitious undertaking for a nation, one that can inspire us and systemically change the way we live on this planet. I also shared it because there are stigmas about working with both public and private sectors, and to some extent they're based in fact. Excessive bureaucracy and red tape can be pervasive in the public sector; excessive freedom and greed can be over the top in the private one. In this unique case, the UAE isn't too different from the most profitable companies in the world, like Apple and Amazon—they all have money, are driven by innovation, and strive to provide value to their various forms of stakeholders.

What I've learned is that favorable outcomes are never about stereotypes of the different sectors or industries we work in. Results come back to leaders at all levels and the intentions that guide them. Leaders who carefully choose their greenhouse conditions effect the biggest changes—achieving a positive impact for their people rather than causing a negative one by leading for their ME, not for all. The lines between public and private orgs, society, and our planet are blending to a point where we can plainly see we're all interconnected...as people.

We've seen happiness and well-being become imperatives in more and more companies, and in similar ways we've seen nations like the UAE, Bhutan, Finland, Iceland, Denmark, Costa Rica, and the Netherlands prioritize programs that create better lives for their citizens. While divided nations and politics will always exist, this keeps me opti-realistic that people will focus on what's most important for humanity and the planet as we externalize our shared beliefs and values. Whether we're a prime minister or government worker, employer or employee, we will keep nudging toward positivity as we realize we're simultaneously citizens and customers in our own greenhouses—and we're all in service of one another.

As a pandemic, economic instability, climate change, and Walt Disney keep reminding us, it's a small world after all.

It's hard not to get overwhelmed when contemplating the global effects of climate change, which seem to be mounting every day. But imagine if you were to turn off that noise from time to time without guilt. Not because you want to hide from reality, but because information, misinformation, and disinformation can go only so far in helping you *do* something about it.

Then imagine, in these quiet moments, that you could wake up every morning, show up to work, and—without even pausing to think about global issues—*know with peace and assurance* that you're affecting the planet positively. In such a way that by the time your head hits the pillow that night, you confidently know that your mere and mighty existence is making a difference. By showing up with your whole, purposeful self, you sleep knowing you've nudged the world to a better place.

This may seem like just another sound bite of crazy talk misinformation floating on the interwebs, but I know that this is happening *every day*. And if you commit to doing the work, not just at your job but *within yourself*, you can manifest it too.

RIPPLE TO THE PLANET: ONE MAN'S JOURNEY TOWARD PURPOSEFUL HAPPINESS

Sam Kass admits he wasn't born with a passion to care for people or the planet. Judging a book by its cover, you could easily mistake him for a rugby player who gets sent into the game with minutes left on the clock to mow everyone down and score a win. He's tenacious and determined, and you instinctually know he'll get the job done. You just don't know what carnage will be left at the end, on either team.

But if you were to read the pages of Sam's book, you'd see his bulldog nature on the outside is complemented by a boyish curiosity about anything new—people, experiences, places, ideas—and a shit ton of ambition and heart. You'd probably be mildly shocked that his curiosity eventually led him to become President Obama's senior policy advisor for nutrition policy, executive director for First Lady Michelle Obama's Let's Move! campaign, and an assistant chef in the White House.

I met Sam when Danny and Annie (the dynamic duo from Starbucks) brought together a motley crew of personalities and backgrounds to help take on the next level of innovation projects at the coffee company. After doing a Purpose + Values exercise with him, I quickly figured out that underneath the exterior of a bulldog needing a dog treat, Sam had a soft side. That's what happens when you corral everyone in a room and make a safe space for them to share their life's highs and lows and to get current on their Purpose + Values.

I learned how Sam had gone from the Obama administration to other endeavors like launching Trove, a food tech consulting company created to transform health, climate, and the planet through food, and becoming a partner in a venture capital fund designed to support and develop projects focusing on transparency, health, and sustainability in the global food system.

But if you ask him how he describes himself now, he'll just say, "I'm that food policy guy that cooked dinner for the Obamas, and now I'm trying to be an investor." In his tone of voice, you can hear how he's trying to prove himself all over again. It may seem unbelievable with all the street, foodie, and Washington, D.C., cred he has under his belt that he's still wondering how he can make a sustainable impact on the world. Although he's still striving, he has realized how transformative it has been to turn his passion into purpose.

And with that, he knew he had the courage to take more risks in life, to go on another spin in his own hero's journey.

Growing up, Sam wasn't sure what he wanted to do in life. These are oftentimes the stories I love the most. He just knew passion wasn't "coming out of the sky" for him. But he also knew he was good at baseball and eventually wanted to learn how to cook. Instead of going the traditional culinary school route, he shared his interest with friends, and after a series of introductions—a "my friend's husband's uncle's son's mailman's cousin has a restaurant" type of thing—he found himself in Vienna training under "this maniac on a sick racing bike" who happened to be the chef Christian Domschitz.

"It was a disaster," Sam said, "but I learned a ton." Sam got paid in food as he accumulated cooking knowledge. He barely had any money, he lived off his meager savings, and the work and exhaustion kicked his ass...but he was happy.

He eventually realized he didn't want to spend his life cooking for rich people. Instead he saw food as a bridge to exploring health and environmental issues. It wasn't an overnight realization by any means, but a cycle through his hero's journey. And by taking those steps with curiosity, he finally realized those perfectly made crème brûlées weren't cutting it for him. His passion was in food policy and politics.

Without consciously thinking he was going to directly affect the planet in positive ways, he finally realized his purpose in climate change and health. Everything he has been doing since then has been around these big ideas. In 2015, he won the James Beard Foundation Award for his work in health and diet—a prestigious award he hadn't set out to win.

The World Economic Forum named him to the 2017 class of Young Global Leaders. With our team at Starbucks, he's been playing an integral part in the company, envisioning and committing to a Planet Positive future, which includes new investments in eco-friendly operations, regenerative agricultural practices, and a new menu capped by 2030 environmental goals to reduce Starbucks's carbon, water, and waste footprints.

Not bad for a bulldog with a big heart who didn't have a passion for the planet not that long ago. Even though he continues to take his life in new directions and feels like he's starting all over again, he also knows it was his curiosity that led to his purpose and a more profound sense of what he values today.

You don't have to be a sixteen-year-old Greta Thunberg stunning the UN Climate Action Summit to feel like you're making a difference in climate change. Greta's voice keeps reverberating around the world, but what most of us haven't heard are the day-to-day things she lives with.

In her words: "I was diagnosed with Asperger's syndrome, OCD, and selective mutism. That basically means I only speak when I think it's necessary. Now is one of those moments."[85]

This statement represents her vulnerable and honest acceptance of the wholeness of who she is—body, head, and heart. She continued with a call to action that called out everyone for thinking and saying but not doing: "I think that in many ways, we autistic are the normal ones, and the rest of the people are pretty strange, especially when it comes to the sustainability crisis, where everyone keeps saying that climate change is an existential threat and the most important issue of all and yet they just carry on like before."

She kept it real by stating the truth of her authentic ME and keeping her advocacy of climate change action—her purpose—as the focal point.

You don't have to be on the level of Sir David Attenborough to make a point either. But you can keep sharing your personal wealth of knowledge, as he did most recently in his book and documentary *A Life on Our Planet* (unbeknownst to me until writing this, we share the same editor ☺). He revealed the raw admission that he lost faith in our future not too long ago. Yet now, in his mid-nineties, he has had a more recent revelation and discovered new hope for humans if we reframe that future: It's not about saving the planet. Or even nature. As we've seen historically, nature always wins because it'll keep regenerating, and the cosmos will continue to exist, so we don't have to worry too much about that.

It's about us. You and me. Making his point concrete and personal, Attenborough asks, "Do we care enough about ourselves to make different choices so that we *as people, with humanity,* can prove we want to survive along with our planet?"

The goal is to wake up knowing, regardless of what bad news might be in the headlines that day, that we're grounded in our internal worlds. That we're putting our time and talents to the best use in service of ourselves, the people we love, and this one and only Earth we live on.

Bring It Back to ME

I watch the ripples change their size
But never leave the stream
—DAVID BOWIE, "CHANGES"

I have said throughout this book that the work is top down, bottom up, and inside out. We've gone from ME to WE to COMMUNITY to SOCIETY and PLANET—and now we come back to the ME. It always comes back to the ME. It's like the IRL (in real life) version of the Choose Your Own Adventure series, if you were lucky enough to read those books growing up. You're still the main character making choices and seeing the actions that come from them, but the big—and pretty significant—difference in this version is that you're making those decisions based on your Purpose + Values. Nothing is scripted for any of us, but if our decisions along the way are based on things that are core to us—our ME—we might just live that life everyone wants...one of meaning, in which we aren't bothered that time's flying by because each moment feels so full. We're assured we did things that made our hearts beat faster, and we can look back without a shred of regret.

It's so easy to look at someone's successful career and think they had it all dialed in. None of them did. But following your curiosity and finding the places where you and others can honor and value your (weird) authentic selves are never bad ways to get to where you want to go. That's what gets you to the highest highs, and through the lowest lows too.

Shawn Achor, one of the most-viewed TED speakers ever, ended up in Flint, Michigan, where he took the positive psychology research he'd been using at companies into low-income public schools to use with teachers. His passion for helping people feel more positive in organizational settings got him excited about making teachers happier. He discovered that not only did the teachers stay longer and have less burnout but also students' test scores rose dramatically. The levels of happiness and optimism among parents and guardians rose as well.

His work with the teachers rippled out as they did random acts of kindness for the community by bringing care packages to road construction crews and children with cancer in hospices. The next year the same people wanted to do something kind for the schools in return. Shawn gets most excited about this type of virtuous circle, one in which the ripples return and keep making an impact. Poverty typically correlates with low test scores, but after a similar intervention in the low-income suburb of Schaumburg outside of Chicago (where a third of the student population came from families below the poverty line), test scores went from the 82nd percentile to the top 2 percent in the nation. Even though Shawn came from the world of organizational training, he saw how he could repurpose his learnings to improve the lives of teachers. This project was especially meaningful to him because both of his parents were educators too.

Hardly anyone thinks about permaculture when they're a kid; most people don't even know what permaculture is. But it's where Tim Chang's purpose has brought him today. Tim is a top investor and partner at Mayfield, one of the oldest venture capital firms in Silicon Valley. But to me he's just one of the nicest guys in the industry, who happens to be a brainiac investor with a heart, a musician with large chest plates who performs in three bands, and someone very good at persuading people to use their superpowers. Even though prior to investing his experience was in operations, product management, and engineering, his latest adventures have him dabbling in permaculture (natural ecosystems that flourish), implementing ways to learn by doing, and creating more regenerative economies.

By using universal patterns and principles in the cosmos, Tim and his buddies are building more sustainable systems as models for economic design. He's crafting economies based in holistic health and wealth, life balance, and right relationships, with participation that is adaptive and responsive.

Like Tim, Jim Kwik could never have predicted where he would end up making an impact. Because he had suffered a traumatic brain injury at the age of five, Jim had focus and memory problems, and teachers had to repeat themselves over and over again. It took him three years longer to learn how to read than everyone else, and he was often teased by classmates. Pointing at him in front of the whole class one day, the teacher said, "That's the boy with the broken brain. Give that boy a break." She had good intentions, but to this day, that sentiment is one Jim remembers: he was the boy with the broken brain.

Recently, Jim sent me a message that his latest book *Limitless* was on the *New York Times* bestseller list and had been the number one nonfiction book on Amazon for the entire week. It even beat out Barack Obama's book, he said in proud disbelief. Being called the boy with the broken brain was one of the lowest lows in his Happiness Heartbeats, but he turned the struggle into strength by studying adult learning theory and multiple intelligences theory. "I wanted to understand how the brain works," he said, "so I could work my brain so it wouldn't be broken anymore."

After years of learning and working on his memory, Jim came to this conclusion: "It's not how smart you are. It's how are you smart. It's not how smart your team is. It's how are they smart. Everybody has genius inside of them. And when they discover their genius, then we can help develop it. That's why my purpose is teaching other people to learn. Limits are learned, and because they're learned, they can be unlearned too." Now his team's mission is to bring more brains (or butterflies, since we're talking greenhouse ecosystems) online to teach and tackle both their own challenges and the grand challenges this world faces. "That's a really exciting world to be in for us."

You may be reading this list of luminaries and thinking they're lucky to wake up every day and love their work. You may be thinking that this kind of satisfaction is available only to those lucky few—and perhaps not to you. But the reason I'm so passionate about the work I do is that I've seen how people—no matter what role they have in the workplace—can make choices to be the leaders in their lives and ripple their impact from there. Around the world, people from all walks of life find fulfillment in unexpected places and unexpected ways every day.

Naya Camelia, for example, worked at the main airport in Curaçao as the director of HR, org dev, and communications. For ten years her hope was to bring on DH for culture transformation, and when it finally happened, she was thrilled to see the progress. Leadership was aligned, Purpose + Values were in place, and employees were inspired. Then, of course, the pandemic hit. The airport went into survival mode, the CEO left, and layoffs had to happen. As a midlevel strategic director, Naya had options for herself—she could save her job—but something didn't feel right about laying off tactical people when the org needed them most. She volunteered to walk away so her team could stay intact. Led by her purpose, she made a scary move, but she knew it was the right thing to do.

"As difficult as that was, I feel better than ever. My body was telling me, 'Naya, you need to take a break.' I offered ten years of dedication to the org, and now I have the freedom I was looking for."

In that period she got clarity and started her own coaching business. Now her old colleagues are hiring her, and with the economy slowly recovering, she's working on bigger projects. By bringing it back to her ME, she's come to a different part of her greenhouse: "I'm an entrepreneur, and I feel so happy and proud."

Gerard's dad had been suffering from a degenerative disease involving Parkinson's and dementia. When he fell and broke his shoulder, he had to be admitted to a Northwell hospital to recover. While the hospitalization was challenging from Gerard's personal point of view, his dad couldn't stop talking about how fantastic it was for him.

"What is it about your stay that's been so great?" Gerard asked. He was curious to know how anyone could possibly enjoy being in a hospital. His dad didn't skip a beat in responding: "It's because of Luiz."

Luiz wasn't the doctor or nurse. He was the custodian who cleaned his room every day. Luiz made it a point to bring Gerard's dad the sports section of the *New York Times* so he could keep up with the latest news, so they could banter and bond over their favorite team, the Mets. Luiz made him feel safe, at home, and gave him something to look forward to.

These seemingly small acts of kindness are what made the experience big and memorable for Gerard's dad. For the next two and a half years of his life—all the way up until his death—he'd remember these times. Without even planning to do so, Luiz rippled an impact to Gerard's dad, then to Gerard's family and friends, and now to anyone else in the world who hears their story.

Luiz is just one example of the seventy-five thousand Northwell team members who have an opportunity to be health-care heroes. It's people like Luiz who exemplify and truly bring Northwell's culture of C.A.R.E. to life, every single day. They know they have the freedom and trust to influence a circumstance, an experience, and a life (or death) in the best way they know how, no matter how simple or unforeseen the interaction.

Did it make a difference that Northwell Health was committed to a culture that rewards and recognizes people based on their values of C.A.R.E.? Of course. If leaders like Sven Gierlinger (the chief experience officer) didn't walk his talk in personally caring about and prioritizing Northwell's people, patients, and families, Gerard's dad would've had a different experience. And so too might the other 5.5 million patients Northwell serves each year.

That said, even though leadership created the right greenhouse conditions, Luiz and Northwell's other team members consciously keep making the choice to continue working at a place that honors their ME and facilitates these meaningful WE connections. Luiz continues to show up and do his work with passion and empathy, now knowing the full potential of what it means to his team and their patients.

There's a reason why Northwell Health continues to rise on *Fortune*'s Best Companies to Work For list. Every team member, from health practitioner to custodian, believes moments are what make a lasting impact. This knowledge of the ripple effect is what drives them to give everything they've got to every moment they're at work.

EXERCISE 3:
YOUR ME RIPPLE TO SOCIETY + PLANET

Every exercise we've done so far has led up to this.

Take a moment to read and sit with the greenhouse exercise of your ME Purpose + Values, which we did back in Part III.

Then your WE of the teams, company, and orgs you're a part of.

Then your COMMUNITY of customers, partners, and vendors in your ecosystem.

Then the people you touch every day, whether you know them or not. The people you see and talk to directly. Those strangers you'll pass by on the street or the ones who deliver your food. Those strangers on the other side of the world you may never meet, but whom you know you are affecting in a positive way because of your Purpose + Values.

Then ripple that to the greatest greenhouse of all, our planet.

How?

1. Think small. On the micro, short-term, day-to-day side, what's one thing you can do that will have an impact on the thing(s) you enjoy in this world the most? Not the people in it, but the planet itself. Maybe it's basking on the beach, gazing at the stars, camping in the forest, driving through an unexplored national park, or breathing good clean air. Then think of *one* thing you can do today that makes sure you can do that again. Don't overthink these daily actions—it can be as simple as recycling, composting, or reusing your favorite water bottle. When you don't overthink, things are easier to do.

2. Then think medium. The midterm, monthly, or quarterly change you'd like to see in your world. Not *the* world, just *your* world. Perhaps you'd like the chance to travel the world freely, without worrying about a pandemic, internet espionage, or a global recession. To hug your loved ones and high-five your friends without wondering if you're endangering your life, theirs, and others'.

3. Then think big. No, even bigger. But again, not in the whole world, just in *your* world. What is it that you care about *so much* you could spend the rest of your life investing your time in it even if you never saw a financial reward? Something you want to do because it makes you feel *human*? It makes you feel like *you*? It allows you to love authentically because you're at peace with the world's imperfections, and your own personal imperfections too?

This is how the ripple of impact works. You start from your roots, from the most vulnerable, wholesome, and truthful definition of your

ME Purpose + Values. Then you make the sometimes easy, oftentimes hard life choices to be true to that. You stay the course, being your own best and worst critic, trying to be gentle and patient with how you'll succeed and fail along the way, knowing you'll keep getting better at sculpting your ever-evolving ME.

By making these choices, you'll start experiencing—viscerally and cerebrally—the differences within yourself first. Then you'll see with awe how it all emanates out, ripple by ripple, person to person. From your ME to your WE, COMMUNITY, SOCIETY, and PLANET.

When that sense of interconnection permeates your choices, you'll know you're building the right greenhouse for yourself and the society, planet, and people you love.

What's Next?

We all go through multiple cycles in our lives, living out our own work/
life hero's journey. The journey starts with our ME when we get real
with ourselves about our Purpose + Values. The journey ripples out to
the WE of our teams and orgs, then our COMMUNITY as we tend
our greenhouse and help build others' along the way. To keep growing,
we keep in mind what it takes to be meaningfully happy while checking
on the greenhouse conditions to make sure they're still set right.

With ME/WE/COMMUNITY aligned, we know how our ripple
of impact continues to SOCIETY and the PLANET in natural and
instinctive ways, because it comes from the whole of our core.

As you've seen from the stories I've shared in the book, this alignment empowers us to wake up for work every day knowing our mere
and mighty existence is creating a positive impact. That goal is within
reach for all of us.

So what's next now that you have all the tools to do this work?

Go all in.

Even if you don't play poker, this bet—your life and living legacy—
is worth all the chips you have stacked in front of you.

Even if times are good, because we know those unpredictable
events are lurking around the corner.

Even in the worst of times—especially in the worst of times—when we're deep in our darkest wells and have no idea how we'll ever see light again, we can find clarity. Sometimes we keep looking for the light at the end of the tunnel, then realize there's a pilot light already lit inside. I've come to terms with the fact that darkness will always be a part of life, but with every dark day I encounter, I know better where to find the light still flickering. As Bruce Lee expressed it in the writings that helped his daughter understand him more, "Now I see that I will never find the light unless, like the candle, I am my own fuel."

I want to return for a moment to my friend Matt, CEO of Automattic. I've never seen him without his signature calm smile and mellow optimism. But sometimes we forget everyone has their own darkest well. Here's how Matt describes his:

> One of the hardest periods for me was when my father was in the ICU for five weeks. Besides the stress of the situation itself, being almost 24-7 in a hospital room meant I was sleeping poorly and erratically, eating bad hospital food, not exercising, and felt helpless and out of control since there was very little I could do to help my father's health directly. A brain fog set in which made it harder to keep up with what was going on, and I began to be short with those around me.

Matt was in an extreme situation on multiple ends. His dad was on the brink of death, and it was the first time Matt had felt how extreme lack of self-care can affect the body and mind. He had to seriously consider what was most important: spending days with his dad knowing they were probably going to be his last or taking care of himself.

Matt chose to tend his greenhouse first. He took a few hours a day to get outside, exercise, shower at home, eat something healthy, and bring good food back to the hospital. He talked to loved ones about the situation so empathy would help him shoulder the burden they were all facing: "It was still the worst period of my life, but I was able to be a much better version of myself for my family in that difficult time than if I hadn't prioritized that time almost every day."

Then Matt did something counterintuitive. He started to work again. From the outside, one might be quick to judge his actions—who chooses to work while his dad is dying in the hospital, when all of his coworkers told him he didn't have to? But Matt wasn't concerned about what others might think about him; he was tending the greenhouses that mattered to him the most.

"A big source of my happiness is feeling connected to a larger mission and seeing the impact of my work on it," he says. "In the long quiet periods when nothing was happening, instead of stewing in my anxiety, I started to plug back into work, which restored that connection to my amazing colleagues and our shared mission. No one was expecting me to work, and it was completely of my own volition, but having something I could contribute to helped curb those feelings of helplessness and being out of control."

Even in his darkest times, Matt was grounded enough within himself and his higher purpose, which enabled him to be at peace with the darkness of his father's impending death and let in his own light. Guided by his mission at work and the meaningful relationships he had with his colleagues, he brought the senses of control and connectedness back into his life when it felt like he was losing both while his dad was ill.

This story doesn't have a happy ending. Although Matt's father regained lucidity and consciousness, just as Matt and his family were hopeful that he was out of the woods, his father succumbed to the illness and passed. Even though that time in his life was one of his hardest and most heartbreaking, Matt had a positive reflection on the experience: "I was able to maintain the capacity to be there for him in the healthiest way I could in those final days. I am grateful."

Sometimes the fragility of life can seem far away. Sometimes it rings your doorbell when you least expect it. In high school for my buddy Travis. Before his first grandchild was born for my dad. During what might've been the prime of his life for Tony.

Death may seem like a morbid inspiration for life. Before you read this book, going to work might've sounded like a masochistic way to get inspired too. But when you put them side by side—death and work—the juxtaposition brings about a new sense of how what we do with our lives can provide meaning. Meaning comes when you are positively, unshakably assured that you're living your days to their fullest. When you know without a doubt that your greenhouse will grow and that you'll help many others grow too.

Of course, you can finish reading this book, implement none of these changes, and go back to your life as it was in 2020 Before COVID. You may do pretty well. You may get to everything you wanted and check it off your to-do list of accomplishments. There are many ways to live life, but the most raw, real, and vulnerable question is whether this is *the* way you *want* to live it.

Not doing the work to condition your greenhouse might be easy in the short term, but you'll eventually have to answer to yourself. Were you living for what you wanted, or what others expected of you? Doing deeper-dive self-exploration and team collaboration might be hard in the short, medium, and long term, but you'll know, with a sense of peace, that you gave it your all before whatever realm is next.

When it comes to the highest stakes of life, going all in isn't just the safest, it's the wisest bet you'll ever make.

The (Not So) End

When Tony passed at the end of 2020, I lost one of my soulmates, conversations without boundaries, and quiet observations on life's randomness. Just when I thought a monstrous year couldn't bring any more disbelief and heartache, my world was somersaulting once again. I hit a newfound low on my Happiness Heartbeats that I had never known could exist. It made me reflect on the highs and lows Tony and I had gone through together and our shared curiosity about humans, happiness, and wholeness at work.

I'll miss his attempts to be funny and punny because he knew I'd shake my head, smile, and sigh. His random magic tricks, his desire to come up with new hacks for everything, and the big pots of soup he made so he could share with others. Most of all, I'll miss his legendary hugs and our times of playful ease when he didn't feel like he had to be "on."

After years of processing the deaths of my dad and Travis, Tony's death felt like a test to see if I understood the beauty of what life, and therefore death, could bring if I truly embraced both. Every encounter I've had with loss continues to cement my commitment to never look back with regret so that I'm not fearing a life unlived. I again felt the conviction that we're not defined by the day we enter the world or the day we leave it for another but by what we do in between. I've learned that time doesn't heal all wounds but the residual scars remind us how much we've changed over time. I happily let go of the idea that

I wouldn't get to know my dad any better after his death, because the more I have grown, the more I have gotten to know him too.

The self-inquiry following each loss has taught me that the beauty of life comes when we can welcome every emotion that arrives at our door as an expected visitor. When our foundation is strong enough to host all the emotions at the same time—bliss and pain, joy and fear, serenity and grief—our internal pilot light shines even brighter. Even as loss digs deep wells inside us, we become wiser about the wider spectrum of our highs and lows and how complex our souls truly are.

Growing up, I remember getting a piece of candy after funeral services and being told by adults that I had to eat it immediately. I thought it was a bonus for being good, like getting a lollipop after going to the dentist. But I later learned it's a Chinese tradition for bringing in the sweet to take the bitter away. I've found a purposeful life isn't too far from that tradition: you take the sweet with the bitter and move on to another day, at peace with both lingering tastes.

As Jack Kerouac described in *On the Road*, there are people who "burn, burn, burn, like fabulous yellow roman candles exploding like spiders across the stars and in the middle you see the blue centerlight pop and everybody goes 'Awww!'" These words summarize my dad, Tony, and Travis. And I know they also describe people you know in your life. Because I believe they describe who we *all* are inside. YOU are this thing too. We don't have to be the extrovert in the room to be a fabulous roman candle. Whether we're an introvert, an extrovert, or a combination of both, our journey is about understanding the ways in which we let that centerlight pop and shine. The ways in which we can do so while feeling heard, understood, and, most of all...loved.

I've come away from the pain of loss and erratic edges of sorrow. But I've also grown from the ecstatic highs of climbing mountains, building greenhouses where people love what they do, and feeling the incomparable bonds of human connection. Every experience gives me an abiding belief that the practices I've shared in this book are good, right, and needed to navigate this unpredictable world. Now more than ever, I know there are no limits to the highs and lows that life will bring, and it's on us to illuminate what's already inside.

Even though we can't forecast when the next drought or flood in our greenhouse will be, we can be sure it will come and that when it does, we can use our simple but mighty superpowers as humans—like being courageous enough to ask a coworker you hardly know "Are you OK?" if it seems they're not—to lift each other up.

As the *Powers of Ten* documentary illustrates, each of us can feel like both the smallest speck and the biggest force in our personal universe, all at the same time. Our world is made up of people, companies, communities, society, and the planet, and all of it is changing in this Adaptive Age. But what's most important is that with commitment to our greenhouses, we can maintain a sense of connection between each of us and the cosmos that surrounds us.

It's worth the time and effort to be archaeologists and architects in our lives. We need to dig deep within ourselves, unearth our Purpose + Values, and design our lives so we can see that purpose and those values in the work we do. We need to make these changes to find happiness for ourselves and for the people we love on the planet we live on.

In the changing world, the danger of losing ourselves to the chaos is high. But because of the profound potential for connectedness as humans, we're on the brink of fulfilling, actualizing, and transcending more than we've ever been able to in the past. Simply because we can now see the lines and dots connecting people and ecosystems, biodiversity and DEIB, work and life. When we feel resonance, we know things are falling into place.

Connection is how we will survive and thrive as a species on this planet. This is how we will live the future of work right now. This is how we'll wake up every day feeling recognized, respected, and celebrated enough to help restore a society that at times can feel broken.

When we understand our *why*, we adapt knowing there's more

to life than just existing. Because it's about living, loving, and being human.

After Tony's passing I wanted to reexamine the ways to express this potential and the steps we need to take to find collective meaning. As I wrote this book, I would take an occasional break and look up and catch sight of the words on my mantel, one that encapsulates what I've been sharing with you:

LIVE YOUR LOVING LEGACY.

There were times when I thought there was no possible way I could do justice to this book. Or to Tony's legacy. Or to everyone's stories, which were shared with honesty and trust. Or to my team, which has given every bit of blood, sweat, and smiles to help build our company. Given all that's happened, there's no doubt writing this book has been one of the hardest mountains I've had to climb.

But I've been on hard treks before. I had no idea how deeply my 2002 trip to Tanzania was going to be etched in my memory. I don't think Tony did either. At the time it felt like the world was falling apart. I saw the extremes of excess and greed at the height of the dot-com daze, with the roller coaster ending in me getting kicked off the ride by getting laid off. 9/11 and the fall of the Twin Towers tested my sense of what "reality" was anymore. Then my absolute worst fear—having to live without loved ones I couldn't imagine life without—came knocking on my door when my dad was diagnosed with stage III colon cancer.

The money, title, and status of my job in the first dot-com boom felt good in the moment, but they just left me with an emptiness that made me wonder how I was going to fill it. I had no idea where I wanted to go; I just knew I didn't want to go back to the same work world I had come from. There had to be more. I just had no clue what that was going to be.

So I decided to do something out of my element. I decided to climb a mountain—proverbially and physically. I remembered a copy of Hemingway's *The Snows of Kilimanjaro* sitting on my dad's bookshelf when I was growing up, so I told my dad I was going to try to get to the top. He was getting gradually sicker during that time, but it made him smile. He said, "Take lots of pictures." I pinged Tony to see if he wanted to go with me, and even though it was one of the most stressful times in his life with Zappos, he was down.

That trip was one of the most grueling yet spiritual experiences I'd ever had. In the days before our hike, we had to acclimatize, so we walked around the town of Arusha and its neighborhoods. We visited with families living in huts made of mud and straw, generously offering the little they had in the form of tea or a biscuit. Even though they didn't have much material wealth, they seemed to have an intrinsic happiness. Crow's-feet wrinkles etched happiness in the corners of their eyes. Not the pseudo smiles people oftentimes put on at work or on the street, the ones we had sadly become accustomed to.

For me, those moments of human connection brought back a sense of what happiness and humanity could mean. Those people had no idea who we were or why we were there, but they made us feel welcomed and gave us a sense of belonging. Sitting with them restored my faith that there was meaning and purpose out there. I took it upon myself to figure out what that meant for me.

The trek itself felt like a geology book that had come to life. Between rain forest, desert, and glacial snow at the top, every day felt like a different movie set. We went from *Gorillas in the Mist* to Luke and Leia in the desert of *Star Wars*. We climbed for five days into thinner and thinner air. On the predawn morning of our sixth day, we were set to summit. It felt like we had just laid down in an attempt to sleep when our guide yelled outside the tent, "Let's go!"

While it was still pitch-black outside, we went up through a series of switchbacks of volcanic scree—small broken rocks that mean for every three steps you go up, you slide back one or two. It was like climbing on

Corn Pops, and the altitude was hitting us harder with every step. We reached the milestone of Stella Point, where we paused to see the sunrise put a slow spotlight on the snows of Kilimanjaro. I said to myself: *Hi, Dad.*

After another hour of hiking, we could finally see the famed flags of the summit, Uhuru Peak, in the far distance. There was only about a hundred yards separating us from the highest point in Africa when my legs started feeling as if they were fifty pounds each. I remembered our guide teaching us polepole—Swahili for "slowly, slowly"—when we first started our hike from basecamp. I finally knew what he meant. Breathing was getting harder as oxygen was getting lower, and after every step it felt like it took a minute to muster the energy to take another. It was such a bizarre notion to visually see the summit and wonder if I had it in me to get there.

With every bit of my body, mind, and expletives from the soul, we made it. I looked at Tony with delirious joy and a smile. He was wearing sunglasses and looked like all he wanted was to get off that damn mountain. Little did I know it was because he was crying. It was the first time I'd ever known him to. As he described in *Delivering Happiness*, he couldn't believe he'd made it: "I remember thinking that this entire experience was by far the hardest thing I had ever done in my life. It was testing every ounce of willpower I had." In that moment he realized to himself, *Anything is possible.*

Writing this book, especially right now, has strangely felt the same. But this time, I'm the one crying as I'm writing this.

Beyond Happiness was my latest Mount Kilimanjaro, and I wasn't sure if I'd be able to summit. For both journeys, I did all I could to get to the goal because I believed I could. But damn, I had no idea how hard it was going to be to get there. Kili seemed like a countryside hill compared to this.

But instead of scaling a mountain, the hope of this book was for me to scale my purpose. If I could choose a superpower, it'd be the ability to sit down with everyone in the world until they know I see the light in them. I'd help share their light and impact with everyone else in the world by meaningfully connecting everyone's greenhouses. That's my purpose in life, and it may evolve, but I'll keep tending it until the day my own greenhouse passes on too.

If this book will further that purpose in some way, then all of this has been worthwhile.

It's been just about twenty years since that trek on Mount Kili. My spectrum of highs and lows has widened in unimaginable ways, and I feel my heart has expanded because of it. The biggest difference between then and now is that I know I've taken more steps toward embracing whatever life may bring with love and compassion, in awe of what is possible when we do it . . . together.

> Out beyond ideas of wrongdoing and rightdoing, there is
> a field. I'll meet you there.
>
> —RUMI

I will always meet you there.

Addendum

I'd love to remain a part of your hero's journey as you develop greenhouses for yourselves and others. For more resources or to share your story with me, come by www.jennlim.com and www.deliveringhappiness.com. You can share your own ME/WE/COMMUNITY alignment (or misalignment) experiences, your living legacy, or the ripples of impact you're making. Together we can increase the impact of our ripples more than ever before.

One of my favorite core values at DH is "inspire and be inspired."

Thank you, in advance, for inspiring me.

Acknowledgments

Writing a book can be one of the most solitary things to do but it actually takes a village. Working on this one made me realize how deep and big my village is. It's not easy to thank everyone who has impacted a project as immersive as this, and it makes me empathize with Oscar winners who are supposed to thank everyone in forty-five seconds then get cut off midspeech by the orchestra. Luckily for me, books don't have the same constraint. There are just too many people I'm deeply grateful for and even if you're not mentioned here, I hope I've been living by my everyday goal to share my gratitude directly with you along the way!

To my book pod—Jennie Nash (part book coach, part therapist) and Lotus Wong (part DH coach|sultant®, part book doula)—thank you for your supreme endurance and unyielding support in a trek we'll never forget. To my agent Lisa Queen and book whisperer Will Schwalbe, if it wasn't for your wisdom and belief in me, there wouldn't have been a new summit. To my executive editor Gretchen Young and assistant editor Haley Weaver, thank you for your support during one of my most challenging times and the sincere attentiveness to get this book as right as it can be in the time we had. To Euge, Sitos, AJ, Snd, Ana, JMan, Karissa, M&M (Mat and Mark) and your teams, thank you for hopping on the next leg of a book tour without hesitation or knowing the destination.

As I've shared, the point of this book was to bring the spotlight to all the companies, organizations, and people that continue to pioneer with self-awareness and purpose. This is the work my team at

Delivering Happiness (DH)—my work family—does every day. An immense thank-you for *everyone* who's been a part of DH since we were born; for your dedication in growing the company and being the Sherpas who keep spreading happiness, humanity, and wholeness around the world. We've weathered so much and without your sweat, support, and smiles, this wouldn't have been possible.

To our DH clients and partners—my gratitude goes first to the trust you continue to give us in taking on one mountain at a time, knowing we'll keep summiting new ones together, and second to allowing me to share your inspiring stories.

To my dear friends—thank you for sharing your most personal stories with trust and confidence that I would do them right, for the greater goal to be in service of others.

This book also wouldn't have been the same without the enduring friendships and fond memories I have with the Hsieh family, Zappos, and Downtown Project. You were and always will be a part of DH and me.

I've been blessed by this extended village, and still in disbelief how lucky I am for my closest one. To my brother James for being the first person to seed the idea that I can be true to myself and do simple yet iconoclastic things. From the time we were kiddos to the last page of this book, you were my cheerleader, meta-guide, and rock. I wish everyone could have a James in their village. To my eldest brother, Ken, for introducing me to raves when they were still underground and inspiring me by being the philosophical doer in life. To Jo and Olivia for keeping my brothers in line based on how you believe life should be. To my aunt Avery for teaching me how to read when I felt inept because I couldn't figure it out. To my goddaughters, nephews, and nieces, thank you for teaching me by being your authentic MEs every day. To my Mom for continuing to pave the beaten yet beautiful path of how we can all love, drive each other crazy, and learn with grace and beauty.

To my PO3!—Power of Three!—Eleen and Clara, thank you for making our truddy (triple buddy) feel like we can skip through any barrier in the world, no matter how big or how many come our way. To Five, thank you for grounding me with your steadfast support and reminding me what's possible without needing to sweat it. To Patrice, Clara, and Vahn, thank you for podding it up during COVID for sanity and insanely delicious food for so many Fridays. To Bruce, my Dutch English BFF, thank you for being my partner in knowing when to "get me coat" forever. To Molly and Kelly, thank you for inspiring and broadening my understanding of life.

I'm sure the Oscar instrumental music started a while ago and I'm sure I've left so many names out—people I've been inspired by and love deeply. My last bit of gratitude goes to every single person I've met (and haven't yet) who contributes to the present and future of your villages and our humanity.

Notes

1. Steve Jobs, "2005 Stanford Commencement Address," June 12, 2005, Stanford University, transcript and video, 15:04. Available at: <https://news.stanford.edu /2005/06/14/jobs-061505/> [Accessed 7 March 2021].

2. Vinge, Vernor. 1993. *The Coming Technological Singularity*. Department of Mathematical Sciences, San Diego State University. Available at: <https://edoras .sdsu.edu/~vinge/misc/singularity.html> [Accessed 8 May 2021].

3. Klaus Schwab, "The Fourth Industrial Revolution: What It Means, How to Respond," *Agenda* (blog), World Economic Forum, January 14, 2016. Available at: <https://www.weforum.org/agenda/2016/01/the-fourth-industrial-revolution -what-it-means-and-how-to-respond/> [Accessed 7 March 2021].

4. Diamandis, Peter H. 2012. *Abundance: The Future Is Better than You Think*. New York: Free Press.

5. Demetrios Pogkas, Claire Boston, Shannon Harrington, Josh Saul, and Davide Scigliuzzo, "The Covid Bankruptcies: Guitar Center to Youfit," *Tracking COVID-19* (blog), Bloomberg, July 9, 2020. Available at: <https://www.bloomberg .com/graphics/2020-us-bankruptcies-coronavirus/> [Accessed 13 May 2021].

6. Minda Zetlin, "The CEO Who Pays a $70,000 Minimum Wage Says Billionaires Should Do This with Their Money," *Icons & Innovators* (blog), *Inc.*, February 25, 2021. Available at: <https://www.inc.com/minda-zetlin/dan-price-70000 -minimum-wage-ceo-billionaire-tax-philanthropy-washington-state-hb-1406 .html> [Accessed 8 March 2021].

7. "Your Special Blend: Rewarding Our Partners," Starbucks, 2014. Available at: <https://globalassets.starbucks.com/assets/589a80b922dd41809f7058eb146338cb .pdf> [Accessed 8 March 2021].

8. Pogkas, "The Covid Bankruptcies: Guitar Center to Youfit."

9. Matt Stevens, "Starbucks C.E.O. Apologizes After Arrests of 2 Black Men," *New York Times*, April 15, 2018. Available at: <https://www.nytimes.com /2018/04/15/us/starbucks-philadelphia-black-men-arrest.html> [Accessed 13 May 2021].

10. Quentin Fottrell, "Starbucks Drops to Lowest Consumer-Perception Level Since November 2015," *Personal Finance* (blog) MarketWatch, April 21, 2018. Available at: <https://www.marketwatch.com/story/starbucks-drops-to-lowest-consumer -perception-level-since-november-2015-2018-04-18> [Accessed 13 May 2021].

11. Rebecca Ungarino, "Starbucks Jumps to Record High after Beating on Earnings and Raising Guidance," *Markets Insider* (blog), *Insider*, April 25, 2019. Available at: <https://markets.businessinsider.com/news/stocks/starbucks-stock-hits -record-after-earnings-beat-raising-guidance-2019-4-1028140841> [Accessed 8 March 2021].

12. Taylor Borden, Allana Akhtar, Joey Hadden, and Debanjali Bose, "The Coronavirus Outbreak Has Triggered Unprecedented Mass Layoffs and Furloughs. Here Are the Major Companies That Have Announced They Are Downsizing Their Workforces," *Insider*, October 8, 2020. Available at <https://www.businessinsider.com /coronavirus-layoffs-furloughs-hospitality-service-travel-unemployment-2020>.

13. Amelia Lucas, "Starbucks Says It Lost $3 Billion in Revenue in Latest Quarter Due to Coronavirus Pandemic," CNBC, June 10, 2020. Available at: <https:// www.cnbc.com/2020/06/10/starbucks-says-it-lost-3-billion-in-revenue-in-latest -quarter-due-to-coronavirus-pandemic.html> [Accessed 13 May 2021].

14. Connor Perrett, "Starbucks Stores Are Reopening, But Fearful Employees Say They'd Rather Collect Unemployment Than Risk Their Health Returning to Work—Except They Can't," *Insider*, May 3, 2020. Available at: <https://www .businessinsider.com/starbucks-workers-afraid-to-work-will-go-without-pay -2020-5> [Accessed 13 May 2021].

15. Justin Bariso, "Starbucks CEO's Emotionally Intelligent Pandemic Response," Inc .com, April 20, 2020. Available at: <https://www.inc.com/justin-bariso/starbucks -ceos-letter-to-employees-about-covid-19-is-a-master-class-in-emotional -intelligence.html> [Accessed 13 May 2021].

16. Sophie Lewis, "Starbucks Commits to Paying All Workers for 30 Days—Even If They Don't Go to Work During Coronavirus," CBS News, 2020. Available at: <https://www.cbsnews.com/news/coronavirus-starbucks-pay-all-workers-30 -days-stay-home-pandemic/> [Accessed 13 May 2021].

17. Nick G., "101 Artificial Intelligence Statistics [Updated for 2021]," *Blog*, TechJury. Available at: <https://techjury.net/blog/ai-statistics/#gref> [Accessed 7 March 2021].

18. World Economic Forum, *The Future of Jobs Report 2020*, October 2020. Available at: <https://cn.weforum.org/reports/the-future-of-jobs-report-2020> [Accessed 7 March 2021].

19. Arianna Huffington, "The S.E.C. Makes History with a Major New Rule on Human Capital," *Wisdom* (blog), Thrive Global, February 23, 2021. Available at: <https://thriveglobal.com/stories/arianna-huffington-recognizing-employee -well-being-key-performance/> [Accessed 26 March 2021].

20. Dr. Saul McLeod, "Maslow's Hierarchy of Needs," Simply Psychology, updated December 29, 2020. Available at: <https://www.simplypsychology.org/maslow .html>. [Accessed 5 March 2021].

21. "Rising Inequality Affecting More than Two-Thirds of the Globe, but It's Not Inevitable: New UN Report," UN News, January 21, 2020. Available at: <https:// news.un.org/en/story/2020/01/1055681> [Accessed 8 March 2021].

22. Marguerite Ward, "The Upskilling Economy: 7 Companies Investing Millions of Dollars in Retraining American Workers so They Can Find Better Jobs," *Better Capitalism* (blog), *Insider*, November 2, 2020. Available at: <https://www.busi nessinsider.com/companies-investing-retraining-upskilling-reskilling-2020-10> [Accessed 8 March 2021].

23. Chamberlain, Andrew, and Zanele Munyikwa. 2020. *What's Culture Worth? Stock Performance of Glassdoor's Best Places to Work 2009 to 2019.* Available at: <https://www.glassdoor.com/research/stock-returns-bptw-2020/#> [Accessed 26 March 2021].

24. Catherine Yoshimoto and Ed Frauenheim, "The Best Companies to Work for Are Beating the Market," *Commentary* (blog), *Fortune*, February 27, 2018. Available at: <https://fortune.com/2018/02/27/the-best-companies-to-work-for-are -beating-the-market/> [Accessed 26 March 2021].

25. Jacob Morgan, "Why the Millions We Spend on Employee Engagement Buy Us So Little," *Harvard Business Review*, March 10, 2017. Available at: <https:// hbr.org/2017/03/why-the-millions-we-spend-on-employee-engagement-buy -us-so-little#> [Accessed 13 May 2021].

26. Mark C. Crowley, "The Proof Is In The Profits: America's Happiest Companies Make More Money," *Fast Company*, February 22, 2013. Available at: <https:// www.fastcompany.com/3006150/proof-profits-americas-happiest-companies -also-fare-best-financially> [Accessed 8 March 2021].

27. Fink, Larry. 2019. *Larry Fink's 2019 Letter to CEOs.* BlackRock. Available at: <https://www.blackrock.com/americas-offshore/en/2019-larry-fink-ceo-letter> [Accessed 8 March 2021].

28. Thomas W. Malnight, Ivy Buche, and Charles Dhanaraj, "Put Purpose at the Core of Your Strategy," *Harvard Business Review*, September–October 2019. Available at: <https://hbr.org/2019/09/put-purpose-at-the-core-of-your-strategy> [Accessed 8 March 2021].

29. Janeane Tolomeo, "New Report: Workplace Well-Being and Business Value," *Lead* (blog), Indeed.com, July 29, 2020. Available at: <https://www.indeed.com /lead/cultivating-workplace-happiness> [Accessed 22 March 2021].

30. Jim Harter and Annamarie Mann, "The Right Culture: Not Just about Employee Satisfaction," *Workplace* (blog), Gallup, April 12, 2017. Available at: <https:// www.gallup.com/workplace/236366/right-culture-not-employee-satisfaction .aspx> [Accessed 7 March 2021].

31. "Stress in the Workplace: Survey Summary," American Psychological Association, March 2011. Available at: <https://www.apa.org/news/press/releases/phwa-survey-summary.pdf> [Accessed 7 March 2021].

32. Csikszentmihalyi, Mihaly. 1990. *Flow: The Psychology of Optimal Experience*. New York: Harper & Row.

33. Morgan McFall-Johnsen, "21 Science 'Facts' You Might Have Learned in School That Aren't True," *Science* (blog), *Insider*, July 24, 2020. Available at: <https://www.businessinsider.com/science-facts-from-school-not-true-2019-9#myth-dinosaurs-were-scaly-earthy-colored-lizards-3> [Accessed 22 March 2021].

34. Ryan, Richard M., and Edward L. Deci. 2001. "On Happiness and Human Potentials: A Review of Research on Hedonic and Eudaimonic Well-Being." *Annual Review of Psychology* 52, no. 1: 141–166. Available at: <https://doi.org/10.1146/annurev.psych.52.1.141> [Accessed 22 March 2021].

35. McFall-Johnsen, "21 Science 'Facts' You Might Have Learned in School That Aren't True."

36. Alanna Petroff, "Volkswagen Scandal May Cost Up to $87 Billion," *CNN Business* (blog), CNN, October 2, 2015. Available at: <https://money.cnn.com/2015/10/02/news/companies/volkswagen-scandal-bp-credit-suisse/> [Accessed 8 March 2021].

37. Conley, Chip. 2014. *Emotional Equations: Simple Steps for Creating Happiness + Success in Business + Life*. New York: Atria Books.

38. Seligman, Martin E. P. 2013. *Flourish: A Visionary New Understanding of Happiness and Well-Being*. New York: Atria Books.

39. Karyn Twaronite, "The Surprising Power of Simply Asking Coworkers How They're Doing," *Harvard Business Review*, February 28, 2019. Available at: <https://hbr.org/2019/02/the-surprising-power-of-simply-asking-coworkers-how-theyre-doing> [Accessed 8 March 2021].

40. BetterUp. 2021. *The Value of Belonging at Work: New Frontiers for Inclusion in 2021 and Beyond*. Available at: <https://www.betterup.com/en-us/resources/reports/the-value-of-belonging-at-work-the-business-case-for-investing-in-workplace-inclusion> [Accessed 8 March 2021].

41. Jacob Morgan, "The 5 Types of Organizational Structures: Part 2, 'Flatter' Organizations," *Leadership* (blog), *Forbes*, July 8, 2015. Available at: <https://www.forbes.com/sites/jacobmorgan/2015/07/08/the-5-types-of-organizational-structures-part-2-flatter-organizations/?sh=1a9ff81a6dac> [Accessed 8 March 2021].

42. Adam Jezard, "Depression Is the No. 1 Cause of Ill Health and Disability Worldwide," *Agenda* (blog), World Economic Forum, May 18, 2018. Available at: <https://www.weforum.org/agenda/2018/05/depression-prevents-many-of-us-from-leading-healthy-and-productive-lives-being-the-no-1-cause-of-ill-health-and-disability-worldwide/> [Accessed 8 March 2021].

43. Hill, Terrence D., Krysia N. Mossakowski, and Ronald J. Angel. 2007. "Relationship Violence and Psychological Distress among Low-Income Urban Women." *Journal of Urban Health* 84, no. 4: 537–551. Available at: <https://www.ncbi.nlm.nih.gov/pmc/articles/PMC2219565/> [Accessed 8 March 2021].

44. Brie Weiler Reynolds, "FlexJobs, Mental Health America Survey: Mental Health in the Workplace," *Blog*, FlexJobs, August 21, 2020. Available at: <https://www.flexjobs.com/blog/post/flexjobs-mha-mental-health-workplace-pandemic/?utm_source=cj&utm_medium=VigLink&utm_campaign=affiliates&cjevent=96b064487d7811eb82ab00520a1c0e13> [Accessed 8 March 2021].

45. Adam Hickman and Ben Wigert, "Lead Your Remote Team Away from Burnout, Not Toward It," *Workplace* (blog), Gallup, June 15, 2020. Available at: <https://www.gallup.com/workplace/312683/lead-remote-team-away-burnout-not-toward.aspx> [Accessed 8 March 2021].

46. Saez, Emmanuel. 2020. *Striking It Richer: The Evolution of Top Incomes in the United States (Updated with 2018 Estimates)*, Econometrics Laboratory, University of California, Berkeley. Available at: <https://eml.berkeley.edu/~saez/saez-UStopincomes-2018.pdf> [Accessed 8 March 2021].

47. Campbell, Joseph. 2004. *The Hero with a Thousand Faces*. Princeton, N.J.: Princeton University Press.

48. "Be Pitiful." January 26, 1898. *Zion's Herald* 76, no.4: 101. Boston: ProQuest American Periodical Series. Translated for semantic change.

49. Motoko Rich, "Why Is This Man Smiling?" *New York Times*, April 8, 2011, Fashion. Available at: <https://www.nytimes.com/2011/04/10/fashion/10HSEIH.html> [Accessed 8 March 2021].

50. Ware, Bronnie. 2012. *The Top Five Regrets of the Dying*. Carlsbad, California: Hay House, Inc.

51. Oprah Winfrey, "Eulogy for Rosa Parks," delivered October 31, 2005, Metropolitan AME Church, Washington, DC. Available at: <https://www.americanrhetoric.com/speeches/oprahwinfreyonrosaparks.htm/> [Accessed 8 March 2021].

52. Christopher John Farley, "'Oh Wow': What Do Steve Jobs's Last Words Really Mean?" *Wall Street Journal*, October 31, 2011, transcript and video, 4:11. Available at: <https://www.wsj.com/articles/BL-SEB-67713> [Accessed 8 March 2021].

53. Laloux, Frédéric. 2014. *Reinventing Organizations*. 1st ed. Brussels, Belgium: Nelson Parker.

54. Robert Gabsa and Shruti Rastogi, "Take Care of Your People, and They'll Take Care of Business," *Workplace* (blog), Gallup, June 23, 2020. Available at: <https://www.gallup.com/workplace/312824/care-people-care-business.aspx> [Accessed 23 March 2021].

55. Carol Dweck, "Carol Dweck Revisits the 'Growth Mindset,'" *EducationWeek*, September 22, 2015, Student Well-Being. Available at: <https://www.edweek.org/leadership/opinion-carol-dweck-revisits-the-growth-mindset/2015/09> [Accessed 24 March 2021].

56. Kate Heinz, "Dangers of Turnover: Battling Hidden Costs," Built In, March 22, 2020. Available at: <https://builtin.com/recruiting/cost-of-turnover> [Accessed 24 March 2021].

57. Twaronite, "The Surprising Power of Simply Asking Coworkers How They're Doing."

58. Lieberman, Matthew D. 2014. *Social: Why Our Brains Are Wired to Connect.* New York: Crown.

59. Nick Tate, "Loneliness Rivals Obesity, Smoking as Health Risk," *Health & Balance* (blog), WebMD, May 4, 2018. Available at: <https://www.webmd.com/balance/news/20180504/loneliness-rivals-obesity-smoking-as-health-risk> [Accessed 8 March 2021].

60. Jennifer Robison, "The Business Case for Well-Being," Gallup, June 9, 2010. Available at: <https://news.gallup.com/businessjournal/139373/Business-Case-Wellbeing.aspx> [Accessed 8 March 2021].

61. David Greene, Scott Horsley, and William Spriggs, "Minority Workers See Highest Levels of Unemployment from COVID-19 Crisis," June 5, 2020, from *Morning Edition*, radio program, MP3 audio and transcript, 6:25. Available at: <https://www.npr.org/2020/06/05/870227952/minority-workers-see-highest-levels-of-unemployment-from-covid-19-crisis> [Accessed 24 March 2021].

62. Anu Madgavkar, Olivia White, Mekala Krishnan, Deepa Mahajan, and Xavier Azcue, "COVID-19 and Gender Equality: Countering the Regressive Effects," McKinsey & Company, July 15, 2020. Available at: <https://www.mckinsey.com/featured-insights/future-of-work/covid-19-and-gender-equality-countering-the-regressive-effects> [Accessed 24 March 2021].

63. "Labor Force Statistics from the Current Population Survey," United States Bureau of Labor Statistics, last modified April 2, 2021. Available at: <https://www.bls.gov/web/empsit/cpsee_e16.htm> [Accessed 24 March 2021].

64. Vivian Hunt, Dennis Layton, and Sara Prince, "Why Diversity Matters," McKinsey & Company, January 1, 2015. Available at: <https://www.mckinsey.com/business-functions/organization/our-insights/why-diversity-matters> [Accessed 25 March 2021].

65. Google, *Google Diversity Annual Report 2020.* Available at: <https://diversity.google/annual-report/> [Accessed 25 March 2021].

66. Intel Corporation, *2019 Annual Intel Diversity and Inclusion Report*, 2019. Available at: <https://www.intel.com/content/www/us/en/diversity/diversity-inclusion-annual-report.html> [Accessed 26 March 2021].

67. "Real Values." 2021. Jobs.netflix.com. Available at: <https://jobs.netflix.com/culture> [Accessed 11 May 2021].

68. "How Intelligent Are Whales and Dolphins?" Whale and Dolphin Conservation. Available at: <https://us.whales.org/whales-dolphins/how-intelligent-are-whales-and-dolphins/> [Accessed 24 March 2021].

69. "Starbucks Solidifies Pathway to a Planet Positive Future," *Starbucks Stories & News* (blog), Starbucks.com, December 9, 2020. Available at: <https://stories .starbucks.com/stories/2020/starbucks-solidifies-pathway-to-a-planet-positive -future/> [Accessed 13 May 2021].

70. Schultz, Howard, and Kevin Johnson. 2016. *2016 Annual Letter to Shareholders.* Starbucks Coffee Company. Available at: <https://s22.q4cdn.com/869488222 /files/doc_financials/annual/2016/2016-Annual-Letter-to-Shareholders.PDF> [Accessed 25 March 2021].

71. JUST Capital, "Here's Exactly How 7 CEOs Are Putting Stakeholder Capitalism into Practice," JUST Capital, February 26, 2020. Available at: <https://just capital.com/news/how-ceos-are-putting-stakeholder-capitalism-into-practice/> [Accessed 24 March 2021].

72. Capgemini Digital Transformation Institute, *Loyalty Deciphered—How Emotions Drive Genuine Engagement*, 2017. Available at: <https://www.capgemini .com/wp-content/uploads/2017/11/dti_loyalty-deciphered_29nov17_final.pdf> [Accessed 24 March 2021].

73. "About," Universum Global, 2021. Available at: <https://universumglobal.com /about-universum/> [Accessed 8 March 2021].

74. *Forbes Kazakhstan.* 2020. Available at: <https://forbes.kz/archive/155> [Accessed 26 March 2021].

75. Rosalind Brewer, "Spelman College Commencement Address," May 20, 2018, Spelman College, video, 23:54. Available at: <https://www.spelman.edu/commencement /commencement-speaker/past-commencement-speakers/rosalind-brewer> [Accessed 8 March 2021].

76. "Bigfork, MT," Data USA. Available at: <https://datausa.io/profile/geo /bigfork-mt#> [Accessed 27 March 2021].

77. Sy, Stephanie, and Leah Nagy. "Asian American Community Battles Surge in Hate Crimes Stirred from COVID-19." *PBS NewsHour*, March 16, 2021. Transcript and video, 7:58. Available at: <https://www.pbs.org/newshour/show /asian-american-community-battles-surge-in-hate-crimes-stirred-from-covid -19> [Accessed 25 March 2021].

78. Suyin Haynes, "'This Isn't Just a Problem for North America.' The Atlanta Shooting Highlights the Painful Reality of Rising Anti-Asian Violence around the World," *Time*, March 22, 2021. Available at: <https://time.com/5947862 /anti-asian-attacks-rising-worldwide/> [Accessed 25 March 2021].

79. Kellie Hwang, "The Most-Viewed GoFundMe Right Now Is for S.F. Asian American Woman Who Fought Off Attacker," *San Francisco Chronicle*, March 19, 2021. Available at: <https://www.sfchronicle.com/local/article/The-most -viewed-GoFundMe-right-now-is-for-S-F-16036503.php> [Accessed 26 March 2021].

80. Tensie Whelan and Carly Fink, "The Comprehensive Business Case for Sustainability," *Harvard Business Review*, October 21, 2016. Available at: <https://hbr

.org/2016/10/the-comprehensive-business-case-for-sustainability> [Accessed 26 March 2021].

81. "Government's Mission Is to Create Conditions Conducive for Happiness of Individuals, Families and Employees, and to Promote Positivity: Mohammed bin Rashid," United Arab Emirates Ministry of Cabinet Affairs. Available at: <https://www.uaecabinet.ae/en/details/news/governments-mission-is-to-create-conditions-conducive-for-happiness-of-individuals-families-and-employees-and-to-promote-positivity-mohammed-bin-rashid> [Accessed 8 March 2021].

82. International Telecommunication Union, United Nations Economic Commission for Europe, and United Nations Human Settlements Programme, *Smart Dubai Happiness Meter in Dubai, United Arab Emirates*, October 2019. Available at: <http://www.itu.int/pub/T-TUT-SMARTCITY-2019-2> [Accessed 26 March 2021].

83. "National Wellbeing Strategy 2031 Introduces a New Approach for Government Work," Media, National Program for Happiness and Wellbeing, June 12, 2019. Available at: <https://www.hw.gov.ae/en/news/national-wellbeing-strategy-2031-introduces-a-new-approach-for-government-work> [Accessed 25 March 2021].

84. "National Program for Happiness and Wellbeing Launches Business for Wellbeing Council," Media, National Program for Happiness and Wellbeing, December 18, 2019. Available at: <https://www.hw.gov.ae/en/news/national-program-for-happiness-and-wellbeing-launches-business-for-wellbeing-council> [Accessed 25 March 2021].

85. Wikipedia, s.v. "Greta Thunberg," last modified April 20, 2021, 17:50. Available at: <https://en.wikipedia.org/wiki/Greta_Thunberg> [Accessed 24 March 2021].

Index

REALIZE YOUR RIPPLE
OF IMPACT

For book resources, events, speaking, exec coaching, and more...

connect at <u>JennLim.com</u>

Inspire Leaders to Be Their Best Selves to Do Their Best Work. Make an Impact by Going Beyond Happiness.

DH is the world's first culture coach|sulting® company that's helped hundreds of organizations use the science of happiness to co-create adaptable organizations that grow people, profits, and purpose so they not just survive, but thrive.

Workshops | Courses | Keynotes | coach|sulting®

See what a culture that goes beyond happiness can do for purpose, people, and profits at **DeliveringHappiness.com**